Congressional Budget Justification
Department of State, Foreign Operations, and Related Programs
Table of Contents

iii

ACCOUNT TABLES

Additional volumes to follow:

Congressional Budget Justification
Appendix 1: Department of State Operations Fiscal Year 2015

Congressional Budget Justification
Appendix 2: Foreign Operations Fiscal Year 2015

Congressional Budget Justification
Appendix 3: Foreign Operations – Regional Perspectives Fiscal Year 2015

STATE OPERATIONS and FOREIGN ASSISTANCE REQUEST

($000)

	FY 2013 Enduring Actual	FY 2013 OCO Actual	FY 2013 Actual Total[1]	FY 2014 Estimate Enduring	FY 2014 Estimate OCO	FY 2014 Estimate Total	FY 2015 Request Enduring	FY 2015 Request OCO	FY 2015 Request Total	Increase / Decrease
INTERNATIONAL AFFAIRS (Function 150) and International Commissions (Function 300)	**41,196,503**	**10,822,173**	**52,018,676**	**44,330,857**	**6,520,000**	**50,850,857**	**44,214,093**	**5,912,525**	**50,126,618**	**(724,239)**
INTERNATIONAL AFFAIRS (Function 150 Account) Only	**41,083,539**	**10,822,173**	**51,905,712**	**44,204,940**	**6,520,000**	**50,724,940**	**44,098,460**	**5,912,525**	**50,010,985**	**(713,955)**
Total – State Department and USAID (including 300)	**38,096,969**	**10,808,531**	**48,905,500**	**40,301,120**	**6,509,584**	**46,810,704**	**40,308,118**	**5,912,525**	**46,220,643**	**(590,061)**
STATE OPERATIONS & RELATED ACCOUNTS	13,098,085	4,604,740	17,702,825	13,875,323	1,817,703	15,693,026	14,618,891	2,021,125	16,640,016	946,990
STATE OPERATIONS	12,359,736	4,592,572	16,952,308	13,115,259	1,807,287	14,922,546	13,862,331	2,021,125	15,883,456	960,910
Administration of Foreign Affairs	8,812,550	4,496,367	13,308,917	9,788,858	1,732,887	11,521,745	9,584,025	1,871,125	11,455,150	(66,595)
State Programs	6,523,801	3,178,992	9,702,793	6,660,071	1,391,109	8,051,180	6,838,910	1,553,425	8,392,335	341,155
Diplomatic and Consular Programs[2]	6,467,427	3,178,992	9,646,419	6,583,171	1,391,109	7,974,280	6,782,510	1,553,425	8,335,935	361,655
Ongoing Operations	5,126,217	2,269,613	7,395,830	4,715,920	490,835	5,206,755	4,654,395	563,719	5,218,114	11,359
Worldwide Security Protection	1,341,210	909,379	2,250,589	1,867,251	900,274	2,767,525	2,128,115	989,706	3,117,821	350,296
Capital Investment Fund	56,374	-	56,374	76,900	-	76,900	56,400	-	56,400	(20,500)
Embassy Security, Construction, and Maintenance[3]	1,582,247	1,237,536	2,819,783	2,399,351	275,000	2,674,351	2,016,900	260,800	2,277,700	(396,651)
Ongoing Operations	912,722	1,237,536	2,150,258	785,351	275,000	1,060,351	799,400	10,800	810,200	(250,151)
Worldwide Security Upgrades	669,525	-	669,525	1,614,000	-	1,614,000	1,217,500	250,000	1,467,500	(146,500)
Other Administration of Foreign Affairs	706,502	79,839	786,341	729,436	66,778	796,214	728,215	56,900	785,115	(11,099)
Conflict Stabilization Operations (CSO)[4]	21,594	8,075	29,669	21,800	8,500	30,300	-	-	-	(30,300)
Office of the Inspector General	59,575	56,944	116,519	69,406	49,650	119,056	73,400	56,900	130,300	11,244
Educational and Cultural Exchange Programs[5]	559,180	14,820	574,000	560,000	8,628	568,628	577,900	-	577,900	9,272
Representation Expenses[6]	7,660	-	7,660	8,030	-	8,030	7,679	-	7,679	(351)
Protection of Foreign Missions and Officials	25,633	-	25,633	28,200	-	28,200	30,036	-	30,036	1,836
Emergencies in the Diplomatic and Consular Services[7]	8,552	-	8,552	9,242	-	9,242	7,900	-	7,900	(1,342)
Buying Power Maintenance Account[8]	-	-	-	-	-	-	-	-	-	-
Repatriation Loans Program Account[9]	1,651	-	1,651	1,537	-	1,537	1,300	-	1,300	(237)
Payment to the American Institute in Taiwan[10]	22,134	-	22,134	31,221	-	31,221	30,000	-	30,000	(1,221)
International Chancery Center[11]	523	-	523	-	-	-	533	-	533	533
Foreign Service Retirement and Disability Fund	-	-	-	-	-	-	-	-	-	-
International Organizations	3,290,126	96,205	3,386,331	3,031,281	74,400	3,105,681	4,035,914	150,000	4,185,914	1,080,233
Contributions to International Organizations (CIO)	1,376,338	96,205	1,472,543	1,265,762	74,400	1,340,162	1,517,349	-	1,517,349	177,187
Contributions for International Peacekeeping Activities (CIPA)[12]	1,913,788	-	1,913,788	1,765,519	-	1,765,519	2,518,565	-	2,518,565	753,046
Peacekeeping Response Mechanism	-	-	-	-	-	-	-	150,000	150,000	150,000
Related Programs	144,096	-	144,096	169,203	-	169,203	126,759	-	126,759	(42,444)
The Asia Foundation	16,139	-	16,139	17,000	-	17,000	12,000	-	12,000	(5,000)

STATE OPERATIONS and FOREIGN ASSISTANCE REQUEST
($000)

	FY 2013 Enduring Actual	FY 2013 OCO Actual	FY 2013 Actual Total[1]	FY 2014 Estimate Enduring	FY 2014 Estimate OCO	FY 2014 Estimate Total	FY 2015 Request Enduring	FY 2015 Request OCO	FY 2015 Request Total	Increase / Decrease
Center for Middle Easter-Western Dialogue	96	-	96	90	-	90	83	-	83	(7)
Eisenhower Exchange Fellowship Program	191		191	400	-	400	400	-	400	-
Israeli Arab Scholarship Program	13		13	13	-	13	26	-	26	13
East-West Center	15,855		15,855	16,700	-	16,700	10,800	-	10,800	(5,900)
National Endowment for Democracy	111,802		111,802	135,000	-	135,000	103,450	-	103,450	(31,550)
International Commissions (Function 300)	**112,964**	**-**	**112,964**	**125,917**	**-**	**125,917**	**115,633**	**-**	**115,633**	**(10,284)**
International Boundary and Water Commission - Salaries and Expenses	41,162	-	41,162	44,000	-	44,000	45,415	-	45,415	1,415
International Boundary and Water Commission - Construction	27,620	-	27,620	33,438	-	33,438	26,461	-	26,461	(6,977)
American Sections	**11,312**	**-**	**11,312**	**12,499**	**-**	**12,499**	**12,311**	**-**	**12,311**	**(188)**
International Joint Commission	6,787	-	6,787	7,664	-	7,664	7,413	-	7,413	(251)
International Boundary Commission	2,206	-	2,206	2,449	-	2,449	2,525	-	2,525	76
Border Environment Cooperation Commission	2,319	-	2,319	2,386	-	2,386	2,373	-	2,373	(13)
International Fisheries Commissions	**32,870**	**-**	**32,870**	**35,980**	**-**	**35,980**	**31,446**	**-**	**31,446**	**(4,534)**
Broadcasting Board of Governors	**709,306**	**4,180**	**713,486**	**729,080**	**4,400**	**733,480**	**721,260**	**-**	**721,260**	**(12,220)**
International Broadcasting Operations	702,632	4,180	706,812	721,080	4,400	725,480	716,460	-	716,460	(9,020)
Broadcasting Capital Improvements	6,674	-	6,674	8,000	-	8,000	4,800	-	4,800	(3,200)
Other Programs	**29,043**	**7,988**	**37,031**	**30,984**	**6,016**	**37,000**	**35,300**	**-**	**35,300**	**(1,700)**
United States Institute of Peace	29,043	7,988	37,031	30,984	6,016	37,000	35,300	-	35,300	(1,700)
FOREIGN OPERATIONS	**26,483,794**	**7,327,133**	**33,810,927**	**28,719,308**	**5,129,593**	**33,848,901**	**27,921,291**	**3,891,400**	**31,812,691**	**(2,055,525)**
U.S Agency for International Development	**1,204,349**	**246,457**	**1,450,806**	**1,222,169**	**91,038**	**1,313,207**	**1,503,916**	**65,000**	**1,568,916**	**255,709**
USAID Operating Expenses (OE)	1,037,068	242,183	1,279,251	1,059,229	81,000	1,140,229	1,318,816	65,000	1,383,816	243,587
Conflict Stabilization Operations (CSO)	-	-	-	-	-	-	-	-	-	-
USAID Capital Investment Fund (CIF)	123,134	-	123,134	117,940	-	117,940	130,815	-	130,815	12,875
USAID Inspector General Operating Expenses	44,147	4,274	48,421	45,000	10,038	55,038	54,285	-	54,285	(753)
Bilateral Economic Assistance	**15,946,523**	**5,188,054**	**21,134,577**	**16,787,609**	**3,894,165**	**20,681,774**	**16,471,852**	**2,778,400**	**19,250,252**	**(1,431,522)**
Global Health Programs (USAID and State)[13]	8,065,888	-	8,065,888	8,439,450	-	8,439,450	8,050,000	-	8,050,000	(389,450)
Global Health Programs - USAID	[2,626,059]	-	[2,626,059]	[2,769,450]	-	[2,769,450]	[2,680,000]	-	[2,680,000]	[-89,450]
Global Health Programs - State	[5,439,829]	-	[5,439,829]	[5,670,000]	-	[5,670,000]	[5,370,000]	-	[5,370,000]	[-300,000]
Development Assistance (DA)	2,717,671	-	2,717,671	2,507,001	-	2,507,001	2,619,984	-	2,619,984	112,983
International Disaster Assistance (IDA)	799,468	750,927	1,550,395	876,828	924,172	1,801,000	665,000	635,000	1,300,000	(501,000)
Transition Initiatives (TI)[14]	47,604	21,224	68,828	48,177	9,423	57,600	67,600	-	67,600	10,000
Complex Crises Fund (CCF)[15]	9,496	43,498	52,994	20,000	20,000	40,000	30,000	-	30,000	(10,000)
Development Credit Authority - Subsidy (DCA)	[40,000]	-	[40,000]	[40,000]	-	[40,000]	[40,000]	-	[40,000]	-
Development Credit Authority - Administrative Expenses	7,880	-	7,880	8,041	-	8,041	8,200	-	8,200	159
Economic Support Fund (ESF)[16,17,18,19]	2,573,587	3,293,886	5,867,473	2,932,967	1,656,215	4,589,182	3,398,694	1,678,400	5,077,094	487,912

STATE OPERATIONS and FOREIGN ASSISTANCE REQUEST
($000)

	FY 2013 Enduring Actual	FY 2013 OCO Actual	FY 2013 Actual Total[1]	FY 2014 Estimate Enduring	FY 2014 Estimate OCO	FY 2014 Estimate Total	FY 2015 Request Enduring	FY 2015 Request OCO	FY 2015 Request Total	Increase / Decrease
Democracy Fund	108,960	-	108,960	130,500	-	130,500	-	-	-	(130,500)
Migration and Refugee Assistance (MRA)[17]	1,590,146	1,078,519	2,668,665	1,774,645	1,284,355	3,059,000	1,582,374	465,000	2,047,374	(1,011,626)
U.S. Emergency Refugee and Migration Assistance (ERMA)	25,823	-	25,823	50,000	-	50,000	50,000	-	50,000	-
Independent Agencies	**1,258,585**	**-**	**1,258,585**	**1,329,700**	**-**	**1,329,700**	**1,422,100**	**-**	**1,422,100**	**92,400**
Peace Corps	356,015	-	356,015	379,000	-	379,000	380,000	-	380,000	1,000
Millennium Challenge Corporation	852,728	-	852,728	898,200	-	898,200	1,000,000	-	1,000,000	101,800
Inter-American Foundation	21,361	-	21,361	22,500	-	22,500	18,100	-	18,100	(4,400)
U.S. African Development Foundation	28,481	-	28,481	30,000	-	30,000	24,000	-	24,000	(6,000)
Department of Treasury	**35,552**	**1,474**	**37,026**	**23,500**	**-**	**23,500**	**23,500**	**-**	**23,500**	**-**
International Affairs Technical Assistance	24,160	1,474	25,634	23,500	-	23,500	23,500	-	23,500	-
Debt Restructuring	11,392	-	11,392	-	-	-	-	-	-	-
International Security Assistance	**6,900,352**	**1,891,148**	**8,791,500**	**7,366,063**	**1,144,390**	**8,510,453**	**6,766,580**	**1,048,000**	**7,814,580**	**(695,873)**
International Narcotics Control and Law Enforcement (INCLE)[15,18,21]	1,005,611	853,067	1,858,678	1,005,610	344,390	1,350,000	721,911	396,000	1,117,911	(232,089)
Nonproliferation, Antiterrorism, Demining and Related Programs (NADR)	560,270	114,592	674,862	630,000	70,000	700,000	605,400	-	605,400	(94,600)
Peacekeeping Operations (PKO)[20,21]	287,508	202,689	490,197	235,600	200,000	435,600	221,150	115,000	336,150	(99,450)
International Military Education and Training (IMET)[14,16,20]	100,432	-	100,432	105,573	-	105,573	107,474	-	107,474	1,901
Foreign Military Financing (FMF)[14,16,20]	4,946,531	720,800	5,667,331	5,389,280	530,000	5,919,280	5,110,645	537,000	5,647,645	(271,635)
Multilateral Assistance	**2,875,204**	**-**	**2,875,204**	**3,010,749**	**-**	**3,010,749**	**2,873,943**	**-**	**2,873,943**	**(136,806)**
International Organizations and Programs[13]	326,651	-	326,651	344,020	-	344,020	303,439	-	303,439	(40,581)
International Financial Institutions (IFIs)	**2,548,553**	**-**	**2,548,553**	**2,666,729**	**-**	**2,666,729**	**2,570,504**	**-**	**2,570,504**	**(96,225)**
International Bank for Reconstruction and Development	180,993	-	180,993	186,957	-	186,957	192,921	-	192,921	5,964
International Development Association (IDA)	1,351,018	-	1,351,018	1,355,000	-	1,355,000	1,290,600	-	1,290,600	(64,400)
African Development Bank	30,717	-	30,717	32,418	-	32,418	34,119	-	34,119	1,701
African Development Fund (AfDF)	163,449	-	163,449	176,336	-	176,336	195,000	-	195,000	18,664
Asian Development Bank	101,190	-	101,190	106,586	-	106,586	112,194	-	112,194	5,608
Asian Development Fund	94,937	-	94,937	109,854	-	109,854	115,250	-	115,250	5,396
Inter-American Development Bank	107,110	-	107,110	102,000	-	102,000	102,020	-	102,020	20
Enterprise for the Americas Multilateral Investment Fund	14,995	-	14,995	6,298	-	6,298	-	-	-	(6,298)
IDA Multilateral Debt Relief Initiative	-	-	-	-	-	-	78,900	-	78,900	78,900
AfDF Multilateral Debt Relief Initiative	-	-	-	-	-	-	13,500	-	13,500	13,500
Global Environment Facility (GEF)	124,840	-	124,840	143,750	-	143,750	136,563	-	136,563	(7,187)
Clean Technology Fund	175,283	-	175,283	184,630	-	184,630	201,253	-	201,253	16,623
Strategic Climate Fund	47,374	-	47,374	49,900	-	49,900	63,184	-	63,184	13,284
International Fund for Agricultural Development	28,481	-	28,481	30,000	-	30,000	30,000	-	30,000	-
Global Agriculture and Food Security Program	128,165	-	128,165	133,000	-	133,000	-	-	-	(133,000)
Transfer to Multilateral Trust Funds[19]	-	-	-	50,000	-	50,000	-	-	-	(50,000)
Middle East and North Africa Transition Fund	-	-	-	-	-	-	5,000	-	5,000	5,000

STATE OPERATIONS and FOREIGN ASSISTANCE REQUEST
($000)

	FY 2013 Enduring Actual	FY 2013 OCO Actual	FY 2013 Actual Total[1]	FY 2014 Estimate Enduring	FY 2014 Estimate OCO	FY 2014 Estimate Total	FY 2015 Request Enduring	FY 2015 Request OCO	FY 2015 Request Total	Increase / Decrease
International Monetary Fund	-	-	-	-	-	-	16,000	-	16,000	16,000
Export & Investment Assistance	(1,336,771)	-	(1,336,771)	(997,482)	-	(997,482)	(1,156,600)	-	(1,156,600)	(159,118)
Export-Import Bank	(1,053,137)	-	(1,053,137)	(841,500)	-	(841,500)	(1,021,200)	-	(1,021,200)	(179,700)
Overseas Private Investment Corporation (OPIC)	(331,103)	-	(331,103)	(211,055)	-	(211,055)	(203,100)	-	(203,100)	7,955
U.S. Trade and Development Agency	47,469	-	47,469	55,073	-	55,073	67,700	-	67,700	12,627
Related International Affairs Accounts	80,765	-	80,765	85,100	-	85,100	88,785	-	88,785	3,685
International Trade Commission	78,866	-	78,866	83,000	-	83,000	86,459	-	86,459	3,459
Foreign Claims Settlement Commission	1,899	-	1,899	2,100	-	2,100	2,326	-	2,326	226
Department of Agriculture	1,533,859	-	1,533,859	1,651,126	-	1,651,126	1,585,126	-	1,585,126	(66,000)
P.L. 480, Title II	1,359,358	-	1,359,358	1,466,000	-	1,466,000	1,400,000	-	1,400,000	(66,000)
McGovern-Dole International Food for Education and Child Nutrition Programs	174,501	-	174,501	185,126	-	185,126	185,126	-	185,126	-
Rescissions										
Total Rescissions State Operations	-	(1,109,700)	(1,109,700)	-	(427,296)	(427,296)	-	-	-	427,296
Diplomatic & Consular Programs (D&CP)	-	(1,109,700)	(1,109,700)	-	(427,296)	(427,296)	-	-	-	427,296
Ongoing Operations Worldwide	-	(1,109,700)	(1,109,700)	-	(427,296)	(427,296)	-	-	-	427,296
Worldwide Security Protection	-	-	-	-	-	-	-	-	-	-
Total Rescissions Foreign Operations	(400,000)	-	(400,000)	(23,000)	-	(23,000)	-	-	-	23,000
Export & Investment Assistance	(400,000)	-	(400,000)	(23,000)	-	(23,000)	-	-	-	23,000
Export-Import Bank	(400,000)	-	(400,000)	(23,000)	-	(23,000)	-	-	-	23,000

Footnotes

1/ The FY 2013 Actual Enduring reflects the full-year continuing resolution, reduced by the 0 032% for Security Category accounts and 0 02% for Non-Security accounts, as well as sequestration The FY 2013 Actual OCO reflects the full year Continuing Resolution reduced by sequestration

2/ The FY 2013 Actual reflects the following transfers: $450,000 transferred to Embassy Security Construction and Maintenance; $21 6 million transferred to Conflict Stabilization Operations; $5 5 million transferred to Educational and Cultural Exchange Programs; $730,000 transferred to Representation Expenses; $13 4 million from Buying Power Maintenance Account; $2 1 million transferred to Payment to the American Institute in Taiwan; and $100,000 transferred from Contributions to Peacekeeping Activities to the Diplomatic and Consular Programs The FY 2014 level reflects the following transfers: $21,800,000 transferred to Conflict Stabilization Operations; and $730,000 transferred to Representation Expenses

3/ The FY 2013 Actual includes $450,000 transferred from Diplomatic and Consular Programs to Embassy Security, Construction, and Maintenance

4/ The FY 2013 Actual level includes $21 6 million transferred from Diplomatic and Consular Programs to Conflict Stabilization Operations; the FY 2014 level includes $21 8 million transferred from Diplomatic and Consular programs

5/ The FY 2013 Actual includes $5 5 million transferred from Diplomatic and Consular Programs to Educational and Cultural Exchange Programs

6/ The FY 2013 Actual includes $730,000 transferred from Diplomatic and Consular Programs to Representation Expenses; the FY 2014 level includes $730,000 transferred from Diplomatic and Consular Programs

7/ The FY 2013 Actual level includes $277,000 transfer from Emergencies in the Diplomatic & Consular Services to Repatriation Loans Program Account

8/ The FY 2013 Actual level includes $13 4 million transferred to Diplomatic and Consular Services from Buying Power Maintenance Account

9/ The FY 2013 Actual includes $277,000 transferred from Emergencies in the Diplomatic and Consular Services to Repatriation Loans Program Account

10/ The FY 2013 Actual level includes $2 1 million transferred from Diplomatic and Consular Programs to Payment to the American Institute in Taiwan

11/ Authority requested to spending funding is derived from a reserve, authorized by section 4 of the International Chancery Center that consists of proceeds from past leases to foreign governments and one international organization

12/ The FY 2013 Actual level includes $100,000 transferred from Contributions to Peacekeeping Activities to the Diplomatic and Consular Programs

13/ The FY 2013 Enduring Actual level reflects the transfer of $4 4 million from the International Organizations and Programs account to the Global Health Programs - USAID account

STATE OPERATIONS and FOREIGN ASSISTANCE REQUEST
($000)

	FY 2013 Enduring Actual	FY 2013 OCO Actual	FY 2013 Actual Total[1]	FY 2014 Estimate Enduring	FY 2014 Estimate OCO	FY 2014 Estimate Total	FY 2015 Request Enduring	FY 2015 Request OCO	FY 2015 Request Total	Increase/ Decrease

14/ The FY 2013 OCO Actual level reflects the transfer of $15 million from the Foreign Military Financing account to the Transition Initiatives account

15/ The FY 2013 OCO Actual level reflects the transfer of $15 million from the International Narcotics Control and Law Enforcement account to the Complex Crises Fund account

16/ The FY 2013 OCO Actual level reflects the transfer of $223 667 million from the Foreign Military Financing account to the Economic Support Fund account

17/ The FY 2013 OCO Actual level reflects the transfer of $35 5 million from the Migration and Refugee Assistance account to the Economic Support Fund account

18/ The FY 2013 OCO Actual level reflects the transfer of $25 78 million from the International Narcotics Control and Law Enforcement account to the Economic Support Fund account

19/ FY 2014 Estimate levels include an anticipated transfer of $50 million from the Economic Support Fund account to the Multilateral Development Banks in accordance with sec 7060(c)(8) of the Consolidated Appropriations Act, 2014

20/ The FY 2013 OCO Actual level reflects the transfer of $87 14 million from the Foreign Military Financing account to the Peacekeeping Operations account

21/ The FY 2013 OCO Actual level reflects the transfer of $38 62 million from the International Narcotics Control and Law Enforcement account to the Peacekeeping Operations account

Statement of Performance

Performance Analysis

The diplomacy and development efforts of the Department of State and U.S. Agency for International Development (USAID) continue to make significant strides toward a more secure, democratic and prosperous world for the benefit of the American people and the international community. The Department and USAID have developed more relevant, measureable, and outcome oriented indicators that are used to assess progress against prior-year performance through examining trend data. The results of these efforts to improve strategic planning and performance management throughout the Department and USAID, both domestically and abroad, are detailed in the accompanying State Operations and Foreign Assistance Appendices of the Congressional Budget Justification (CBJ).

The FY 2014 - 2017 Joint State and USAID Strategic Plan

The establishment of the FY 2014-2017 Joint State and USAID Strategic Plan (JSP) reiterates the commitment of the Department and USAID to joint planning to implement foreign policy initiatives and investing effectively in foreign assistance programs. Moreover, the JSP will be used to inform the second Quadrennial Diplomacy and Development Review (QDDR). The JSP will be published at www.performance.gov concurrently with the FY 2015 Annual Performance Plan (APP) in March 2014.

Strategic Objectives

The strategic objectives of the JSP will serve as the primary basis for performance measurement, strategic analysis, and decision making for the Department and USAID. The strategic objectives will be expanded upon in the FY 2015 APP and will align with performance goals and a limited number of two-year Agency Priority Goals (APGs) supported by metrics that describe how the Department and USAID will advance the JSP goals.

Performance Goals

The GPRA Modernization Act of 2010 requires that agencies tie their annual performance information to the strategic objectives identified in their strategic plan. The primary method for accomplishing this link is through performance goals, which identify the specific, measurable, and attributable level of performance that the Department and USAID will strive to achieve and to which the agencies can be held accountable. The performance goals in the JSP will provide measurable progress towards the achievement of the strategic objectives in the Plan and reflect the Department and USAID strategic and management priorities. The majority of the performance goals will be measured annually; five of the performance goals have been identified as APGs and will have data available on a quarterly basis. Further information about the strategic goals and objectives of the new JSP is located on www.Performance.gov.

Performance Planning and Reporting

The performance indicators featured in Appendix 1 and Appendix 2 of the CBJ constitute the FY 2013 Annual Performance Report (APR) for the Department of State and USAID. The FY 2013 APR will close out performance reporting under the current goal structure. A new reporting framework of performance goals and performance indicators aligned to the FY 2014-2017 JSP will commence with the FY 2014 APR. The FY 2015 APP will consist of a series of performance plans that are organized around each strategic objective from the new JSP. It will outline performance goals, associated indicators, and accountable bureaus and offices responsible for accomplishing each performance goal. Concurrent with the release of theCBJ, the Department of State and USAID publish the joint FY 2015 Annual Performance Plan (APP) on www.performance.gov.

Evaluation

The Department and USAID have made major progress on putting in place frameworks for implementation of performance and impact evaluations as well as streamlined performance metrics that support evidence-based analysis and active use of performance information, including information from evaluations. These evaluations are used to determine what is working and what is not, which in turn provides evidence for programmatic and budgetary decisions.

The focus of the Department since issuance of the new evaluation policy in February 2012 has been capacity building and training of Department personnel to effectively plan for, execute, and manage evaluations. At the end of 2013 State completed or had in process over 70 evaluations and has over 100 planned for 2014. Further information about the Department's evaluation policy is located at www.state.gov/s/d/rm/rls/evaluation/2012/184556.htm.

To ensure country programs and strategies are achieving results, USAID introduced a new evaluation policy in 2011 that has been called "a model for other federal agencies" by the American Evaluation Association.. Under this policy, high-quality evaluations are completed for every major project and conducted by independent third parties. Findings must be action-oriented and should identify ways to apply the lessons learned. Based on these and other criteria, USAID had completed or had in process 350 evaluations by the end of FY 2013 and has close to 300 evaluations planned for FY 2014. More than 50 percent of completed evaluations led staff to make mid-course corrections and more than a third led to budgetary changes. USAID's commitment to evaluation is to improve development outcomes as well as to improve accountability. To ensure data is publicly available, USAID has built an accessible website where evaluations can be read and easily shared. Further information about USAID evaluations is located at www.usaid.gov/evaluation.

In summary, the Department of State and USAID engage in a variety of data collection, monitoring, evaluation, and analytical activities to assess progress against our goals and objectives, and to inform our programmatic and budgetary decisions.

This page intentionally left blank.

FY 2015 INTERNATIONAL AFFAIRS ENDURING PROGRAMS

Department of State
Summary of Appropriations
Enduring Budget

($ in thousands)	FY 2013 Actual	FY 2014 Estimate	FY 2015 Request	Increase / Decrease
Administration of Foreign Affairs	**8,812,550**	**9,788,858**	**9,584,025**	**-204,833**
State Programs	6,523,801	6,660,071	6,838,910	178,839
Diplomatic and Consular Programs[1/]	6,467,427	6,583,171	6,782,510	199,339
Ongoing Operations	5,126,217	4,715,920	4,654,395	-61,525
Worldwide Security Protection	1,341,210	1,867,251	2,128,115	260,864
Capital Investment Fund	56,374	76,900	56,400	-20,500
Embassy Security, Construction, and Maintenance[2/]	1,582,247	2,399,351	2,016,900	-382,451
Ongoing Operations	912,722	785,351	799,400	14,049
Worldwide Security Upgrades	669,525	1,614,000	1,217,500	-396,500
Other Administration of Foreign Affairs	706,502	729,436	728,215	-1,221
Conflict Stabilization Operations[3/]	21,594	21,800	0	-21,800
Office of Inspector General	59,575	69,406	73,400	3,994
Educational and Cultural Exchange Programs[/4]	559,180	560,000	577,900	17,900
Representation Expenses[5/]	7,660	8,030	7,679	-351
Protection of Foreign Missions and Officials	25,633	28,200	30,036	1,836
Emergencies in the Diplomatic and Consular Service[6/]	8,552	9,242	7,900	-1,342
Buying Power Maintenance Account[7/]	0	0	0	0
Repatriation Loans Program Account[8/]	1,651	1,537	1,300	-237
Payment to the American Institute in Taiwan[9/]	22,134	31,221	30,000	-1,221
Foreign Service Retirement and Disability Fund (non-add)	*158,900*	*158,900*	*158,900*	*0*
International Chancery Center[10/]	523	0	533	533
International Organizations	**3,290,126**	**3,031,281**	**4,035,914**	**1,004,633**
Contributions to International Organizations	1,376,338	1,265,762	1,517,349	251,587
Contributions for International Peacekeeping Activities[11/]	1,913,788	1,765,519	2,518,565	753,046
International Commissions (Function 300)	**112,964**	**125,917**	**115,633**	**-10,284**
International Boundary and Water Commission - S&E	41,162	44,000	45,415	1,415
International Boundary and Water Commission - Construction	27,620	33,438	26,461	-6,977
American Sections	11,312	12,499	12,311	-188
International Joint Commission	6,787	7,664	7,413	-251
International Boundary Commission	2,206	2,449	2,525	76
Border Environment Cooperation Commission	2,319	2,386	2,373	-13
International Fisheries Commissions	32,870	35,980	31,446	-4,534
Related Programs	**144,096**	**169,203**	**126,759**	**-42,444**
The Asia Foundation	16,139	17,000	12,000	-5,000
Center for Middle Eastern-Western Dialog	96	90	83	-7
Eisenhower Exchange Fellowship Program	191	400	400	0
Israeli Arab Scholarship Program	13	13	26	13
East-West Center	15,855	16,700	10,800	-5,900
National Endowment for Democracy	111,802	135,000	103,450	-31,550
TOTAL, Department of State Appropriations	**12,359,736**	**13,115,259**	**13,862,331**	**747,072**

Summary of Appropriations Footnotes:

1/ FY 2013 Actual reflects the following transfers: $450,000 transferred to Embassy Security, Construction, and Maintenance; $21.6 million transferred to Conflict Stabilization Operations; $5.5 million transferred to Educational and Cultural Exchange Programs; $730,000 transferred to Representation Expenses; $13.4 million from Buying Power Maintenance Account; $2.1 million transferred to Payment to the American Institute in Taiwan; and $100,000 transferred from Contributions to Peacekeeping Activities. The FY 2014 level reflects the following transfers: $21,800,000 transferred to Conflict Stabilization Operations; and $730,000 transferred to Representation Expenses.

2/ The FY 2013 Actual includes $450,000 transferred from Diplomatic and Consular Programs to Embassy Security, Construction, and Maintenance.

3/ The FY 2013 Actual level includes $21.6 million transferred from Diplomatic and Consular Programs to Conflict Stabilization Operations; the FY 2014 level includes $21.8 million transferred from Diplomatic and Consular Programs.

4/ The FY 2013 Actual includes $5.5 million transferred from Diplomatic and Consular Programs to Educational and Cultural Exchange Programs.

5/ The FY 2013 Actual includes $730,000 transferred from Diplomatic and Consular Programs to Representation Expenses; the FY 2014 level includes $730,000 transferred from Diplomatic and Consular Programs.

6/ The FY 2013 Actual level includes $277,000 transfer from Emergencies in the Diplomatic & Consular Services to Repatriation Loans Program Account.

7/ The FY 2013 Actual level includes $13.4 million transferred to Diplomatic and Consular Programs from Buying Power Maintenance Account.

8/ The FY 2013 Actual level includes $277,000 transfer to Repatriation Loans Program Account from Emergencies in the Diplomatic & Consular Services.

9/ The FY 2013 Actual level includes $2.1 million transferred from Diplomatic and Consular Programs to Payment to the American Institute in Taiwan.

10/ Authority requested to spending funding is derived from a reserve, authorized by section 4 of the International Chancery Center that consists of proceeds from past leases to foreign governments and one international organization.

11/ The FY 2013 Actual level includes $100,000 transferred from Contributions to Peacekeeping Activities to the Diplomatic and Consular Programs.

Diplomatic and Consular Programs

($ in thousands)	FY 2013 Actual[1]/	FY 2014 Estimate[2]/	FY 2015 Request	Increase / Decrease
Diplomatic and Consular Programs	9,646,419	7,974,280	8,335,935	361,655
Enduring[1][2]/	6,467,427	6,583,171	6,782,510	199,339
Ongoing Operations	5,126,217	4,715,920	4,654,395	-61,525
Worldwide Security Protection	1,341,210	1,867,251	2,128,115	260,864
Overseas Contingency Operations[3]/	3,178,992	1,391,109	1,553,425	162,316
Ongoing Operations	2,269,613	490,835	563,719	72,884
Worldwide Security Protection	909,379	900,274	989,706	89,432

1/ FY 2013 Actual reflects the following transfers: $450,000 transferred to Embassy Security, Construction, and Maintenance; $21.6 million transferred to Conflict Stabilization Operations; $5.5 million transferred to Educational and Cultural Exchange Programs; $730,000 transferred to Representation Expenses; $13.4 million transferred from Buying Power Maintenance Account; $2.1 million transferred to Payment to the American Institute in Taiwan; and $100,000 transferred from Contributions to Peacekeeping Activities.

2/The FY 2014 level reflects the following transfers: $21,800,000 transferred to Conflict Stabilization Operations; and $730,000 transferred to Representation Expenses.

3/ The FY 2013 Actual includes $2.5 million transferred from Diplomatic and Consular Programs OCO to Educational and Cultural Exchange Programs.

The FY 2015 enduring budget request for Diplomatic and Consular Programs (D&CP) – the State Department's principal operating appropriation – totals $6.8 billion. This funding provides for the core people, infrastructure, and programs that conduct official U.S. relations with foreign governments and international organizations, as well as to support U.S. businesses and to reach foreign audiences through public diplomacy. The request supports the Department's global engagement, as a national security institution, and builds relationships with other nations to advance American interests and values.

D&CP - Ongoing Operations

The D&CP request provides $4.7 billion for Ongoing Operations. This funding supports essential diplomatic personnel and programs worldwide. It also supports the infrastructure for U.S. Government agencies and employees at 275 diplomatic and consular posts in 190 countries around the globe.

The current services request provides funding to support D&CP-funded bureaus and programs at their FY 2014 operating level, supports the recurring costs for constructed overseas facilities, and reflects efficiency savings adjustments in support of the President's focus on fiscal discipline and spending restraint. Bureaus and programs continue to pursue efficiency savings to offset the impact of domestic and overseas inflation. It also supports cost for the American pay increase, locally engaged wage increases, absorption of other inflationary costs and adjustment of resources associated with payroll execution.

Requested program changes continue priority domestic and overseas initiatives, including Economic Statecraft, Asia Rebalance, and Cyber Security. The Department's core staffing levels reflect a lower rate of growth, with funding for 53 new Department positions, including 43 Foreign Service positions and 10 Civil Service positions. The Department's "Economic Statecraft" initiative comprises the largest segment of this growth including 23 new positions with a particular emphasis on Euro-Asian, Near East Asia, and

Latin American countries. The Department's Economic Statecraft efforts, coordinated through the Bureau of Economic and Business Affairs, complement the five overarching goals of the SelectUSA program, which seeks to highlight the advantages the United States offers as a location for business and investment. Additional focus is placed on alternative and renewable energy, power generation markets, and cyber-security issues including 11 new positions for the Energy Bureau and three for the Secretary's Coordinator for Cyber Issues office. Other personnel-related increases over FY 2014 include the creation and implementation of the Centralized Overseas Retirement Development (CORD) account that will address the FSN/LES liabilities among the 230 varied retirement plans.

The request includes a total of $521.2 million for public diplomacy to further U.S. foreign policy goals by informing and influencing foreign opinion. Public diplomacy efforts include countering misinformation about U.S. society and policies, strengthening relationships between Americans and foreign publics, and shaping worldwide information campaigns on issues such as climate change, food security, water, and global health. The public diplomacy request includes resources for three positions that support the Asia Rebalance initiative. Funding for a new rapid response program is requested to advance people-to-people relationships around the world in countries experiencing conflict or crisis, dramatic leadership transition, and significant societal transformation for exchange activities.

This request also continues the Department's Security Realignment initiative, shifting 421 positions and $141.8 million from Ongoing Operations to Worldwide Security Protection (WSP) for costs associated with International Cooperative Administrative Support Services (ICASS) Marine Security Guard detachments, and overseas security positions reporting to Diplomatic Security.

D&CP - Category Descriptions

Human Resources: $2,334 million
These resources support American Salaries for overseas and domestic positions, the Human Resources Bureau (HR), and the Foreign Service Institute. American salary costs for Public Diplomacy and Worldwide Security Protection are included in this category.

In fulfillment of the Department's goals, HR will address critical human capital areas:
- Effectively recruiting, hiring, developing and assigning employees in order to strengthen U.S. diplomacy.
- Aligning staffing with critical foreign policy objectives.
- Improving IT infrastructure and Shared Services capabilities to ensure efficient delivery of HR services.

The Department will also continue its support of FSI's strong partnerships with regional centers in Frankfurt, Ft. Lauderdale, Charleston, Manila and Bangkok, providing cost effective and efficient training opportunities under FSI auspices to the Department's worldwide workforce.

Overseas Program: $1,839 million
These resources support the Department's global diplomacy efforts, including the following bureaus and offices: African Affairs, East Asian and Pacific Affairs, European and Eurasian Affairs, International Organizations Affairs, Office of the Medical Director, Near Eastern Affairs, South and Central Asian Affairs, and Western Hemisphere Affairs; as well as related costs for post-assignment travel and local staff separation liabilities.

The resources included in this category are responsible for managing U.S. foreign policy through bilateral and multilateral relationships. Bureaus will continue political and economic reporting and analysis of interest to the U.S. Funding will support hosting of and participation in various international workshops, meetings and multilateral activities in the U.S. and abroad. This request regularizes resources associated with the Conflict Stabilization Operations into the D&CP request, consistent with recent Congressional action

This category includes $387.9 million for bureau-managed Public Diplomacy programs and operations. The Department's public diplomacy program makes significant contributions to U.S. foreign policy and national security. One of its key tasks is the strategic development of prolific people-to-people relationships around the world that persuasively advocates U.S. foreign policy goals and quickly counters misinformation about U.S. society and policies.

Diplomatic Policy and Support: $795.7 million
These resources support the Department's central policy and management functions, including the following bureaus and offices: Office of the Secretary; Consular Affairs; Democracy, Human Rights, and Labor; Political-Military Affairs; International Security and Nonproliferation; Public Affairs; Office to Monitor and Combat Trafficking in Persons; Legislative Affairs; Chief of Protocol; the Under-Secretary for Management; Budget and Planning; Comptroller and Global Financial Services; Administration; Information Resource Management; Oceans and International Environmental and Scientific Affairs; Office of Population & International Migration; Arms Control, Verification and Compliance; Economic and Business Affairs; Energy Resources; Intelligence and Research; and the Office of the Legal Adviser.

Offices and bureaus within this category are responsible for many of the activities that support the Department's global footprint. For instance, the Bureau of Administration manages the Department's global supply chain, including transportation of goods, diplomatic pouches and mail, and acquisition of goods and services from several U.S. and foreign locations. This bureau provides a viable platform for the diplomatic component of smart power, maintaining energy efficient, sustainable, secure, and functional facilities in the U.S. and overseas for State and other agency employees. As of FY 2013, the Department was pleased to report that 48 percent of its owned and delegated domestic real estate portfolio had been certified by independent parties (e.g., LEED, Green Globes, Energy Star) as sustainable and/or energy efficient, exceeding the goal established by the Office of Management and Budget and the Council of Environmental Quality.

The request includes resources to support new positions for the Office of the Coordinator for Cyber Issues; technology upgrades for the Operations Center; grants officer representatives within the Bureau of Democracy Human Rights and Labor; and enhancements to the Joint Financial Management System. The request also includes funding for four positions for the Bureau of Intelligence and Research (INR). Three positions will support INR's increasing cyber requirements and one will ensure timely intelligence support to Department policymakers.

Security Programs: $1,814 million
These resources support the Department's security programs and policies. This includes the Bureau of Diplomatic Security (DS), the Bureau of Counterterrorism, the Office of Foreign Missions, and security components of the Office of the Medical Director, Bureau of Administration, Bureau of Intelligence and Research, Bureau of International Security and Non-Proliferation, Bureau of Information Resource Management, Bureau of Human Resources, regional bureaus, and the Foreign Service Institute.

This enduring request provides $2.1 billion, for DS and partner bureaus to help ensure the security of diplomatic and consular personnel, property, and information. WSP funding supports ongoing core functions such as the worldwide local guard program, high threat protection needs, security technology, armored vehicles, cyber security, and diplomatic couriers. WSP funding will address security challenges in dangerous places where diplomatic operations are most critical, through the following program priorities:

Effective and Efficient Risk-Based Security: DS will continue increasing efficiency by calling on the skills of partner agencies in the design and implementation of joint security efforts. DS will build on the successes in researching and developing solutions and technologies that can be leveraged by DS's skilled personnel. Further, DS will maximize the use of the Department's performance management culture by evaluating large programs in keeping with the DS Evaluation Plan.

Provide Robust Information Security Protection: Cyber security is a highly important mission in support of diplomacy. DS stays vigilant in monitoring network traffic, detecting and responding to cyber security incidents, ensuring compliance with Department regulations, and identifying potential system security vulnerabilities. DS assesses emerging security technologies that protect the Department's technology assets and allow users the flexibility needed to keep pace with changing environments.

Threat Investigation and Analysis (TIA): Aside from managing the 24/7 DS Command Center, TIA directs, coordinates, and conducts counterterrorism, and protective intelligence investigations and intelligence analysis involving terrorist threats, incidents, and/or hostile activities directed against all U.S. government personnel, facilities, and interests abroad under the authority of the Chief of Mission (COM), as well as the Secretary of State, Department of State employees and property domestically, U.S. foreign policy interests, and foreign diplomatic officials and facilities located in the United States. Through several initiatives and programs, including the Overseas Security Advisory Council, the Security Environment Threat List, Rewards for Justice, and the Joint Terrorism Task Force, TIA assists foreign governments and private companies, as well as other U.S. government agencies, on issues related to terrorism, global and domestic.

Countermeasures (C): C leverages the latest physical and technical countermeasures for use in facilities around the world to protect against a wide range of security threats. C is responsible for the management and direction of the development of standards, policies, and procedures associated with these countermeasures. Moreover, C supports the operability of technical security equipment at all Department of State overseas missions using staff at 77 engineering services centers, offices, and technical security offices worldwide. C deploys physical security systems such as armored vehicles, blast and ballistic-resistant perimeter guard towers, access controls such as vehicle barriers, anti-climb and anti-ram fences, temporary modular protection systems designed to mitigate blast, overhead and forced entry/blast resistant threats, vehicular anti-ram barriers, and compound access control enclosures.

C will continue to innovate, building on the success initiatives of such as the Streetscape Vehicular Anti-Ram and Landscape Vehicular Anti-Ram programs. These barriers answered an industry-wide call to merge perimeter security with the environment. DS designed and tested anti-ram terrain features, boulders, lampposts, bus shelters and benches. Other development and successful testing include the DS non-proprietary Modular Guard Tower System and the Hardened Alternative Trailer System (HATS). Finally, the Diplomatic Courier Service will continue to provide its unique service of secure and expeditious delivery of classified and sensitive material to our U.S. missions abroad.

High Threat Programs (HTP) and International Programs (IP): As U.S. diplomacy pursues in challenging security environments, DS will provide necessary security support. In light of global events in 2012, DS created HTP. HTP's focus is to provide critical security support in high threat/high risk posts. While HTP and IP handle different posts based on threat level, the general duties carried out by the directorates are similar. HTP and IP administer vital security programs such as the Local Guard Program, Surveillance Detection, and Residential Security that support the implementation of U.S. foreign policy at overseas missions. HTP and IP also work to continue critical contract oversight and management of private security contractors working overseas.

Training (T): T, in coordination with the Foreign Service Institute, develops and implements training and professional development programs for the Department and other U.S. government personnel and dependents deployed overseas. DS will continue to prepare foreign affairs and other U.S. government personnel posted overseas under Chief of Mission (COM) authority through the Foreign Affairs Counter Threat (FACT) course to the best of DS' resources.

DS will continue to increase the number of DS special agents trained in the High Threat Tactical Course (HTTC). DS provides strategic security support through its Office of Mobile Security Deployments. Through the Office of Anti-Terrorism Assistance (ATA), DS builds the law enforcement and counterterrorism capacities of partner nations. ATA also manages the Special Program for Embassy Augmentation and Response (SPEAR), which supports foreign guards and police who help to protect US missions abroad. Through the Weapons of Mass Destruction Countermeasures Program, DS personnel train COM personnel how to best protect themselves in the event of Chemical, Biological, Radiological, or Nuclear (CBRN) attack. Additionally, the Department of Homeland Security established DS as a Center of Excellence for instructor-led cyber security training in 2010. DS continues to provide comprehensive role-based cyber security education and training programs to secure infrastructure design and development, incident analysis, and defensive skills and capabilities of Department personnel and those of other agencies.

Security Infrastructure (SI): SI is responsible for the initial and periodic vetting of all employees and contractors whose positions require security clearances, access to sensitive intelligence, or public trust certifications. It is also responsible for the security of classified and sensitive information produced or retained in the Department's information technology systems, and the physical and cyber security of Top Secret/Sensitive Compartmented Information produced or retained in the Department's intelligence systems and holdings. The Office of Personnel Security and Suitability conducts 36,000 personnel security investigations each year to ensure that granting an individual access to classified information is clearly consistent with the interests of national security. The Office of Computer Security ensures the Department's need for a safe and secure communications platform from which to conduct diplomacy. The office protects over 125,000 IT assets at 275 diplomatic and consular posts around the globe.

Domestic Operations (DO): DO manages a full spectrum of criminal and special investigations to include violations of laws regarding U.S. passports and visas, defensive counterintelligence programs, and interagency liaison functions in the areas of law enforcement and counterintelligence. DO is the entity overseeing the responsibility for the safety and security of the Secretary of State, Deputy Secretaries of State, U.S. Permanent Representative to the United Nations, certain visiting foreign dignitaries, and other persons of interest. It is also responsible for protecting resident foreign diplomatic personnel, embassies, and consulates. DO is the U.S. lead for security planning for major international events such as the Olympics, World Cup, and other global events attended by heads of state and other diplomatic dignitaries. DO manages the protective security support programs for over 100 Department sites, including numerous annexes in the greater Washington area, as well as passport and Office of Foreign Missions (OFM) offices throughout the United States.

WSP Partner Bureaus: WSP funding also supports IRM's information technology security and information assurance programs, domestic emergency management planning conducted by the Bureau of Administration, Operational Medicine support to high threat posts provided by MED, and National Level Exercise support coordinated by CT.

Resource Detail - Funding Category for D&CP

($ in thousands)	FY 2013 Actual[1]/	FY 2014 Estimate[2]/	FY 2015 Request	Increase / Decrease
Total Diplomatic and Consular Programs	**6,467,427**	**6,583,171**	**6,782,510**	**199,339**
Human Resources	**2,388,085**	**2,431,191**	**2,334,377**	**-96,814**
American Salaries, Central Account	2,195,984	2,256,396	2,164,477	-91,919
Public Diplomacy American Salaries (non-add)	*130,136*	*131,713*	*133,306*	*1,593*
Iraq Operations American Salaries (non-add)	*350*	*-*	*-*	*-*
WSP - American Salaries (non-add)	*216,963*	*255,866*	*331,885*	*76,019*
Foreign Service Institute	77,761	67,522	59,826	-7,696
Human Resources	114,340	107,273	103,405	-3,868
Human Resources Initiative	-	-	6,669	6,669
Overseas Programs	**1,886,549**	**1,661,631**	**1,838,543**	**176,912**
African Affairs	228,206	208,118	211,111	2,993
Ambassador's Fund for Cultural Preservation	5,750	5,750	5,750	-
Centralized Overseas Retirement Development	-	-	33,300	33,300
Conflict Stabilization Operations	-	-	43,900	43,900
East Asian and Pacific Affairs	190,780	169,713	167,441	-2,272
European and Eurasian Affairs	353,251	332,654	317,959	-14,695
FSN Separation Liability Trust Fund	35,675	7,048	7,048	-
International Conferences	18,160	17,256	17,256	-
International Organization Affairs	29,092	26,277	25,937	-340
Medical Director	21,047	22,532	21,864	-668
Near Eastern Affairs	215,638	126,158	187,872	61,714
Iraq Operations (non-add)	*60,878*	*-*	*62,287*	*62,287*
Post Assignment Travel	183,347	169,345	173,345	4,000
South and Central Asian Affairs	99,933	55,343	88,576	33,233
Western Hemisphere Affairs	164,038	151,848	149,263	-2,585
Public Diplomacy	341,632	369,589	387,921	18,332
Diplomatic Policy and Support	**915,325**	**783,387**	**795,652**	**12,265**
Administration (including GSA Rent)	436,793	320,067	330,404	10,337
GSA Rent (non-add)	*166,148*	*169,652*	*173,142*	*3,490*

($ in thousands)	FY 2013 Actual[1]/	FY 2014 Estimate[2]/	FY 2015 Request	Increase / Decrease
Arms Control, Verification and Compliance	14,600	13,904	14,413	509
Budget and Planning	-	6,839	10,651	3,812
Chief of Protocol	4,345	2,698	2,703	5
Comptroller and Global Financial Services	81,187	73,973	76,029	2,056
Consular Affairs (excluding Border Security Program)	-	-	-	-
Democracy, Human Rights and Labor	9,332	11,627	13,657	2,030
Economic and Business Affairs	7,234	8,208	8,421	213
Energy Resources	4,421	4,188	5,088	900
Information Resource Management	202,030	193,423	175,804	-17,619
Intelligence and Research	13,662	15,908	18,399	2,491
International Security and Nonproliferation	17,289	16,289	16,698	409
Legal Advisor	13,759	12,841	12,848	7
Legislative Affairs	3,457	2,329	2,332	3
Management	4,969	4,257	4,259	2
Oceans and International Environmental and Scientific Affairs	14,392	15,898	15,917	19
Political-Military Affairs	9,682	9,201	10,347	1,146
Population & International Migration	657	628	634	6
Public Affairs	13,830	13,123	13,141	18
Trafficking in Persons	3,142	2,204	2,205	1
Office of the Secretary	53,697	55,782	61,702	5,920
Security Programs	**1,277,468**	**1,706,962**	**1,813,938**	**106,976**
Counterterrorism	13,828	9,870	9,875	5
Diplomatic Security	131,223	77,940	-	-77,940
Iraq Operations (non-add)	*21,246*	-	-	-
Office of Foreign Missions	8,170	7,767	7,833	66
Worldwide Security Protection	1,124,247	1,611,385	1,796,230	184,845
WSP Current Services - Bureau Managed (non-add)	*1,138,281*	*1,124,247*	*1,648,327*	*524,080*
WSP Program Changes (non-add)	*-14,034*	*487,138*	*147,903*	*-339,235*

1/ The FY 2013 Actual reflects the following transfers: $13.4 million transferred from the Buying Power Maintenance Account; $730,000 transferred to Representation Expenses; $2.1 million transferred to the Payment to the American Institute in Taiwan; $450,000 transferred to Embassy Security, Construction, and Maintenance; $5.5 million transferred to Educational and Cultural Exchange Program; $21.6 million transferred to Conflict Stabilization Operations; and $100,000 transferred from Contributions to Peacekeeping Activities.

2/ FY 2014 Estimate reflects the following transfers: $730,000 transferred to Representation Expenses; $21.8 million transferred to Conflict Stabilization Operations.

Resource Detail - Highlights of Budget Changes for D&CP

	D&CP Direct	D&CP PD	D&CP Ongoing Operations (Direct & PD)	Worldwide Security Protection	D&CP Total
FY 2014 Estimate	$4,214,618	$501,302	4,715,920	$1,867,251	6,583,171
Built-in Changes					
Base Adjustments	**-108,494**	**0**	**-108,494**	**0**	**-108,494**
Facility Operating Cost	6,506	0	6,506	0	6,506
Operational Level Adjustment	-115,000	0	-115,000	0	-115,000
Anticipated Wage & Price Requirements	**54,427**	**9,761**	**64,188**	**39,505**	**103,693**
American Pay Increase	24,841	1,422	26,263	5,900	32,163
Locally Engaged Staff Wage and Step Increase	25,996	4,117	30,113	15,546	45,659
Overseas Price Inflation	0	2,961	2,961	11,258	14,219
Domestic Inflation & Absorption of Current Services	100	1,261	1,361	6,043	7,404
GSA Rents	3,490	0	3,490	758	4,248
Total, Built-in Changes	**-54,067**	**9,761**	**-44,306**	**39,505**	**-4,801**
Total, Current Services	**4,160,551**	**511,063**	**4,671,614**	**1,906,756**	**6,578,370**
Program Changes					
Human Resources	-30,243	0	-30,243	0	-30,243
Overseas Programs	72,808	10,164	82,972	0	82,972
Diplomatic Policy and Support	7,910	0	7,910	0	7,910
Security Programs	-77,858	0	-77,858	221,359	143,501
Total, Program Changes	**-27,383**	**10,164**	**-17,219**	**221,359**	**204,140**
Total	**4,133,168**	**521,227**	**4,654,395**	**2,128,115**	**6,782,510**

1/ FY 2014 Estimate reflects the following transfers: $730,000 transferred to Representation Expenses; $21.8 million transferred to Conflict Stabilization Operations.

IT Central Fund

($ in thousands)	FY 2013 Actual	FY 2014 Estimate	FY 2015 Request	Increase / Decrease
Capital Investment Fund	56,374	76,900	56,400	-20,500
Expedited Passport Fees	167,756	163,181	160,387	-2,794
Total IT Central Fund	224,130	240,081	216,787	-23,294

The Department of State's FY 2015 request of $56.4 million for the Capital Investment Fund (CIF) will support greater consolidation, improve efficiency, and support enhanced customer service; modernization of critical information technology systems and infrastructure; and maintain essential services that provide critical IT functions to both domestic and foreign consumers. Combined with Expedited Passport Fees collected by the Department, the IT Central Fund will provide a total of $216.8 million for priority IT investments and modernization activities.

Department of State's Information Technology Strategic Plan (ITSP) FY 2014 through FY 2016 continues the Department's vision of positioning secure information technology as a critical enabler of U.S. diplomacy and the protection of national and economic security interests. This new Plan focuses on five strategic goals:

- Goal 1: Mobile Diplomacy - ensures that our diplomats can securely use mobile devices and access Information Technology (IT) systems and data anytime, anywhere. Sub-goals are:

    Goal 1.1 – End User Devices

    Goal 1.2 – Access

    Goal 1.3 – Applications

- Goal 2: Digital Diplomacy - enhances collaboration and information sharing among our internal and external stakeholders ensuring that our diplomats and development experts can communicate securely. Sub-goals are:

    Goal 2.1 – External Outreach and Collaboration

    Goal 2.2 – Foreign Affairs Agency Collaboration and Knowledge Management

    Goal 2.3 – Next generation e-mail and information management

    Goal 2.4 – Analytics for collaboration

- Goal 3: Mission and Management systems – modernizes and integrates enterprise applications to exploit technology, provide comprehensive functional capabilities, and enhance services to U.S. citizens and other stakeholders.   Sub-goals are:

    Goal 3.1 – Public services

    Goal 3.2 – Integration

    Goal 3.3 – Rapid application evolution

- Goal 4: Global Infrastructure - provides a secure, robust, worldwide, web-based infrastructure to U.S. agencies operating overseas under Chief of Mission authority as well as State employees.   Sub-goals are:

> Goal 4.1 – Foreign Affairs Network (FAN)
>
> Goal 4.2 – Cloud Computing
>
> Goal 4.3 – Green IT
>
> Goal 4.4 – Life-cycle Management
>
> Goal 4.5 – Cyber Security

- Goal 5: IT Leadership – ensures effective governance of IT resources focusing on accountability for performance and service delivery with a highly trained workforce. Sub-goals are:

> Goal 5.1 – Governance
>
> Goal 5.2 – Centralized shared services
>
> Goal 5.3 – Enhanced customer service
>
> Goal 5.4 – Workforce development and training

The Department's IT environment will deliver a set of vital tools and information products to reach the foreign public and engage effectively in the global competition for ideas and values. State will capitalize on secure mobile technologies, social media, knowledge management tools, enterprise system monitoring, and the integration of core IT systems to provide better information analysis and a more productive work environment. The infrastructure will support other U.S. Government agencies operating overseas through an environmentally sustainable, cost-efficient, integrated platform that promotes inter-agency collaboration and coordination. The following FY 2015 priorities include:

- Expanding the use of mobile technology, to include a diversified catalog of secure end-user services and devices.
- Continuing the development of the FAN. This extends cloud Infrastructure as a Service (IaaS) to other Federal agencies operating overseas.
- Continuing the development of the Department's private cloud computing service, providing a full range of infrastructure, software, and data services to internal and external customers. This includes leveraging continued investments in the Enterprise Server Operations Centers (ESOCs) data center consolidation initiative, and the modernization of our global network infrastructure.
- Continuing the modernization of the Department's major functional systems, which operate as enterprise-wide centrally managed shared services (e.g. logistics, financial management, and human resource management), with data standardization, system interoperability, integrated management reporting and mobile delivery.
- Continuing the investment in global training for IT specialists and end users, focusing on use of distance learning, online courses, and knowledge sharing.

IT Central Funds by Goal

($ in thousands)	FY 2013 Actual	FY 2014 Estimate	FY 2015 Request	Increase / Decrease
Goal One: Mobile Diplomacy	**46,363**	**70,866**	**61,722**	**-9,144**
Foreign Post Telephones	280	3,300	3,570	270
Global IT Modernization	45,822	62,487	53,775	-8,712
Mobile Computing	261	5,079	4,377	-702
Goal Two: Digital Diplomacy	**40,766**	**19,396**	**14,158**	**-5,238**
Department SharePoint Services	4,238	2,543	1,943	-600
Emergency Health Record (EMR)	-	-	4,615	4,615
Enterprise Application Integration (EAI)	696	885	-	-885
Enterprise Data Warehouse	2,471	2,500	2,500	-
Global eTravel (GeT) Program	4,500	3,968	2,100	-1,868
Messaging Services, Email, and Remote Connectivity	15,657	9,500	3,000	-6,500
Post Administrative Software Suite (PASS)	10,655	-	-	
Goal Two Other[1]/	2,549	-	-	-
Goal Three: Mission and Management Systems	**53,582**	**62,355**	**57,929**	**-4,426**
Integrated Logistics Management System (ILMS)	20,210	20,000	19,612	-388
Global Foreign Affairs Compensation System (GFACS)	17,839	13,140	20,481	7,341
Support for Legacy Compensation System	1,597	6,630	6,130	-500
Integrated Personnel Management System (IPMS)	5,309	6,410	6,622	212
Joint Financial Management System (JFMS)	6,257	5,119	2,778	-2,341
Centralizing Financial Systems	-	3,248	-	-3,248
Mandatory Compliance	-	1,500	-	-1,500
Maximo Asset Management Software	-	1,366	-	-1,366
Goal Three Other[2]/	2,370	4,942	2,306	-2,636
Goal Four: Global Infrastructure	**69,519**	**72,649**	**71,524**	**-1,125**
Bandwidth Management Services	9,127	-	-	-
Enterprise Server Operations Center (ESOC)	18,768	29,908	23,500	-6,408
Enterprise Software Licensing and Maintenance	27,814	27,904	39,046	11,142
Foreign Affairs Network (FAN)	5,509	5,250	3,750	-1,500

($ in thousands)	FY 2013 Actual	FY 2014 Estimate	FY 2015 Request	Increase / Decrease
Internet Protocol Version 6 (IPv6)	-	3,500	2,500	-1,000
Goal Four Other[3]/	8,301	6,087	2,728	-3,359
Goal Five: IT Leadership	**13,900**	**14,815**	**11,454**	**-3,361**
FSI Corporate Systems - STMS	4,374	2,000	1,300	-700
FSI Instructional Support (SAIT)	3,175	4,000	4,000	-
FSI Learning Infrastructure	2,513	3,000	3,000	-
E-Gov Lines of Business	642	815	654	-161
IT Capital Planning	3,196	5,000	2,500	-2,500
Total IT Central Fund	**224,130**	**240,081**	**216,787**	**-23,294**

1/ Goal Two Other includes $1,098,000 for e-Diplomacy, $1,298,000 for Video Conferencing, and $153,000 for Voice Technology for FY 2013.

2/ Goal Three Other includes $1,806,000 for Central Resource Management System (CRMS) and $500,000 for the Innovation Fund in FY 2015. The Centralizing Financial Systems, Mandatory Compliance, and Maximo Asset Management Software programs have been removed from the IT Central Fund.

3/ Goal Four Other includes $3,590,000 for Enterprise Network Management, $104,000 for Domestic Technical Services, $1,155,000 for Public Key Infrastructure (PKI), and $3,452,000 for Secure Voice Program in FY 2013. Goal 4 Other includes $6,085,000 for Beltsville Information Management Center (BIMC) and $2,000 for Domestic Technical Services in FY 2014. The FY 2015 Request includes $1,778,000 for Information Assurance and $950,000 for BIMC.

Border Security Program

($ in thousands)	FY 2013 Actual	FY 2014 Estimate	FY 2015 Request	Increase / Decrease
Border Security Program	2,723,661	2,876,933	3,204,254	327,321

The FY 2015 request provides $3.2 billion for the Border Security Program (BSP). The Department of State's Border Security Program (BSP) provides protection to Americans overseas and contributes to the security of the nation's borders. The program is managed by the Bureau of Consular Affairs (CA), and is a core element of the coordinated national effort to deny individuals who threaten the country entry into the United States, while facilitating the entry of legitimate travelers.

The BSP uses revenue from consular fees and surcharges to fund consular programs and activities. These fees include Machine Readable Visa fees; Western Hemisphere Travel Surcharges; a Passport Security Surcharge; Immigrant Visa Security Surcharge; Diversity Immigrant Visa Security Surcharge; and H-1B and L Fraud Prevention and Detection Fees.

The FY 2015 request provides for the consular services outlined below, including overseas citizen services, consular facility costs, and investigative resources to support the Visa and Passport Security Strategy.

CONSULAR PROJECT INITIATIVES: $2,018.6 million

Consular Systems Technology: $277.1 million
Consular Systems Technology (CST) supports worldwide consular information systems operations, maintenance, and modernization. CST includes several major investments, including Consular One, which consolidates and modernizes all consular applications under a common IT application framework, enabling the Department to improve system functionality and add new consular capabilities. CST also manages several application packages to support citizens with unplanned or emergency needs; support task force groups in Washington, DC, and overseas when a crisis arises that endangers citizens' lives; and to maintain the Department's website, which provides extensive data on travel requirements, in-country conditions, and options for American citizens residing abroad who require assistance from the local consulate or embassy.

Domestic Executive Support Costs: $32.8 million
Domestic Executive Support supports the domestic executive offices associated with the development, broad supervision, and coordination of the worldwide consular programs and policy for the Bureau of Consular Affairs. Funding supports operational costs for CA's Front Office, Office of Policy Coordination, Office of the Comptroller, and the Executive Office.

Document Integrity, Training and Anti-Fraud Programs: $15.0 million
This initiative supports enhanced U.S. border protection and security through strengthening the integrity of U.S. visas and passports in addition to fraud prevention as it relates to Overseas Citizen Services issues. Funding will continue to support passport and visa fraud prevention as well as expanded H-1B and L visa fraud detection efforts.

Visa Processing: $73.4 million
The Visa Office is the Department's central authority on the visa function and handles all aspects of the visa issuance process. FY 2015 funding will support ongoing operations at the National Visa Center

(NVC), the Kentucky Consular Center (KCC) and the Visa Office headquarters operations in Washington, DC. In FY 2015, the Department will partner with the National Counterterrorism Center to implement a new visa screening program aiming to significantly decrease administrative processing time for hundreds of thousands of nonimmigrant visas.

Passport Directorate: $709.4 million
The Passport Directorate line item includes activities previously included under Passport Operations, Passport Facilities, and Consular Affairs Domestic Support (now renamed Passport Support). The Passport Directorate provides accurate and secure U.S. Passport documents, responds effectively to the needs of U.S. passport customers, and strengthens management and delivery capabilities.

In FY 2015, the Department estimates passport workload will be 15.8 million travel documents (13.9 million passport books and 1.9 million passport cards). The Department will begin phased implementation of the new, more secure, Next Generation Passport, which will be developed in FY 2014.

Presenting up-to-date, comfortable, and safe spaces for the public at agencies is one of many facets in providing a positive customer experience. Passport Facilities costs include maintenance services, renovations, telephone systems, utilities, furniture, and office equipment. The FY 2015 Request will maintain the infrastructure of existing passport agencies nationwide.

American Citizen Services (ACS): $8.6 million
The safety and welfare of American citizens abroad, particularly in times of crisis, is one of the Department's core duties. Funding in FY 2015 will allow the Department to engage in bilateral and multilateral meetings to strengthen crisis assistance to citizens; monitor international compliance with treaties such as the Hague Abduction Convention; train federal, state, and local officials on consular notification and access issues, and operate routine programs such as voter assistance. FY 2015 funding will also allow ACS to meet its protection responsibilities for American citizens overseas through programs for crisis management, protection of children, victims of crime, and U.S. citizens residing and traveling abroad, voter assistance programs, and emergency support to destitute American citizens.

Consular Affairs Overseas Support: $902.3 million
This activity covers overseas expenses of the Border Security program. These costs include start-up and recurring costs for overseas staff such as program support costs for visa consumables and supplies (visa foils and card stock); the Global Support Services (GSS); International Cooperative Administrative Support Services (ICASS); CA Post Allotments (collection of MRV bank fees from applicants; and equipment for consular agents; and support for Consular Management Assessment Team (CMAT); LES and U.S. Direct Hire non-salary support; and consular-related human resources support.

BORDER SECURITY STAFF/AMERICAN SALARIES (AMSALS): $570.1 million

Border Security staff costs include domestic and overseas positions in the Bureau of Consular Affairs and Diplomatic Security. Funding also covers selected domestic positions supporting consular activities within the Department's Operations Center, Bureau of Administration, Bureau for Counterterrorism, Office of the Legal Advisor, Foreign Service Institute, and Information Resource Management. The FY 2015 request will fund 153 new positions to support the BSP, including 86 domestic consular positions, 10 Assistant Regional Security Officer-Investigator (ARSO-I) positions for Diplomatic Security, and 57 overseas consular officer positions, of which up to 35 may be Limited Non-career Appointments (LNAs). The overseas positions are necessary to keep pace with demand, workload, and the Department's ability to continue meeting the President's goal to interview 80 percent of applicants within three weeks as established by Executive Order 13597. The domestic positions will to support consular programs managed within CA.

BORDER SECURITY SUPPORT/DEPARTMENT OF STATE PARTNERS: $458.6 million

Bureau of Administration (A): $60.2 million
The Bureau of Administration manages the rent and leasing for all consular domestic facilities including CA's headquarters building (SA-17) in Washington, DC. Funding for A bureau also supports facilities maintenance, custodial services, and utilities costs for the Portsmouth Consular Center (PCC), the Kentucky Consular Center (KCC), and the Charleston Regional Center (CRC).

Diplomatic Security (DS): $59.4 million
DS uniformed protection officers guard all domestic CA facilities. In addition, DS plays an important role in border security by coordinating and facilitating investigations involving U.S. passports and visas. DS investigates and coordinates fraudulent issuance, acquisition, and use of U.S. passports; and international visa fraud cases including fraudulent issuance, procurement, counterfeiting and forgery of U.S. visas. In coordination with CA, DS also investigates fraudulent document vendors, bribery, alien smuggling or trafficking involving U.S. visas, and allegations of corruption by American employees and LES. Beginning in FY 2015, the BSP will fund $0.5 million for law enforcement activity previously funded through the Emergencies in the Diplomatic and Consular Service (EDCS) appropriation.

Foreign Service Institute (FSI): $5.7 million
FSI provides consular training in domestic and overseas classes, conferences, on-line courses, language training, leadership and workshops. Training supports shifting consular workload and changes in consular systems applications and other technology. The training targets consular officers, consular agents, LES, and systems staffs who support automated consular systems. The courses cover the protection of American citizens abroad, including crisis planning and victim assistance, visa adjudication policies and procedures, interviewing techniques, name checks, fraud prevention, and leadership and management principles. FSI also provides leadership and management training and foreign language proficiency through language studies for overseas consular staff. To improve workflow efficiencies, funding for training associated with existing overseas consular positions is now reflected in CA Overseas Support.

Information Resource Management (IRM): $67.7 million
IRM provides systems technology and backbone support for critical visa and passport systems. These resources directly support domestic and overseas initiatives such as Network Services, Enterprise Server Operations Center (ESOC) Hosting Services, Global IT Modernization (GITM) Program, SharePoint, and SMART.

Office of the Legal Advisor (L): $0.2 million
L provides legal advice and services to Consular Affairs and other Department of State bureaus and officials on consular-related matters. L supports interagency efforts and international negotiations concerning visas; immigration, repatriation, sharing of information with foreign governments; parole, citizenship, and passport issues; the protection of and provision of benefits and services to U.S. citizens abroad; international children's issues; international judicial assistance; and the performance of other consular functions by U.S. consular officers or U.S. protecting powers abroad. This request provides funding for L/CA staff support costs.

Overseas Building Operations (OBO): $236.5 million
The FY 2015 resources fund the cost of all residential and functional lease space for consular officers overseas. This includes $119 million to fund CA's share of the Department's Capital Security Cost Sharing (CSCS) program, based on the same calculations of 'per desk' cost applied to all CSCS agencies. This contribution to CSCS will continue in future years.

American Institute in Taiwan (AIT): $1.1 million
These funds provide $6.1 million to normalize AIT's consular operations to match worldwide process and systems, particularly in light of Taiwan's acceptance into the Visa Waiver Program and the resulting drop in fees collected by AIT.

Repatriation Loans: $0.8 million
The BSP will fund the administrative expenses for the Repatriation Loans program, which assists destitute Americans abroad, who have no other source of funds to return to the U.S. Funds will allow the Department to administer the program from approval to final payoff at a level consistent with expected loan volume.

Charleston Global Financial Services (CGFS): $1.0 million
CGFS provides certain financial services in support of consular-related activities, (e.g., vouchering, payroll processing, accounts payable/receivable). Funding for CGFS was previously included under the CA-managed Overseas Support line.

Post Assignment Travel: $25.9 million
This line item reflects Post Assignment Travel costs for overseas consular personnel, including training, travel, and change of station costs, which are crucial to staffing overseas missions with trained personnel.

FBI FINGERPRINT CHECKS REIMBURSEMENT: $157.0 million

The FY 2015 Request includes funding for the Department to reimburse the Federal Bureau of Investigation (FBI) for fingerprint and name check clearances for visa applicants.

Working Capital Fund

($ in thousands)	FY 2013 Actual	FY 2014 Estimate	FY 2015 Request	Increase / Decrease
Working Capital Fund	1,292,977	1,322,452	1,301,915	-20,537

The Working Capital Fund (WCF) does not receive direct appropriations. Revenues are generated in the WCF from the sale of goods and services to the Department and other federal agencies. The revenue collected from these customers is used to pay for the acquisition of resources needed to ensure the continuous operation of the various WCF activities. Further, in exchange for goods and services, resources from the initial/additional investment are expended and subsequently are reimbursed from funded customer orders. The economies of scale achieved through WCF activities are a significant advantage in controlling costs, avoiding duplication, and achieving service standards.

The WCF allows the use of business practices to improve operations, provide support, and reduce costs in accordance with government rules, regulations, and laws. The offices that operate WCF cost centers do not have the same latitude as commercial businesses, but they act similar to businesses because they charge customers for services and use revenue to fund their activities. The Working Capital Fund operates under the legal authority of 22 U.S.C. 2684. The WCF FY 2015 decrease is primarily due to the downward glide path of operations in Iraq and Afghanistan under the Aviation WCF.

Embassy Security, Construction and Maintenance

($ in thousands)	FY 2013 Actual[1]/	FY 2014 Estimate	FY 2015 Request	Increase / Decrease
Embassy Security, Construction and Maintenance	2,819,783	2,674,351	2,277,700	-396,651
Enduring	1,582,247	2,399,351	2,016,900	-382,451
Ongoing Operations	912,722	785,351	799,400	14,049
Worldwide Security Upgrades	669,525	1,614,000	1,217,500	-396,500
Overseas Contingency Operations[2]/	1,237,536	275,000	260,800	-14,200

1/ The FY 2013 Actual includes $450,000 transferred from D&CP to Embassy Security, Construction, and Maintenance.

2/ OCO justification is provided in the OCO section.

The Bureau of Overseas Buildings Operations (OBO), funded through the Embassy Security, Construction, and Maintenance (ESCM) appropriation, is responsible for providing U.S. Diplomatic and Consular missions overseas with secure, safe, and functional facilities to assist them in achieving the foreign policy objectives of the United States.

The work supported by this request is vital, as over 86,000 U.S. Government employees from more than 30 agencies at 275 diplomatic and consular posts depend on the infrastructure OBO provides and maintains. OBO is focused on several priorities to ensure that the President, the Secretary, and other U.S. government agencies have the tools and platform to be effective in their mission. Following the September 2012 attacks on several embassies and the subsequent recommendations of the Accountability Review Board (ARB), the Department has undertaken a worldwide review of its overall security posture to identify and implement additional measures to bolster the security of our facilities and personnel where necessary. The FY 2015 Request supports $2.2 billion for the construction of new secure facilities, consistent with the recommendations of the ARB.

OBO is focused on four priority goals that advance diplomatic readiness and are aligned with the Department's strategic goals. They are:

- **Capital Security Construction** – Award capital security construction projects which have been listed in the Department's Long-Range Plan (LRP) after consultation with other agencies, and complete the construction on-time and within budget. The program will provide new facilities that are secure, safe, and functional for U.S. Government employees to pursue the national interests of the United States.

- **Compound and Physical Security** – Provide physical security and compound security upgrades to Department overseas facilities to protect employees from terrorist and other security threats. This also includes security upgrades for soft targets such as schools, recreational facilities, and residences.

- **Maintenance of Assets** – Maintain, repair, and rehabilitate overseas diplomatic and consular facilities in an effective manner that enhances the quality of life of employees while allowing them to perform their duties in secure, safe, and functional facilities.

- **Asset Management** – Acquire, dispose of, and manage the Department's overseas real property in a professional manner that meets Department needs and is performed on terms favorable to the U.S. Government.

The FY 2015 Request is $2.0 billion and 1,020 positions, a decrease of $382 million below the FY 2014 Estimate. The decrease largely reflects progress toward normalization of the Capital Security Cost Sharing funding level called for by the Benghazi Accountability Review Board. In FY 2015, CSCS allocations that had been borne by the Department of State will now be cost-shared across defense and law enforcement agencies as well as other international affairs programs including fee-funded activities.

The FY 2015 Request of $2.0 billion includes $1.2 billion to continue the Worldwide Security Upgrade Program, including the continuation of the Capital Security and Maintenance Cost Sharing Programs; $126 million for the Repair and Construction Program; and $673 million to support operating elements.

The Request reflects a $2.2 billion Capital Security Construction program for the construction of new secure facilities overseas. The request includes $987 million in ESCM Worldwide Security Upgrade appropriations. When combined with Capital Security Cost Sharing (CSCS) contributions from other agencies and other reimbursements (including the realignment of Consular Affairs' Border Security Program fee revenues), the request will provide a total of $2.0 billion for up to six new construction projects; as well as Marine Security Guard Quarters and site acquisitions for future plans. The ESCM OCO request includes $250 million that supports the ARB-recommended total of $2.2 billion.

In addition, the WSU request includes the Compound Security Program and Maintenance Cost-Sharing. The $101 million for Compound Security continues to upgrade security for high risk diplomatic facilities and soft targets, such as schools and recreation facilities. The Maintenance Cost Sharing (MCS) program will address facility needs at posts that will not receive a NEC in the near future. The $130 million provided under the MCS initiative is to extend the useful life of existing infrastructure and protect the U.S. long-term investment in new facilities. This request will be combined with $134 million from other cost sharing contributions, for a total of $264 million.

The ESCM request further provides $799 million for Ongoing Operations. The funding will support real property management, including administration of leaseholds, and other vital ongoing activities. These activities include repair and construction, program development and support, construction and security management, and maintenance and renovation of the Department's facilities at locations in the United States.

Office of Inspector General

($ in thousands)	FY 2013 Actual[1]/	FY 2014 Estimate	FY 2015 Request	Increase / Decrease
Office of Inspector General	116,519	119,056	130,300	11,244
Enduring	59,575	69,406	73,400	3,994
Overseas Contingency Operations	56,944	49,650	56,900	7,250
Special Inspector General for Afghanistan Reconstruction	48,039	49,650	56,900	7,250
Special Inspector General for Iraq Reconstruction	5,776	-	-	-
Office of the Inspector General - MERO	3,129	-	-	-

1/ In FY 2013, funding was provided for the Special Inspector General for Iraq Reconstruction to sunset operations. In FY 2014, and FY 2015, funding is provided for the Special Inspector General for Afghanistan Reconstruction (SIGAR) and is included in the Overseas Contingency Operations (OCO) chapter.

The Office of Inspector General's (OIG) mandate encompasses all domestic and overseas activities, programs, and missions of the Department and the Broadcasting Board of Governors (BBG). OIG's overarching goal for FY 2015 is to effect positive change by being a valued resource to the Department and BBG in promoting U.S. interests and sustained leadership, with specific emphasis on the following:

- **Relevance:** OIG's work will be directed by Department and BBG priorities, including those identified in the Quadrennial Diplomacy and Development Review (QDDR). OIG's work will emphasize critical, resource-intensive programs and operations in the frontline states; global issues; the effectiveness of foreign assistance programs; regional management activities and the use of new technologies and innovative approaches; priority posts and bureaus; and the Department's coordination with other U.S. Government agencies.

- **Value Added:** OIG will recommend actions that correct identified vulnerabilities and result in savings, cost recoveries, funds put to better use, restitutions and fines, prevention of losses, and improved efficiencies and security.

- **Usefulness:** OIG products will assist decision makers in improving programs and making the most effective spending decisions in an environment of increasingly constrained financial resources.

- **Timeliness:** OIG will continually strive to reduce the time for completing its audits, inspections, and reviews by using appropriate technologies to start jobs sooner, finish them quicker, and disseminate the results broadly and rapidly.

The FY 2015 enduring request of $73.4 million supports the activities of the Department's Inspector General. These activities include audits, investigations, and inspections of worldwide operations and programs of the Department and the BBG. Such activities assist in improving the economy, efficiency, and effectiveness of operations, as well as in detecting and preventing fraud, waste, and mismanagement. The request will also provide the Department's full contribution to the Council of the Inspectors General on Integrity and Efficiency. Included in the enduring request is an increase of $4 million for current staffing wage and inflation increases, the new Office of Special Projects, and funding for the Kuwait office which is currently scheduled to begin in FY 2015.

Educational and Cultural Exchange Programs

($ in thousands)	FY 2013 Actual[1]	FY 2014 Estimate	FY 2015 Request	Increase / Decrease
Educational and Cultural Exchange Programs	574,000	568,628	577,900	9,272
Enduring	559,180	560,000	577,900	17,900
Overseas Contingency Operations[2]	14,820	8,628	-	-8,628

1/ The FY 2013 Actual includes $5.5 million transferred from Diplomatic and Consular Programs to Educational and Cultural Exchange Programs.

2/The FY 2013 Actual includes $2.5 million transferred from Diplomatic and Consular Programs OCO to Educational and Cultural Exchange Programs.

The Department of State's Educational and Cultural Affairs Academic Programs, Professional and Cultural Exchanges, Performance and Alumni Activities, and Exchanges Support further U.S. foreign policy goals promoting increased understanding among nations. Exchange activities play a critical role towards increased U.S. security and economic development via "soft" public diplomacy approaches. ECA programs support the Department's foreign policy priorities by leveraging American education, society and culture as 21st Century diplomatic tools, facilitating increased connections among the American people and peoples around the world.

Academic Programs include the J. William Fulbright Educational Exchange Program, which provide U.S. and foreign students and scholars the opportunity to pursue degrees, teach, and conduct research in foreign and U.S. universities. The FY 2015 Fulbright program request focuses resources on South-East Asia and sub-Saharan Africa.

Educational advising is critical to the success of global academic exchange participants, supporting outreach to foreign students as they apply to U.S. universities. English language programs help train and develop foreign teachers of English, send Americans overseas to teach English and train instructors, teach English to disadvantaged students, and provide language learning materials and resources. Additional academic programs such as the Benjamin A. Gilman International Scholarship Program provide opportunities for American participants in financial need to study abroad.

The Academic Programs request includes three new initiatives. The Young African Leaders Initiative (YALI) will invest in a new generation of Young African leaders, shaping the continent's future, and reinforcing the Department's commitment to an enduring partnership between the United States and Africa. A companion program, the Young South-East Asian Leaders Initiative (YSEALI), increases outreach to emerging regional actors in Asia. A new Special Academic Exchanges activity, the Fulbright University – Vietnam supports academic freedom and autonomy in developing new curricula.

Professional and Cultural Exchanges include the International Visitors Leadership Program, bringing thousands of foreign leaders to the United States for intensive short-term professional exchanges to interact with their American counterparts, gaining first-hand knowledge about the United States. Citizen Exchanges Program participants partner with an extensive network of organizations and experts from across the United States to conduct professional fellowships and arts, sports, and high school exchange programs focused on current and future leaders. The request includes the J. Christopher Stevens Virtual Exchange Initiative in honor of the late Ambassador, expanding outreach to high-priority youth populations in both the United States and Middle Eastern and North African countries.

Exchanges Rapid Response (ERR). The Fiscal Year 2015 request includes a new program activity focused on exchange activities that respond rapidly to countries experiencing conflict or crisis, dramatic leadership transition, and significant societal transformation for exchange activities.

Program and Performance includes funding for necessary performance monitoring and evaluation as well as for alumni activities. The request includes expanded alumni activities to ensure that exchange participants continue engagement with the United States once actual exchanges cease.

Exchanges Support funding is requested to support all domestic staff and support costs managed by the ECA Bureau, as well as government-wide exchanges coordination.

Resource Detail – ECE Activities

($ in thousands)	FY 2013 Actual	FY 2014 Estimate	FY 2015 Request	Increase / Decrease
Academic Programs	**308,354**	**307,766**	**313,439**	**5,673**
Fulbright Program	236,432	234,666	204,200	-30,466
Students, Scholars, Teachers, Humphrey, Undergraduates	236,432	234,666	204,200	-30,466
Global Academic Exchanges	52,673	53,970	62,989	9,019
Educational Advising and Student Services	11,591	12,185	17,204	5,019
English Language Programs	41,082	41,785	41,785	-
American Overseas Research Centers	-	-	4,000	4,000
Special Academic Exchanges	19,249	19,130	46,250	27,120
American Overseas Research Centers	3,620	4,000		-4,000
South Pacific Exchanges	435	435	350	-85
Timor Leste Scholarship Program	435	435	350	-85
Mobility (Disability) Exchange Clearinghouse	450	450	450	-
Tibet Fund	574	710	500	-210
Fulbright University - Vietnam	-	-	2,500	2,500
Benjamin A. Gilman Scholarship Program	10,800	12,100	12,100	-
George Mitchell Fellowship Program	435			-
Young African Leaders Initiative	2,500	1,000	20,000	19,000
Young South-East Asian Leaders Initiative	-	-	10,000	10,000
Professional and Cultural Exchanges	**186,428**	**188,734**	**180,509**	**-8,225**
International Visitor Leadership Program	86,811	89,372	89,665	293
International Visitor Leadership Program	86,811	89,372	89,665	293
Citizen Exchange Program	95,957	98,787	85,286	-13,501
Professional/Cultural/Youth	95,957	98,787	85,286	-13,501

($ in thousands)	FY 2013 Actual	FY 2014 Estimate	FY 2015 Request	Increase / Decrease
Special Professional and Cultural Exchanges	3,660	575	5,558	4,983
J. Christopher Stevens Virtual Exchange	3,000	-	5,000	5,000
Youth Science Leadership Institute of the Americas	130	-	-	-
Ngwang Choephel Fellows (Tibet)	530	575	558	-17
Program and Performance	**3,798**	**3,500**	**6,252**	**2,752**
Evaluation	1,321	1,218	1,252	34
Alumni	2,477	2,282	5,000	2,718
Exchanges Rapid Response (ERR)	**-**	**-**	**18,000**	**18,000**
Exchanges Rapid Response	-	-	18,000	18,000
Exchanges Support	**60,600**	**60,000**	**59,700**	**-300**
Total	**559,180**	**560,000**	**577,900**	**17,900**

Representation Expenses

($ in thousands)	FY 2013 Actual[1]/	FY 2014 Estimate	FY 2015 Request	Increase / Decrease
Representation Expenses	7,660	8,030	7,679	-351

1/ The FY 2013 Actual includes $730,000 transferred from Diplomatic and Consular Programs to Representation Expenses; the FY 2014 level includes $730,000 transferred from Diplomatic and Consular Programs.

Representational functions convey U.S. foreign policy goals and objectives in both bilateral and multilateral fora. The Department concentrates on representational activities that support U.S. positions on multilateral trade and economic development issues pending before the European Union (EU), the Association of Southeast Asian Nations (ASEAN), the Asia-Pacific Economic Cooperation (APEC), Central American Free Trade Agreement (CAFTA), Free Trade of the Americas (FTAA), African Growth and Opportunity Acts (AGOA) and the North American Free Trade Agreement (NAFTA).

Representation funding is used to establish or consolidate professional relationships with local government counterparts necessary to the performance of official duties; strengthen relationships among individuals (e.g. business and labor leaders) who perform duties such as trade promotion; protection of American business interests; economic, commercial, and labor reporting; and negotiations. Representational funding also supports formal events, such as the installation or inauguration of national leaders, visits of noted personages, recognition of deaths or marriages of prominent citizens, and presentation of credentials to heads of state. For the Foreign Service, the ability to engage partners in an informal setting is an invaluable opportunity to strengthen the U.S. position where interlocutors are not yet ready to be forthcoming in a more formal setting.

The FY 2015 Request is $7.7 million, a $351,000 decrease from FY 2014. Representation activities directly contribute to global engagement with foreign counterparts, thus enabling the environment for diplomacy and development.

Protection of Foreign Missions and Officials

($ in thousands)	FY 2013 Actual	FY 2014 Estimate	FY 2015 Request	Increase / Decrease
Protection of Foreign Missions and Officials	25,633	28,200	30,036	1,836

The FY 2015 request for Protection of Foreign Missions and Officials (PFMO) is $30 million, which is $1.8 million above the FY 2014 level. This increase will provide additional funding for reimbursable expenses to New York City and the surrounding areas, and other state and local governments.

In addition to direct appropriations, the Department requests continuation of legislative authority to transfer expired unobligated balances from the Diplomatic and Consular Programs appropriation to the PFMO account. This transfer authority was originally provided in FY 2014. To extent that such balances are available in future years, they will provide additional resources for the Protection of Foreign Missions and Officials to meet extraordinary protection requirements.

Emergencies in the Diplomatic and Consular Service

($ in thousands)	FY 2013 Actual[1]/	FY 2014 Estimate	FY 2015 Request	Increase / Decrease
Emergencies in the Diplomatic and Consular Service	8,552	9,242	7,900	-1,342

1/ The FY 2013 Actual level includes $277,000 transfer from Emergencies in the Diplomatic & Consular Services to Repatriation Loans Program Account.

EDCS funding is heavily influenced by unpredictable evacuations that may occur as a result of natural disasters, epidemics, terrorist acts, and civil unrest. Recent demands include the earthquakes in Japan and Haiti, and the Arab Spring conflicts which resulted in several large-scale evacuations. In FY 2012, evacuations occurred in Damascus, Syria, Bamako, Mali, Tripoli, Libya, Lahore and Karachi, Pakistan, Tunis, Tunisia, and Khartoum, Sudan. In FY 2013, evacuations occurred in Algiers, Algeria; Bangui, Central African Republic; Bamako, Mali; Niamey, Niger; Tripoli, Libya; Cairo, Egypt; Sanaa, Yemen; and Lahore, Pakistan.

EDCS also funds certain activities relating to the conduct of foreign affairs by senior Administration officials. These activities generally take place in connection with the U.S. hosting of U.S. Government-sponsored conferences, such as the UN and OAS General Assemblies, the G-20 Summit, the Nuclear Security Summit, the U.S.-China Strategic and Economic Dialogue, the Asian-Pacific Economic (APEC) Summit, and the NATO Summit. In FY 2013, the Department's EDCS costs for the APEC Summit exceeded $2 million, and the Department's EDCS costs for the G8 and NATO Summits exceeded $1 million. In FY 2015, the U.S. will begin the two-year Chairmanship of the Arctic Council.

Other EDCS activities include travel of Presidential delegations, official visits and official gifts for foreign dignitaries, Presidential, Vice Presidential, and Congressional travel overseas, representation requirements of senior Department officials, rewards for information on international terrorism, narcotics trafficking, transnational organized crime, and war crimes, as well as the expansion of publicity efforts.

Buying Power Maintenance Account

($ in thousands)	FY 2013 Actual[1]/	FY 2014 Estimate	FY 2015 Request	Increase / Decrease
Buying Power Maintenance Account	-	-	-	-

1/ The FY 2013 Actual level includes $13.4 million transferred to Diplomatic and Consular Programs from Buying Power Maintenance Account.

The Buying Power Maintenance Account (BPMA) is intended to offset adverse fluctuations in foreign currency exchange rates and/or overseas inflationary requirements. The FY 2015 Request does not include an increase in BPMA total appropriated resources. The Department will use existing BPMA balances and related transfer authority to manage exchange rate fluctuations and overseas inflationary adjustments.

Repatriation Loans Program Account

($ in thousands)	FY 2013 Actual[1]	FY 2014 Estimate	FY 2015 Request	Increase / Decrease
Repatriation Loans Program Account	1,651	1,537	1,300	-237

1/ FY 2013 Actual includes $277,292 transferred from Emergencies in the Diplomatic and Consular Services to Repatriation Loans Program Account.

The FY 2015 Repatriation Loans Program Account request is $1.3 million, which is $0.2 million below the FY 2014 estimated level. At the FY 2015 subsidy rate, the appropriated amount will make up 52.65 percent of the total loan level, for a total loan level of up to $2.5 million. These funds will allow the Department of State to subsidize the Repatriation loans program consistent with the Credit Reform Act of 1990. Administrative costs for Repatriation Loans will be funded with fees from the Border Security Program.

Payment to the American Institute in Taiwan

($ in thousands)	FY 2013 Actual[1]	FY 2014 Estimate	FY 2015 Request	Increase / Decrease
Payment to the American Institute in Taiwan	22,134	31,221	30,000	-1,221

1/ FY 2013 Actual includes a transfer in of $2,095,000 from Diplomatic and Consular Programs to Payment to the American Institute in Taiwan.

The Department's FY 2015 request of $30 million for the American Institute in Taiwan (AIT) includes adjustments to maintain current services and continue support for several key initiatives as a result of reduced visa revenue due to Taiwan's entry into the Visa Waiver Program (VWP). In addition to these amounts, consular related expenses for AIT are funded with fee revenue from the Border Security Program.

Foreign Service Retirement and Disability Fund

($ in thousands)	FY 2013 Actual	FY 2014 Estimate	FY 2015 Request	Increase / Decrease
Foreign Service Retirement and Disability Fund	158,900	158,900	158,900	-

This appropriation provides mandatory funding for the Foreign Service Retirement and Disability Fund (FSRDF). The FSRDF includes the operations of two separate retirement systems - the Foreign Service Retirement and Disability System (FSRDS) and the Foreign Service Pension System (FSPS). The FSRDF was established to provide pensions to all eligible retired and disabled members of the Foreign Service who are enrolled in either of the two systems, and certain eligible former spouses and survivors. The purpose of this appropriation is to maintain the required funding level of the FSRDF.

This request serves as one of the resources to finance any unfunded liability created by new or liberalized benefits, new groups of beneficiaries, and salary increases paid from the Fund, and for normal costs not met by employee and employer contributions. The amount of the appropriation is determined by the annual evaluation of the Fund balance derived from current statistical data, which includes Federal pay raise information.

The FY 2015 request for the FSRDF is $158.9 million. This amount includes estimated Foreign Service costs for the Department of $122.5 million and for the United States Agency for International Development of $36.4 million.

Contributions to International Organizations

($ in thousands)	FY 2013 Actual	FY 2014 Estimate	FY 2015 Request	Increase / Decrease
Contributions to International Organizations	1,472,543	1,340,162	1,517,349	177,187
Enduring	1,376,338	1,265,762	1,517,349	251,587
Overseas Contingency Operations	96,205	74,400	-	-74,400

The FY 2015 request of $1.5 billion for Contributions to International Organizations (CIO) provides funding to pay the U.S. share of the assessed budgets of 45 international organizations. U.S. participation in nearly all of these organizations is the result of U.S. ratification of a treaty or convention that commits the United States to pay an assessed contribution.

The Administration's commitment to strengthening and working through international organizations is laid out in the National Security Strategy as a vital component of diplomacy and foreign policy. By combining resources and expertise provided by nations from every part of the world, international organizations undertake coordinated efforts that are an effective alternative to acting unilaterally or bilaterally, especially in the areas of providing humanitarian assistance, eradicating disease, setting food and transportation safety standards, and reaching agreement to impose sanctions on rogue states and actors. International organizations facilitate collective action by the world community to combat violent extremism; limit the spread of nuclear and chemical weapons; achieve balanced and sustainable economic growth; and forge solutions to the threats of armed conflict, hunger, poverty, and climate change.

The Administration is committed to robust multilateral engagement and to promoting U.S. leadership in international organizations as a means of advancing U.S. national security interests and values. For this reason, the Department continues to seek legislation that would provide authority to waive legislative restrictions that prohibit paying U.S. contributions to United Nations (UN) specialized agencies that grant the Palestinians the same standing as member states or full membership as a state. The FY 2015 Budget does not include funding for organizations currently subject to such restrictions, but does include conditional transfer authority should the waiver be enacted. The ability to make such contributions is essential to advancing U.S. interests worldwide and strengthening U.S. global leadership, influence, and credibility. The Administration remains committed to heading off any new efforts by the Palestinians to seek such membership in organizations across the UN system.

International organizations offer significant benefits to U.S. taxpayers. Nearly every Federal agency relies on international organizations to help advance foreign and domestic objectives. Countless U.S. businesses and citizens depend on international organizations to reduce barriers to trade, improve border and port security, obtain international patent and trademark protection, set standards for aviation and maritime security, maintain the world's telecommunications networks, harmonize international law in the areas of child custody, support, and international adoption, and disseminate information about the supply and demand of vital commodities such as cotton and coffee. Appendix 1 of the Congressional Budget Justification demonstrates the return on investment that the U.S. taxpayers receive through hundreds of accomplishments that international organizations have achieved in these areas.

Resource Detail – CIO Activities

($ in thousands)	FY 2013 Actual	FY 2014 Estimate	FY 2015 Request	Increase / Decrease
United Nations and Affiliated Agencies				
United Nations Regular Budget	567,946	617,661	620,379	2,718
UN War Crimes Tribunal - Rwanda (UNICTR)	9,731	8,963	5,148	-3,815
UN War Crimes Tribunal - Yugoslavia (ICTY)	16,048	14,299	11,077	-3,222
Int'l Residual Mechanism for Criminal Tribunals (IRM)	3,002	6,781	6,781	-
Food and Agriculture Organization (FAO)	113,639	116,093	118,378	2,285
International Atomic Energy Agency (IAEA)	106,866	115,955	116,319	364
International Civil Aviation Organization (ICAO)	21,497	19,824	18,719	-1,105
International Labor Organization (ILO)	85,492	89,555	90,787	1,232
International Maritime Organization (IMO)	1,290	1,338	1,498	160
International Telecommunication Union (ITU)	10,712	11,152	10,994	-158
UN Educational, Scientific & Cultural Org (UNESCO)[1]/	-	-	-	-
Universal Postal Union (UPU)	2,450	2,526	2,568	42
World Health Organization (WHO)	109,879	109,879	114,105	4,226
World Intellectual Property Organization (WIPO)	1,225	1,278	1,250	-28
World Meteorological Organization (WMO)	15,185	15,898	15,514	-384
Subtotal, United Nations and Affiliated Agencies	**1,064,962**	**1,131,203**	**1,133,517**	**2,315**
Inter-American Organizations				
Organization of American States (OAS)	48,513	48,513	48,513	-
Pan American Health Organization (PAHO)	65,686	66,086	66,486	400
Inter-American Inst. for Cooperation on Ag. (IICA)	16,359	16,360	16,360	-
Pan American Inst. of Geography and History (PAIGH)	324	324	324	-
Subtotal, Inter-American Organizations	**130,882**	**131,283**	**131,683**	**400**
Regional Organizations				
Org. for Econ. Cooperation and Development (OECD)	82,135	87,425	86,608	-817
North Atlantic Treaty Organization (NATO)	60,542	70,589	72,224	1,635
NATO Parliamentary Assembly (NPA)	1,059	1,233	1,215	-18

($ in thousands)	FY 2013 Actual	FY 2014 Estimate	FY 2015 Request	Increase / Decrease
The Pacific Community (SPC)	1,592	1,660	1,636	-24
Asia-Pacific Economic Cooperation (APEC)	1,032	1,040	1,052	12
Colombo Plan Council Technical Cooperation (CPCTC)	17	17	17	-
Subtotal, Regional Organizations	**146,377**	**161,964**	**162,752**	**788**
Other International Organizations				
Organization Prohibition of Chemical Weapons (OPCW)	20,135	21,252	21,127	-125
World Trade Organization (WTO)	25,481	25,748	24,477	-1,271
Customs Cooperation Council (CCC)	4,080	4,300	4,296	-4
Hague Conference on Private Int'l Law (HCOPIL)	277	292	293	1
International Agency for Research on Cancer (IARC)	1,965	2,104	2,146	42
Int'l Bureau Publication of Customs Tariffs (IBPCT)	171	176	173	-3
Int'l Bureau Permanent Court Arbitration (IBPCA)	57	74	73	-1
International Bureau of Weights and Measures (IBWM)	1,416	1,493	1,503	10
Int'l Ctr Study of Preserv & Restoration Cultural Prpty (ICCROM)	1,055	1,092	1,072	-20
International Coffee Organization (ICO)	624	658	659	1
International Copper Study Group (ICSG)	34	35	41	6
International Cotton Advisory Committee (ICAC)	351	332	333	1
International Grains Council (IGC)	523	579	575	-4
International Hydrographic Organization (IHO)	128	132	130	-2
Int'l Institute Unification of Private Law (IIUPL)	164	174	170	-4
International Lead and Zinc Study Group (ILZSG)	35	35	35	-
International Organization of Legal Metrology (IOLM)	150	154	151	-3
International Renewable Energy Agency (IRENA)	3,553	4,290	4,290	-
International Seed Testing Association (ISTA)	15	14	14	-
International Tropical Timber Organization (ITTO)	285	310	310	-
Int'l Union for Conservation of Nature (IUCN)	530	568	555	-13

($ in thousands)	FY 2013 Actual	FY 2014 Estimate	FY 2015 Request	Increase / Decrease
Int'l Union Protection New Varieties of Plants (UPOV)	289	301	294	-7
World Organization for Animal Health (OIE)	198	214	214	-
Subtotal, Other International Organizations	**61,516**	**64,327**	**62,931**	**-1,396**
Tax Reimbursement Agreements for U.S. Citizens				
Tax Reimbursement Agreements	23,367	26,241	26,466	225
Subtotal, Tax Reimbursement Agreements for U.S. Citizens	**23,367**	**26,241**	**26,466**	**225**
Total Annual Requirements	**1,427,104**	**1,515,019**	**1,517,349**	**2,330**
Adjustment for Exchange Rate and Other Changes	3,684	-24,502	-	24,502
Buydown of FY 2013 Requirements	-69,000	-	-	-
Buydown of FY 2014 Requirements	110,755	-110,755	-	110,755
UN Tax Equilization Fund Credit	-	-39,600	-	39,600
FY 2014 Unfunded Requirements	-	-	-	-
FY 2015 Unfuded Requirements	-	-	-	-
UN Mission in Frontline States (UNAMI/UNAMA) in OCO	-96,205	-74,400	-	74,400
Total Contributions to International Organizations (CIO)	**1,376,338**	**1,265,762**	**1,517,349**	**251,587**

1/ The Administration seeks Congressional support for legislation that would provide authority to waive legislative restrictions that, if triggered, would prohibit paying U.S. contributions to United Nations specialized agencies that grant the Palestinians the same standing as member states or full membership as a state.

Contributions for International Peacekeeping Activities

($ in thousands)	FY 2013 Actual[1]/	FY 2014 Estimate	FY 2015 Request	Increase / Decrease
Contributions for International Peacekeeping Activities	1,913,788	1,765,519	2,518,565	753,046

1/ The FY 2013 Actual level includes $100,000 transferred from Contributions to Peacekeeping Activities to the Diplomatic and Consular Programs.

The Contributions for International Peacekeeping Activities (CIPA) account funds expenses of international peacekeeping activities directed to the maintenance or restoration of international peace and security. United Nations (UN) peacekeeping, which is the principal use for which CIPA funds are utilized, promotes the peaceful resolution of conflict.

The FY 2015 Request of $2.5 billion will provide funds for the U.S. share of assessed expenses for UN peacekeeping operations including the cost to fully meet accrued US commitments for each mission. In FY 2015, it is critical that significant additional funding be provided above the FY 2014 level to address the growth in peacekeeping missions that address complex challenges to international peace and security including those in Somalia, South Sudan, and Mali. Major highlights include:

- UNDOF (Golan), will continue to monitor the Separation Agreement between Israel and Syria in the increasingly challenging and dangerous environment posed by the Syrian civil war. UNDOF grew in strength up to 1,250 (the maximum authorized under the 1974 Disengagement Agreement) due to the dangerous conditions;
- UNMIL (Liberia), as the overall security situation remains stable, the implementation of the security transition plan is expected to continue in 2015, resulting in further decreases in military personnel;
- UNOCI (Cote d'Ivoire), which is implementing a drawdown by reducing military personnel gradually;
- MINUSTAH (Haiti), will complete its reduction of force levels back to pre-earthquake levels, and continue priority efforts to help the Haitian National Police to develop the capacities required to assume responsibility for security;
- UNAMID (Darfur, Sudan), will have consolidated some positions, but remain focused on protecting civilians in the context of ongoing conflict between the Government of Sudan and Darfuri rebels and increased criminal activity due to a lack of rule of law in Darfur;
- UNSOA (Support Office for the African Union Mission in Somalia), will continue to provide a logistical support package for the Africa Union Mission in Somalia (AMISOM) for up to a maximum of 22,126 uniformed personnel including the reimbursement of contingent-owned equipment including force enablers and multipliers. The logistics package provides equipment and support services similar to UN peacekeeping operations. UNSOA is working very closely with the UN Assistance Mission in Somalia (UNSOM) and AMISOM to stabilize political and security conditions in Somalia, in concert with the international community and other UN bodies;
- MONUSCO (Democratic Republic of the Congo (DRC), will continue to focus on its core task of supporting the Congolese government efforts to protect civilians, and will maintain its full authorized strength with the extension of the Intervention Brigade tasked with neutralizing threats from armed groups operating in the eastern DRC. There is a possibility the new mandate will authorize the mission to provide logistical support for elections expected in 2015;
- UNISFA (Abyei, Sudan/South Sudan), the Security Council's May 2013 decision to increase the mission's troop ceiling from 4,200 to 5,326, is consistent with the revised Joint Border Verification Monitoring Mission (JBVMM) implementation plan, will continue to maintain security in the volatile

disputed region of Abyei and to support the JBVMM's work in the 2,000 km-long Safe Demilitarized Border Zone between Sudan and South Sudan;

- UNMISS (South Sudan), will operate with a temporary increase from 7,000 to 12,500 troops in order to respond to the crisis that erupted in South Sudan in December 2013, focusing primarily on the protection of 75,000 civilians sheltering on its compounds; supporting the delivery of humanitarian assistance to more than 650,000 additional people displaced by the conflict; and monitoring and documenting human rights violations;

- MINUSMA (Mali), will continue to stabilize key population centers in northern Mali and support the reestablishment of state authority throughout the country, as well as support national reconciliation efforts. It will also continue to promote and protect human rights, and support humanitarian assistance and cultural preservation. Approximately $100 million of the $390.5 million request for MINUSMA will be used to offset a portion of the FY 2014 unbudgeted assessments for the mission; and

- Mission Monitoring and Effectiveness Support Funds, requested in FY 2013 for the first time, will continue to support costs associated with U.S. oversight of and travel to UN peacekeeping missions at least once a year to review the budgets and effectiveness of the missions.

The FY 2015 Request is based on the United States' scale of assessment rate for calendar year 2014 for UN peacekeeping as specified in the Annex accompanying United Nations General Assembly document A/67/224/Add.1, which is 28.36 percent.

Resource Detail – CIPA Activities

($ in thousands)	FY 2013 Actual	FY 2014 Estimate	FY 2015 Request	Increase / Decrease
Activities				
UN Peacekeeping Force in Cyprus (UNFICYP)	9,366	9,525	9,525	-
UN Disengagement Observer Force (UNDOF)	16,094	17,580	17,580	-
UN Interim Force in Lebanon (UNIFIL)	147,630	156,000	156,000	-
UN Mission Referendum West Sahara (MINURSO)	17,464	17,450	17,450	-
UN War Crimes Tribunal - Yugoslavia (ICTY)	20,230	20,375	13,650	-6,725
UN War Crimes Tribunal Rwanda (ICTR)	13,674	10,550	5,275	-5,275
UN Interim Administration Mission Kosovo (UNMIK)	13,925	13,400	11,000	-2,400
UN Mission in Liberia (UNMIL)	142,742	132,510	120,880	-11,630
UN Operations in Cote d'Ivoire (UNOCI)	175,208	163,000	145,000	-18,000
UN Stabilization Mission in Haiti (MINUSTAH)	184,979	184,000	170,650	-13,350
UN Integrated Mission in Timor-Leste (UNMIT)	1,365	-	-	-
UN-AU Hybrid Mission in Darfur (UNAMID)	400,242	410,351	410,350	-1
UN Support Office for the AU Mission in Somalia (UNSOA)	-	-	165,500	165,500
UN Org. Stabilization Mission in the DRC (MONUSCO)	326,780	438,000	438,000	-

($ in thousands)	FY 2013 Actual	FY 2014 Estimate	FY 2015 Request	Increase / Decrease
Int'l Residue Mechanism for Criminal Tribunals (MICT)	3,873	7,300	14,600	7,300
UN Interim Security Force for ABYEI (UNISFA)	81,216	88,935	92,500	3,565
UN Mission in Southern Sudan (UNMISS)	277,099	303,500	340,000	36,500
UN Supervision Mission in Syria (UNSMIS)	4,774	-	-	-
UN Multidimensional Integrated Stabilization Mission in Mali (MINUSMA)	115,072	250,255	390,505	140,250
Mission Monitoring / Effectiveness Support	100	100	100	-
Subtotal, Activities	**1,951,833**	**2,222,831**	**2,518,565**	**295,734**
Total Annual Requirements	**1,951,833**	**2,222,831**	**2,518,565**	**295,734**
FY 2013 Unobligated (CN 13-249)	72,696	-	-	-
Application of FY 2013 Credits	-112,449	-	-	-
Application of FY 2014 Credits	-	-75,000	-	75,000
FY 2012 Carryforward into FY 2013	-58,128	-	-	-
FY 2013 Carryforward into FY 2014	142,542	-142,542	-	142,542
FY 2013 Rate Adjustment	-38,263	-	-	-
FY 2014 Rate Adjustment (P.L. 113-76, per UNGA Resolution 64-220)	-	-98,600	-	98,600
FY 2013 Rate Adjustment (P.L. 113-6)	-44,343	-	-	-
FY 2014 Rate Adjustment (P.L. 113-76)	-	-141,070	-	141,070
Transfer to D&CP - Mission Monitoring /Effectiveness Support	-100	-100	-	100
Total Contributions for International Peacekeeping Activities (CIPA)	**1,913,788**	**1,765,519**	**2,518,565**	**753,046**

International Boundary and Water Commission

($ in thousands)	FY 2013 Actual	FY 2014 Estimate	FY 2015 Request	Increase / Decrease
International Boundary and Water Commission	68,782	77,438	71,876	-5,562
IBWC - Salaries and Expenses	41,162	44,000	45,415	1,415
IBWC - Construction	27,620	33,438	26,461	-6,977

The International Boundary and Water Commission (IBWC) is a treaty-based organization comprised of U.S. and Mexican Sections. The Sections exercise respective national rights and obligations under U.S.-Mexico boundary and water treaties and related agreements to develop binational solutions to boundary and water problems arising along the 1,952-mile border.

The FY 2015 request for IBWC Salaries & Expenses provides $45.4 million for the staffing, operations and maintenance of headquarters in El Paso, Texas, as well as eight field offices and three satellite offices along the border. These activities afford protection of lives and property from floods in bordering communities. The appropriation provides for the preservation of the international border and addresses binational sanitation issues through wastewater treatment. The appropriation also supports administrative and engineering activities.

The FY 2015 request for IBWC Construction provides $26.5 million for major renovations and construction that enable the storage, distribution, and delivery of international waters in the Rio Grande, Tijuana and Colorado Rivers. The FY 2015 request continues multi-year efforts to improve Rio Grande levees and related flood control structures in the United States. The levees contain about 440 miles of river and interior floodway channel along three unique Rio Grande flood control systems. The funding will also support rehabilitation of the dams for which the IBWC is responsible and renovation of IBWC facilities.

American Sections

($ in thousands)	FY 2013 Actual	FY 2014 Estimate	FY 2015 Request	Increase / Decrease
American Sections	11,312	12,499	12,311	-188
International Joint Commission	6,787	7,664	7,413	-251
International Boundary Commission	2,206	2,449	2,525	76
Border Environment Cooperation Commission	2,319	2,386	2,373	-13

International Joint Commission
The FY 2015 request provides $7.4 million for the International Joint Commission (IJC). This funding will support the activities of the U.S. Section staff in Washington, D.C., and a binational Great Lakes Regional Office in Windsor, Canada.

The IJC was established by the 1909 Boundary Waters Treaty as a cornerstone of U.S.-Canadian relations in the boundary region. Under the treaty, the IJC licenses and regulates certain water resource projects along the border that affect levels and flows on the other side, provides advice to the governments and conducts studies on critical issues of mutual concern, and apportions waters in transboundary river systems.

The IJC also assists in efforts to prevent transboundary air pollution and improve air quality. The IJC's model for preventing and resolving disputes is scientifically based, inclusive, and open to public input. Currently, 17 active boards and task forces, plus various related technical working groups and committees, provide expert advice on both science and policy issues.

International Boundary Commission
The FY 2015 request provides $2.5 million for the International Boundary Commission (IBC). This funding will support the primary mission of the IBC to maintain an effective (accurately delineated and marked) boundary between the United States and Canada as prescribed by the 1925 Treaty of Washington. Maintaining such a boundary ensures the sovereignty of each nation over its territory by clearly establishing where one's rights and responsibilities end, and the other's begin, thus virtually eliminating the potential for serious and costly boundary disputes.

The request will fund IBC operations and six boundary maintenance projects along the 5,525-mile boundary. The IBC maintains more than 5,500 land boundary monuments and more than 2,800 reference monuments. The request will also provide for mapping and maintenance of a Geographical Information System.

Border Environment Cooperation Commission
The FY 2015 request provides $2.4 million for the Border Environment Cooperation Commission (BECC). The funding will continue the BECC's work to improve health and environmental conditions for the U.S.-Mexico border region by strengthening cooperation among interested parties and supporting sustainable projects. A binational institution created in 1993, the BECC assists border communities in developing environmental infrastructure projects that meet certification requirements to be eligible to receive funding from the North American Development Bank or other institutions. These requirements help ensure that projects provide environmental and health benefits and are technically feasible and affordable.

International Fisheries Commissions

($ in thousands)	FY 2013 Actual	FY 2014 Estimate	FY 2015 Request	Increase / Decrease
International Fisheries Commissions	32,870	35,980	31,446	-4,534

The FY 2015 request provides $31.4 million for International Fisheries Commissions (IFC) to fund the U.S. share of operating expenses for ten international fisheries commissions, the International Whaling Commission, two international marine science organizations, the Arctic Council, the Antarctic Treaty, international shark and sea turtle conservation initiatives, travel expenses of the U.S. Commissioners, and compensation payments to non-government employees for the days worked as U.S. Commissioners to the Pacific Salmon Commission.

In most cases, U.S. contributions are mandated by treaties and agreements. Each commission facilitates international cooperation by conducting or coordinating scientific studies of fish stocks and other marine resources and their habitats and establishing common management measures to be implemented by member governments. Many also oversee the allocation of fishing rights to their members.

Full payment of assessments is required to maintain voting privileges and influence in the commissions and organizations to advance the economic and conservation interests of the United States and important constituent groups.

Through the ongoing efforts of the commissions and programs funded by this appropriation, many fishing areas that were nearly depleted are now yielding sustainable catches for U.S. commercial and sport fishermen, and some key endangered populations are recovering. The commercial and recreational fisheries managed by the commissions generate income of $12 billion to $15 billion annually and support thousands of jobs for the United States.

Resource Detail – IFC Activities

($ in thousands)	FY 2013 Actual	FY 2014 Estimate	FY 2015 Request	Increase / Decrease
Inter-American Tropical Tuna Commission (IATTC)	**1,748**	**1,822**	**1,750**	**-72**
Great lakes Fishery Commission (GLFC)	**21,570**	**23,709**	**19,915**	**-3,794**
International Pacific Halibut Commission (IPHC)	**4,172**	**4,350**	**3,950**	**-400**
Pacific Salmon Commission (PSC)	**2,632**	**3,050**	**2,800**	**-250**
Other Marine Conservation Organizations	**2,748**	**3,049**	**3,031**	**-18**
Arctic Council Secretariat	58	125	125	-
Antarctic Treaty Secretariat	60	61	65	4
Commission for the Conservation of Atlantic Marine Living Resources (CCAMLR)	148	156	146	-10
Expenses of the U.S. Commissioners	138	149	140	-9
Int'l Commission for the Conservation of Atlanta Tunas (ICCAT)	212	325	285	-40
Int'l Council for the Exploration of the Sea (ICES)	216	220	222	2
International Sea Turtle Conservation Programs	170	200	200	-
International Shark Conservation Programs	75	100	100	-
International Whaling Commission (IWC)	134	90	90	-
North Atlantic Salmon Conservation Org. (NASCO)	47	44	45	1
North Pacific Anadromous Fish Commission (NPAFC)	180	190	190	-
North Pacific Marine Science Organization (PICES)	124	116	170	54
Northwest Atlantic Fisheries Organization (NAFO)	236	273	275	2
Western &Central Pacifi Fisheries Commission (WCPFC)	950	1,000	978	-22
Total	**32,870**	**35,980**	**31,446**	**-4,534**

The Asia Foundation

($ in thousands)	FY 2013 Actual	FY 2014 Estimate	FY 2015 Request	Increase / Decrease
The Asia Foundation	16,139	17,000	12,000	-5,000

The Asia Foundation (TAF) is a private, non-profit organization that advances U.S. interests in the Asia-Pacific region. Incorporated and headquartered in California, TAF operates programs through 17 offices in Asia. TAF's programs and grants support democratic initiatives, governance and economic reform, expansion of rule of law, women's empowerment, regional cooperation, and peaceful relations between the United States and Asia. Its longstanding and deep relationships with governments and civil society and reform-minded individuals in Asia are unique.

Under the Asia Foundation Act of 1983, appropriated funds are TAF's core funding source. In fact, the USG's investment in TAF leverages over five times as much funding from other sources to support democracy and governance programs. The FY 2015 request of $12 million will enable TAF to continue its work with Asian governments, nongovernmental organizations, and the private sector. This level reflects TAF's growing capacity to generate program funds from other Federal and non-Federal sources.

Center for Middle Eastern-Western Dialogue

($ in thousands)	FY 2013 Actual	FY 2014 Estimate	FY 2015 Request	Increase / Decrease
Center for Middle Eastern-Western Dialogue	96	90	83	-7

The International Center for Middle Eastern-Western Dialogue (the Hollings Center) was established by the Congress in 2004 to further scholarship and implement programs to open channels of communication and deepen cross-cultural understanding between the United States and nations of the Middle East, Turkey, Central and North Africa, Southwest and Southeast Asia and other countries. In FY 2015, $83,000 in estimated earnings from the Hollings Center's trust fund is available for operations, support for conferences, academic programs, and grants. This represents a $7,000 decrease from the FY 2014 enacted level due to interest earnings reestimates. In addition, the Department of State has determined funds previously made available to the Trust Fund principle may be utilized for operations to provide further support to the Hollings Center.

Eisenhower Exchange Fellowship Program

($ in thousands)	FY 2013 Actual	FY 2014 Estimate	FY 2015 Request	Increase / Decrease
Eisenhower Exchange Fellowship Program	191	400	400	-

The Eisenhower Exchange Fellowship Program (EEF) builds international understanding by bringing rising leaders to the United States, and sending their American counterparts abroad, on custom designed professional programs. The EEF trust fund accrues interest earnings to support these exchanges. The FY 2014 estimate will be updated through the year as such earnings are available. The FY 2015 request reflects an estimated $400,000 in projected earnings to be available for obligation to the program.

Israeli Arab Scholarship Program

($ in thousands)	FY 2013 Actual	FY 2014 Estimate	FY 2015 Request	Increase / Decrease
Israeli Arab Scholarship Program	13	13	26	13

The Israeli Arab Scholarship Program (IASP) funds scholarship programs for Israeli Arabs to attend institutions of higher education in the United States. The IASP trust fund will provide an estimated $26,300 in interest earnings in FY 2015 to support such activities to be implemented by the Bureau of Education and Cultural Affairs. Due to the low interest earned by this trust fund, the Department intends to allow for the accumulation of interest and earnings over time to effectively implement the scholarship program. In addition, opportunities for highly qualified Israeli-Arab graduate students to attend institutions of higher education in the U.S. will be executed as part of the Fulbright program.

East-West Center

($ in thousands)	FY 2013 Actual	FY 2014 Estimate	FY 2015 Request	Increase / Decrease
East-West Center	15,855	16,700	10,800	-5,900

The Center for Cultural and Technical Interchange between East and West (East-West Center) was established by the Congress in 1960 to promote understanding and good relations between the United States and the nations of the Asia-Pacific region. Located in Hawaii, the East-West Center has engaged more than 62,000 participants in its programs since its inception, including at the highest political levels in some nations. It draws on extensive individual and institutional ties to work effectively on critical regional issues.

The FY 2015 request of $10.8 supports the East-West Center's Congressionally-mandated public diplomacy mission, helping the U.S. and countries of the Asia Pacific region to understand each other's societies and interests as a means of reducing conflict and advancing U.S. national interests.

National Endowment for Democracy

($ in thousands)	FY 2013 Actual	FY 2014 Estimate	FY 2015 Request	Increase / Decrease
National Endowment for Democracy	111,802	135,000	103,450	-31,550

The National Endowment for Democracy (NED) was established by the Congress in 1983 to strengthen democratic institutions around the world. Through a worldwide grants program, NED assists those working abroad to build democratic institutions and spread democratic values.

NED's four affiliated core institutes – the American Center for International Labor Solidarity, the Center for International Private Enterprise, the International Republican Institute, and the National Democratic Institute – represent public American institutions working in sectors critical to the development of democracy. NED also supports initiatives of nongovernmental organizations fostering independent media, human rights, and other essential democratic elements.

Directed by a bipartisan board, NED makes approximately 1,200 grants per year in nearly 100 countries. NED's grants advance long-term U.S. interests and address immediate needs in strengthening democracy, human rights, and the rule of law.

The FY 2015 request for NED of $103.5 million will enable NED to continue a strong grants program in priority countries and regions, such as the Middle East and North Africa.

Broadcasting Board of Governors

($ in thousands)	FY 2013 Actual	FY 2014 Estimate	FY 2015 Request	Increase / Decrease
Broadcasting Board of Governors	713,486	733,480	721,260	-12,220
International Broadcasting Operations	702,632	721,080	716,460	-4,620
Broadcasting Capital Improvements	6,674	8,000	4,800	-3,200
Overseas Contingency Operations	4,180	4,400	-	-4,400

The FY 2015 request provides $716.5 million for International Broadcasting Operations. Through this appropriation, the Broadcasting Board of Governors (BBG) funds operations of its broadcasting organizations, as well as related program delivery and support activities. The FY 2015 request provides $4.8 million in Broadcasting Capital Improvements funding to maintain the worldwide transmission network of the BBG, including the security requirements of facilities, maintenance, repairs, and improvements to existing systems.

The BBG is an independent Federal entity responsible for all U.S. non-military international broadcasting programs. BBG broadcasting organizations include the Voice of America (VOA), Radio Free Europe/Radio Liberty (RFE/RL), Radio Free Asia (RFA), Radio and TV Marti, and the Middle East Broadcasting Networks (MBN) – Radio Sawa and Alhurra Television.

The BBG mission is to inform, engage, and connect people around the world in support of freedom and democracy. BBG radio, television, and Internet programs reach more than 206 million people each week in 61 languages. By exemplifying free media and free expression, the BBG helps foster and sustain free, democratic societies. Those societies have proven to be more peaceful and stable and rarely threaten their neighbors or offer safe havens for terrorists. Nurturing them is thus a national security imperative, consistent with the President's National Security Strategy.

The FY 2015 Budget Request includes substantial reductions and investments that rebalance BBG resources away from legacy markets (in Europe) and platforms (shortwave and medium wave) and toward current foreign policy priorities (Africa, Asia, and the Middle East) and modern media platforms (FM radio, television, and digital). In keeping with this strategy, the request includes investments to engage audiences in Africa and Southeast Asia, expand English learning programs, and increase and enhance social media presence and products. The request also expands on BBG efforts to transition to digital transmission technology by continuing to evolve away from shortwave radio transmissions.

The BBG will reduce language service duplication in some markets, increasing efficiency and boosting impact, by ensuring coordinated complementary operations and content where two BBG broadcasters co-exist. To afford some of the proposed investments and its transition to digital technology, the BBG proposes significant targeted reductions to administrative costs and to scale back less effective transmissions.

As part of a multi-year strategy to realize efficiencies and cost savings in its Satellite transmission program, the BBG included a $29.9 million funding request through the Opportunity, Growth and Security Initiative. By providing this funding the BBG estimates savings of 31 percent in satellite transmission costs over a seven year period.

United States Institute of Peace

($ in thousands)	FY 2013 Actual	FY 2014 Estimate	FY 2015 Request	Increase / Decrease
United States Institute of Peace	37,030	37,000	35,300	-1,700
Enduring	29,040	30,984	35,300	4,316
Overseas Contingency Operations	7,990	6,016	-	-6,016

The United States Institute of Peace (USIP) is a quasi-federal, independent, nonpartisan institution charged with increasing the nation's capacity to manage international conflict without violence. USIP exemplifies America's commitment to peace and acts daily to uphold that commitment.

The FY 2015 request for USIP provides $35.3 million to engage directly in conflict zones and provide education, training, analysis, and resources to those working for peace.

USIP works with U.S. government partners and non-governmental organizations to advance U.S. strategic interests while helping to protect the vulnerable from conflicts that devastate lives and livelihoods. These conflicts undermine legitimate governments that attempt to resolve disputes through laws rather than arms, and violate universal standards of human dignity. All too often, they sustain extremists and their vicious ideologies. Left unaddressed, these conflicts imperil America's economic and physical security. They threaten values America shares with just societies worldwide. For these reasons, Congress included United States Institute of Peace Act in Title XVII of the Defense Authorization Act of 1985, creating an independent institute to "promote international peace and the resolution of conflicts among the nations and peoples of the world without recourse to violence." The Institute is governed by a 15-member Board. By law, Board members include the Secretary of State, the Secretary of Defense, and the President of the National Defense University along with 12 others appointed by the President of the United States and confirmed by the U.S. Senate.

FOREIGN ASSISTANCE REQUEST
($000)

	FY 2013 Enduring Actual	FY 2013 OCO Actual	FY 2013 Actual Total[1]	FY 2014 Estimate Enduring	FY 2014 Estimate OCO	FY 2014 Estimate Total	FY 2015 Request Enduring	FY 2015 Request OCO	FY 2015 Request Total	Increase / Decrease
FOREIGN OPERATIONS	**26,483,794**	**7,327,133**	**33,810,927**	**28,719,308**	**5,129,593**	**33,848,901**	**27,921,291**	**3,891,400**	**31,812,691**	**(2,055,525)**
U.S Agency for International Development	**1,204,349**	**246,457**	**1,450,806**	**1,222,169**	**91,038**	**1,313,207**	**1,503,916**	**65,000**	**1,568,916**	**255,709**
USAID Operating Expenses (OE)	1,037,068	242,183	1,279,251	1,059,229	81,000	1,140,229	1,318,816	65,000	1,383,816	243,587
Conflict Stabilization Operations (CSO)	-	-	-	-	-	-	-	-	-	-
USAID Capital Investment Fund (CIF)	123,134	-	123,134	117,940	-	117,940	130,815	-	130,815	12,875
USAID Inspector General Operating Expenses	44,147	4,274	48,421	45,000	10,038	55,038	54,285	-	54,285	(753)
Bilateral Economic Assistance	**15,946,523**	**5,188,054**	**21,134,577**	**16,787,609**	**3,894,165**	**20,681,774**	**16,471,852**	**2,778,400**	**19,250,252**	**(1,431,522)**
Global Health Programs (USAID and State)[2]	8,065,888	-	8,065,888	8,439,450	-	8,439,450	8,050,000	-	8,050,000	(389,450)
Global Health Programs – USAID	[2,626,059]	-	[2,626,059]	[2,769,450]		[2,769,450]	[2,680,000]		[2,680,000]	[-89,450]
Global Health Programs - State	[5,439,829]	-	[5,439,829]	[5,670,000]		[5,670,000]	[5,370,000]		[5,370,000]	[-300,000]
Development Assistance (DA)	2,717,671	-	2,717,671	2,507,001		2,507,001	2,619,984		2,619,984	112,983
International Disaster Assistance (IDA)	799,468	750,927	1,550,395	876,828	924,172	1,801,000	665,000	635,000	1,300,000	(501,000)
Transition Initiatives (TI)[3]	47,604	21,224	68,828	48,177	9,423	57,600	67,600	-	67,600	10,000
Complex Crises Fund (CCF)[4]	9,496	43,498	52,994	20,000	20,000	40,000	30,000	-	30,000	(10,000)
Development Credit Authority – Subsidy (DCA)	[40,000]		[40,000]	[40,000]		[40,000]	[40,000]		[40,000]	
Development Credit Authority - Administrative Expenses	7,880	-	7,880	8,041		8,041	8,200		8,200	159
Economic Support Fund (ESF)[5, 6, 7, 8]	2,573,587	3,293,886	5,867,473	2,932,967	1,656,215	4,589,182	3,398,694	1,678,400	5,077,094	487,912
Democracy Fund	108,960	-	108,960	130,500		130,500	-	-	-	(130,500)
Migration and Refugee Assistance (MRA)[6]	1,590,146	1,078,519	2,668,665	1,774,645	1,284,355	3,059,000	1,582,374	465,000	2,047,374	(1,011,626)
U.S. Emergency Refugee and Migration Assistance (ERMA)	25,823	-	25,823	50,000		50,000	50,000	-	50,000	-
Independent Agencies	**1,258,585**	**-**	**1,258,585**	**1,329,700**		**1,329,700**	**1,422,100**	**-**	**1,422,100**	**92,400**
Peace Corps	356,015	-	356,015	379,000		379,000	380,000	-	380,000	1,000
Millennium Challenge Corporation	852,728	-	852,728	898,200		898,200	1,000,000	-	1,000,000	101,800
Inter-American Foundation	21,361	-	21,361	22,500		22,500	18,100	-	18,100	(4,400)
U.S. African Development Foundation	28,481	-	28,481	30,000		30,000	24,000	-	24,000	(6,000)
Department of Treasury	**35,552**	**1,474**	**37,026**	**23,500**	**-**	**23,500**	**39,500**	**-**	**39,500**	**16,000**
International Affairs Technical Assistance	24,160	1,474	25,634	23,500		23,500	23,500		23,500	-
Debt Restructuring	11,392	-	11,392	-		-	-		-	-
International Monetary Fund	-	-	-	-		-	16,000		16,000	16,000
International Security Assistance	**6,900,352**	**1,891,148**	**8,791,500**	**7,366,063**	**1,144,390**	**8,510,453**	**6,766,580**	**1,048,000**	**7,814,580**	**(695,873)**
International Narcotics Control and Law Enforcement (INCLE)[4, 7, 10]	1,005,611	853,067	1,858,678	1,005,610	344,390	1,350,000	721,911	396,000	1,117,911	(232,089)
Nonproliferation, Antiterrorism, Demining and Related Programs (NADR)	560,270	114,592	674,862	630,000	70,000	700,000	605,400	-	605,400	(94,600)
Peacekeeping Operations (PKO)[9, 10]	287,508	202,689	490,197	235,600	200,000	435,600	221,150	115,000	336,150	(99,450)
International Military Education and Training (IMET)	100,432	-	100,432	105,573		105,573	107,474	-	107,474	1,901
Foreign Military Financing (FMF)[3, 5, 9]	4,946,531	720,800	5,667,331	5,389,280	530,000	5,919,280	5,110,645	537,000	5,647,645	(271,635)
Multilateral Assistance	**2,875,204**	**-**	**2,875,204**	**3,010,749**		**3,010,749**	**2,873,943**	**-**	**2,873,943**	**(136,806)**
International Organizations and Programs[2]	326,651	-	326,651	344,020		344,020	303,439		303,439	(40,581)

FOREIGN ASSISTANCE REQUEST
($000)

	FY 2013 Enduring Actual	FY 2013 OCO Actual	FY 2013 Actual Total [1]	FY 2014 Estimate Enduring	FY 2014 Estimate OCO	FY 2014 Estimate Total	FY 2015 Request Enduring	FY 2015 Request OCO	FY 2015 Request Total	Increase / Decrease
International Financial Institutions (IFIs)	**2,548,553**	**-**	**2,548,553**	**2,666,729**	**-**	**2,666,729**	**2,570,504**	**-**	**2,570,504**	**(96,225)**
International Bank for Reconstruction and Development	180,993	-	180,993	186,957	-	186,957	192,921	-	192,921	5,964
International Development Association (IDA)	1,351,018	-	1,351,018	1,355,000	-	1,355,000	1,290,600	-	1,290,600	(64,400)
African Development Bank	30,717	-	30,717	32,418	-	32,418	34,119	-	34,119	1,701
African Development Fund (AfDF)	163,449	-	163,449	176,336	-	176,336	195,000	-	195,000	18,664
Asian Development Bank	101,190	-	101,190	106,586	-	106,586	112,194	-	112,194	5,608
Asian Development Fund	94,937	-	94,937	109,854	-	109,854	115,250	-	115,250	5,396
Inter-American Development Bank	107,110	-	107,110	102,000	-	102,000	102,020	-	102,020	20
Enterprise for the Americas Multilateral Investment Fund	14,995	-	14,995	6,298	-	6,298	-	-	-	(6,298)
IDA Multilateral Debt Relief Initiative	-	-	-	-	-	-	78,900	-	78,900	78,900
AfDF Multilateral Debt Relief Initiative	-	-	-	-	-	-	13,500	-	13,500	13,500
Global Environment Facility (GEF)	124,840	-	124,840	143,750	-	143,750	136,563	-	136,563	(7,187)
Clean Technology Fund	175,283	-	175,283	184,630	-	184,630	201,253	-	201,253	16,623
Strategic Climate Fund	47,374	-	47,374	49,900	-	49,900	63,184	-	63,184	13,284
International Fund for Agricultural Development	28,481	-	28,481	30,000	-	30,000	30,000	-	30,000	-
Global Agriculture and Food Security Program	128,165	-	128,165	133,000	-	133,000	-	-	-	(133,000)
Transfer to Multilateral Trust Funds [8]	-	-	-	50,000	-	50,000	-	-	-	(50,000)
Middle East and North Africa Transition Fund	-	-	-	-	-	-	5,000	-	5,000	5,000
Export & Investment Assistance	**(1,336,771)**	**-**	**(1,336,771)**	**(997,482)**	**-**	**(997,482)**	**(1,156,600)**	**-**	**(1,156,600)**	**(159,118)**
Export-Import Bank	(1,053,137)	-	(1,053,137)	(841,500)	-	(841,500)	(1,021,200)	-	(1,021,200)	(179,700)
Overseas Private Investment Corporation (OPIC)	(331,103)	-	(331,103)	(211,055)	-	(211,055)	(203,100)	-	(203,100)	7,955
U.S. Trade and Development Agency	47,469	-	47,469	55,073	-	55,073	67,700	-	67,700	12,627
Related International Affairs Accounts	**80,765**	**-**	**80,765**	**85,100**	**-**	**85,100**	**88,785**	**-**	**88,785**	**3,685**
International Trade Commission	78,866	-	78,866	83,000	-	83,000	86,459	-	86,459	3,459
Foreign Claims Settlement Commission	1,899	-	1,899	2,100	-	2,100	2,326	-	2,326	226
Department of Agriculture	**1,533,859**	**-**	**1,533,859**	**1,651,126**	**-**	**1,651,126**	**1,585,126**	**-**	**1,585,126**	**(66,000)**
P.L. 480, Title II	1,359,358	-	1,359,358	1,466,000	-	1,466,000	1,400,000	-	1,400,000	(66,000)
McGovern-Dole International Food for Education and Child Nutrition Programs	174,501	-	174,501	185,126	-	185,126	185,126	-	185,126	-
Rescissions										
Total Rescissions Foreign Operations	**(400,000)**	**-**	**(400,000)**	**(23,000)**	**-**	**(23,000)**	**-**	**-**	**-**	**23,000**
Export & Investment Assistance	**(400,000)**	**-**	**(400,000)**	**(23,000)**	**-**	**(23,000)**	**-**	**-**	**-**	**23,000**
Export-Import Bank	(400,000)	-	(400,000)	(23,000)	-	(23,000)	-	-	-	23,000

Footnotes

1/ The FY 2013 Actual Enduring reflects the full-year continuing resolution, reduced by the 0.032% rescission and sequestration The FY 2013 Actual OCO reflects the full year Continuing Resolution reduced by sequestration

2/ The FY 2013 Enduring Actual level reflects the transfer of $4.4 million from the International Organizations and Programs account to the Global Health Programs - USAID account

3/ The FY 2013 OCO Actual level reflects the transfer of $15 million from the Foreign Military Financing account to the Transition Initiatives account

4/ The FY 2013 OCO Actual level reflects the transfer of $15 million from the International Narcotics Control and Law Enforcement account to the Complex Crises Fund account

5/ The FY 2013 OCO Actual level reflects the transfer of $223.667 million from the Foreign Military Financing account to the Economic Support Fund account

6/ The FY 2013 OCO Actual level reflects the transfer of $35.5 million from the Migration and Refugee Assistance account to the Economic Support Fund account

7/ The FY 2013 OCO Actual level reflects the transfer of $25.78 million from the International Narcotics Control and Law Enforcement account to the Economic Support Fund account

8/ FY 2014 Estimate levels include an anticipated transfer of $50 million from the Economic Support Fund account to the Multilateral Development Banks in accordance with sec 7060(c)(8) of the Consolidated Appropriations Act, 2014

9/ The FY 2013 OCO Actual level reflects the transfer of $87.14 million from the Foreign Military Financing account to the Peacekeeping Operations account

10/ The FY 2013 OCO Actual level reflects the transfer of $38.62 million from the International Narcotics Control and Law Enforcement account to the Peacekeeping Operations account

USAID Operating Expenses

($ in thousands)	FY 2013 Actual	FY 2014 Estimate	FY 2015 Request	Increase / Decrease
USAID Operating Expenses	1,279,251	1,140,229	1,383,816	243,587
Enduring	1,037,068	1,059,229	1,318,816	259,587
Overseas Contingency Operations	242,183	81,000	65,000	-16,000

Recognizing that development is essential, along with defense and diplomacy, in advancing U.S. foreign policy and national security interests, the National Security Strategy (NSS) and Presidential Policy Directive (PPD) on Development call for investing in development capabilities and institutions. The FY 2015 U.S. Agency for International Development (USAID) Operating Expenses (OE) request provides that investment in a constrained budget environment. The request includes funding to maintain the strengthened U.S. Direct Hire (USDH) overseas workforce to meet U.S. foreign policy objectives and support Presidential initiatives. It also includes funding to continue the institutionalization of the USAID Forward agenda, which is transforming the Agency by reforming procurement systems, building local capacity in host countries, and pioneering scientific, technological, and innovative approaches to traditional development challenges.

For FY 2015, the $1,318.8 million USAID OE request for enduring operations will fund the administrative costs of managing USAID programs. This amount will allow the Agency to offset the projected decrease in other funding sources, such as recoveries, reimbursements, and trust funds, that support operations while restoring the New Obligation Authority (NOA) needed to maintain its current levels of operations into FY 2015. The OE budget covers salaries and benefits, overseas and Washington operations, and central support, including human capital initiatives, security, and information technology (IT).

FY 2015 funds will also cover salaries, operational expenses, and the operational costs for the enduring programs in the frontline states of Afghanistan, Pakistan, and Iraq. Separately, an additional $65 million is requested in Overseas Contingency Operations (OCO) for extraordinary costs for Afghanistan.

Below are highlights of the FY 2015 enduring request and the $116.1 million in other funding sources USAID expects to have available in FY 2015.

Highlights:

- **Overseas Operations ($762.2 million):** The request includes funding for all USDH salaries and benefits for Foreign Service Officers serving overseas and the costs associated with securing and maintaining mission operations - including the enduring programs in the frontline states of Afghanistan, Pakistan, and Iraq - such as the salaries of local staff, travel, office and residential space, and International Cooperative Administrative Support Services.

- **Washington Operations ($424.5 million):** Funding will cover USDH salaries and benefits for Civil Service and Foreign Service employees working in Washington, general office support, and advisory and assistance services.

- **Central Support ($248.2 million):** The request includes funding for IT, office space, and other mandatory services.

Details of the FY 2015 OCO request of $65 million for USAID OE are addressed in the OCO chapter.

USAID Capital Investment Fund

($ in thousands)	FY 2013 Actual	FY 2014 Estimate	FY 2015 Request	Increase / Decrease
USAID Capital Investment Fund	123,134	117,940	130,815	12,875

The FY 2015 request for the U.S. Agency for International Development (USAID) Capital Investment Fund (CIF) of $130.8 million will support capital investments in information technology (IT), facility construction, and real-property maintenance. The USAID Operating Expenses account funds the annual operating and maintenance costs of information systems and facilities infrastructure.

Highlights:

- **Facility Construction ($95.8 million):** The request will support USAID's full cost of participation in the Capital Security Cost Sharing (CSCS) Program, which is designed to accelerate the construction of new secure, safe, and functional diplomatic and consular office facilities for all U.S. government personnel overseas. Since the FY 2013 CSCS bill was less than the amount appropriated in FY 2013, USAID plans to apply $35.7 million of available resources to fully fund the estimated FY 2015 CSCS bill of $131.5 million. The Secure Embassy Construction and Counterterrorism Act of 1999 (P.L. 106-113) requires USAID to co-locate on new embassy compounds.

- **Information Technology ($27.4 million):** The request will support USAID Forward goals through implementation of the IT Strategic Plan and address Federal priorities, such as the 25 Point Implementation Plan to Reform Federal Information Technology and PortfolioStat. It also will fund investments to standardize and consolidate IT infrastructure to lower operational costs and close the productivity gap by building a "future-ready" workforce equipped with modern tools and technologies. In addition, funding supports the increased use of shared services, with an emphasis on commodity information technology and cyber security, modernization of information systems, and maximization of interoperability and information accessibility per Federal Open Data policies.

- **Real Property Maintenance ($7.6 million):** The request will continue a real property maintenance fund that will allow the Agency to develop and sustain a maintenance-and-repair program for the properties it owns. The fund will reduce the expensive future cost of major repairs, limit health and safety risks, increase efficiencies and protect value, and align with best practices.

USAID Inspector General Operating Expenses

($ in thousands)	FY 2013 Actual	FY 2014 Estimate	FY 2015 Request	Increase / Decrease
USAID Inspector General Operating Expenses	48,421	55,038	54,285	-753
Enduring	44,147	45,000	54,285	9,285
Overseas Contingency Operations	4,274	10,038	-	-10,038

The FY 2015 request of $54.3 million for the Office of Inspector General (OIG) for the U.S. Agency for International Development (USAID) will fund salaries, benefits, and operating expenses for the organization. This funding supports audit and investigative coverage of USAID, United States African Development Foundation (USADF), and Inter-American Foundation (IAF) programs and activities, and includes mandatory audits of these organizations' annual financial statements and information security management.

OIG advances foreign assistance objectives by improving the management and delivery of foreign assistance funds, increasing the efficiency and effectiveness of foreign assistance programs, and deterring and detecting fraud, corruption, criminal activity, and misconduct in the programs, operations, and workforce of the agencies for which it provides oversight. OIG oversight activities help address the heightened risks of fraud and misuse of funds that foreign assistance programs face in international settings where systems of accountability need further strengthening.

This funding level will enable OIG to respond to increasing foreign assistance oversight requirements. Under USAID's Local Solutions initiative, a larger share of foreign assistance funds are expected to be allocated to host governments and to local private sector and nonprofit organizations. This focus on implementing more development programs through host-country systems exposes assistance funds to increased risks. OIG will continue to respond to these risks by intensifying audit coverage of these funds, increasing outreach efforts to implementing partners and beneficiaries, and expanding engagement with local law enforcement, prosecutors, and host-country audit entities.

In addition to addressing risks associated with intensified use of host-country systems, this funding will assist OIG in responding to other developments that increase oversight requirements. The extension of whistleblower protections to contractors and grantees is expected to increase the number of complaints of fraud, waste, and abuse OIG receives. New mandatory OIG reporting requirements associated with these whistleblower protections, protections extended to whistleblower federal employees related to their eligibility to access classified information, and trafficking-in-persons-related activities will also affect OIG's workload. In addition, increased agency efforts to detect insider threats are expected to produce more allegations of employee misconduct.

OIG is working to improve its operations to ensure that it is appropriately structured to respond to evolving operating conditions and oversight requirements. In response to Department of State guidance on staffing in Egypt, OIG is in the process of restructuring its footprint in the Middle East. The anticipated shift in personnel from Cairo to another regional hub is expected to increase OIG operating expenses.

While making these adjustments, OIG will continue to focus on activities with the potential to bring the greatest value to the organizations it serves and remain proactive in keeping customers and stakeholders informed. This funding level will also enable OIG to meet commitments to the Council of the Inspectors General on Integrity and Efficiency.

Global Health Programs

($ in thousands)	FY 2013 Actual[1/]	FY 2014 Estimate	FY 2015 Request	Increase / Decrease
Global Health Programs	8,065,888	8,439,450	8,050,000	-389,450
Global Health Programs - USAID	2,626,059	2,769,450	2,680,000	-89,450
Global Health Programs - State	5,439,829	5,670,000	5,370,000	-300,000

1/ The FY 2013 Enduring Actual level reflects the transfer of $4.4 million from the International Organizations and Programs account to the Global Health Programs - USAID account.

The Global Health Programs account funds health-related foreign assistance managed by the Department of State and the U.S. Agency for International Development (USAID). Investments in global health target the symptoms of and root causes of poverty and provide valuable assistance for U.S. government our partner countries to effectively deliver services, leading to the advancement of basic human rights and dignity. Moreover, these investments protect Americans at home and abroad, strengthen fragile states, promote social and economic progress, and support the rise of capable partners who can help to solve regional and global problems. U.S. government efforts in global health, including the United States' historic commitment to the treatment, care, and prevention of HIV/AIDS, are a signature of American leadership in the world.

The FY 2015 budget reflects a comprehensive and integrated global health strategy toward achieving an AIDS-free generation and ending preventable child and maternal deaths through the Administration's approach under the next phase of the Global Health Initiative (GHI). GHI will continue its drive for maximum impact and to expand its reach by building upon previous GHI investments made through the President's Emergency Plan for AIDS Relief (PEPFAR), the President's Malaria Initiative (PMI), maternal and child health, family planning and reproductive health, tuberculosis, neglected tropical diseases, and other programs. This approach will continue to save millions of lives while fostering sustainable health care delivery systems that can address the full range of developing country health needs. GHI's overall emphases are improving health outcomes through a focus on women, girls, and gender equity; increasing impact through strategic coordination and integration; strengthening and leveraging key multilateral organizations and global health partnerships; encouraging country ownership and investing in country-led plans; building sustainability through investments in health systems strengthening; improving metrics, monitoring, and evaluation; and promoting research, development, and innovation. The Department and USAID remain steadfast in their commitment to enhancing the integration of quality interventions with the broader health and development programs of the U.S. government, country partners, multilateral organizations, and other donors. Responding to global health challenges is a shared responsibility that cannot be met by one nation alone. The United States will remain unremitting in its challenge to the global community that it continue to focus on building healthier, stronger, and more self-sufficient nations in the developing world.

For FY 2015, a total of $8,050 million is requested for Global Health Programs (GHP) under two subaccounts: $2,680 million GHP-USAID for USAID-administered programs and $5,370 million GHP-State for Department of State-administered programs. The programs will focus on three key areas: Ending Preventable Child and Maternal Deaths; Creating an AIDS-free Generation; and Protecting Communities from Infectious Diseases. For all programs, resources will be used to support interventions intended to achieve ambitious global health outcomes. They will be focused toward countries with the highest need, demonstrable commitment to achieving sustainable health impacts, and the greatest potential to leverage U.S. government programs and platforms.

<u>Ending Preventable Child and Maternal Deaths</u>

The world has made remarkable strides in both public and private efforts toward saving the lives of women and children, yet maternal and child mortality remains a critical problem in developing countries. Child deaths decreased by 46 percent from 1990 to 2012, and maternal deaths decreased by 47 percent from 1990 to 2010. While these global mortality declines since 1990 are impressive, recent estimates indicate that each year more than 287,000 still women die from complications during pregnancy or childbirth and there are still 6.6 million deaths of children under five years of age – 43 percent of which are in the first month of life. Approximately three-quarters of these child and maternal deaths are preventable with currently available interventions.

The U.S. government continues to lead the charge in renewing the global effort to end preventable child and maternal deaths. Together with country partners, international organizations and non-governmental organizations from around the globe, the United States is working towards targets that will truly represent an end to preventable child deaths – with all countries having fewer than 20 deaths per 1,000 live births and fewer than 50 maternal deaths per 10,000 live births by 2035. Achieving these goals will save an additional 5 million children's lives each year and decrease by 75 percent the number of women who die from complications during pregnancy on an annual basis.

Ending preventable child and maternal deaths is not an outcome of U.S. government assistance alone nor is it solely the outcome of narrowly defined programs in maternal and child health (MCH). Rather, improvements in mortality outcomes are the result of increasingly effective efforts to link diverse health programs – in MCH, in malaria, in family planning's contribution to the healthy timing and spacing of pregnancy, in nutrition, in HIV/AIDS, and in sanitation and hygiene improvement. All of these efforts contribute to ending preventable child and maternal deaths.

The FY 2015 request provides over $2 billion in pursuit of the aforementioned goals. In addition to this request, the Administration's Opportunity, Growth, and Security Initiative, if enacted, will provide additional funding to expand programs supporting maternal and child survival to further catalyze the global momentum towards ending preventable maternal and child deaths.

Highlights:

Maternal and Child Health (MCH) ($695 million): Funding will support programs that work with country and global partners to increase the wide-spread availability and use of proven life-saving interventions, and to strengthen the delivery systems to help ensure the long term sustainability of these programs. USAID will extend coverage of proven, high-impact interventions to the most vulnerable populations in high-burden countries.

Funding will support a limited set of high-impact interventions that will accelerate the reduction of maternal and newborn mortality, including the introduction and scale-up of new child vaccines. For FY 2015, $200 million is requested within MCH for the GAVI Alliance to support the introduction of new vaccines, especially pneumococcal and rotavirus vaccines that have the greatest potential additional impact on child survival. Other priority child health interventions include essential newborn care; prevention and treatment of diarrheal disease, including increased availability and use of household and community-level water, sanitation, and hygiene; and expanded prevention and treatment of pneumonia, particularly at the community level. With further development of the public-private partnerships "Helping Babies Breathe and Survive and Thrive," the key causes of neonatal mortality, such as birth asphyxia, will receive increased attention. Under the Saving Mothers, Giving Life initiative, the maternal health program will provide support for essential and long-term health system improvements. Its impact will be enhanced through programs aimed at reducing maternal mortality during labor, delivery, and the vital first 48 hours postpartum, when most deaths from childbirth occur – and the highest point of risk during labor and delivery. Resources will be provided to combat maternal mortality with expanded coverage of preventive and life-saving interventions, such as prevention and management of post-partum hemorrhage, hypertensive disorders of pregnancy, and sepsis, as well as contributory causes of maternal death such as anemia. Simultaneously, resources will support efforts to build the health systems capability required to provide functioning referral systems and comprehensive obstetric care. The MCH program will also work to leverage investments in other health programs, particularly family planning and reproductive health, nutrition, and infectious diseases.

Malaria ($674 million): FY 2015 resources will continue to support the comprehensive strategy of the President's Malaria Initiative (PMI), which brings to scale a combination of proven malaria prevention and treatment approaches and integrates, where possible, these interventions with other priority health interventions. According to the World Health Organization's World Malaria Report 2013, the estimated number of malaria deaths in the Africa region has decreased by 54 percent among children under five years of age from 2000 to 2012. The estimated number of malaria cases in all age groups in Africa has dropped from 174 million cases in 2000 to 165 million in 2012. Deaths from malaria in Africa have also decreased in all age groups, from 802,000 in 2000 to 562,000 in 2012. PMI has played a significant role in these reductions. In FY 2013 alone, PMI distributed more than 27 million rapid diagnostic tests and 52 million life-saving antimalarial treatments and protected 45 million people against malaria with insecticide-treated nets or indoor residual spraying.

In PMI-supported countries, there is evidence of positive impacts on malaria-related illness and death. In all 15 of the original PMI countries (Angola, Benin, Ethiopia, Ghana, Kenya, Liberia, Madagascar, Malawi, Mali, Mozambique, Rwanda, Senegal, Tanzania, Uganda, and Zambia) declines in all-cause mortality rates among children under five have been observed – ranging from 16 percent (in Malawi) to 50 percent (in Rwanda).

While a variety of factors are influencing these mortality declines, malaria prevention and control efforts are playing a major role in these reductions. Ninety percent of all malaria deaths occur in sub-Saharan Africa, and the vast majority of these deaths are among children under five. USAID, through PMI, will continue to scale up malaria prevention and control activities and invest in strengthening delivery platforms in up to 24 African countries as well as support the scale-up of efforts to contain the spread of multidrug-resistant malaria in the Greater Mekong region of Southeast Asia and the Amazon Basin of South America. PMI will support host countries' national malaria control programs and strengthen local capacity to expand the use of four highly effective malaria prevention and treatment measures, including indoor residual spraying, long-lasting insecticide-treated mosquito nets, artemisinin-based combination therapies to treat acute illnesses, and interventions to prevent malaria in pregnancy and pilot new proven malaria control strategies as they become available. Funding will also continue to support the development of new malaria vaccine candidates, antimalarial drugs, new insecticides, and other malaria-related research with multilateral donors.

Family Planning and Reproductive Health ($538 million): Funding will support programs that improve and expand access to high-quality voluntary family planning services and information as well as other reproductive health care and priority health services. About 220 million women in the developing world have an unmet need for family planning, resulting in 53 million unintended pregnancies and 25 million abortions annually. In 2012 and 2013, USAID's family planning and reproductive health programs averted more than 12 million unintended pregnancies. Family planning (FP) is an essential intervention for the health of mothers and children, contributing to reduced maternal mortality (through preventing unintended pregnancy), healthier children (through breastfeeding), and reduced infant mortality (through better birth spacing). Activities will be directed toward enhancing the ability of couples to decide the number, timing, and spacing of births and toward reducing abortion and maternal, infant, and child mortality and morbidity. Activities will also support the key elements of successful FP programs, including mobilizing demand for modern family planning services through behavior change communication; commodity supply and logistics; service delivery; policy analysis and planning; biomedical, social science, and program research; knowledge management; and monitoring and evaluation. Priority areas include leveraging opportunities to expand services through MCH and HIV platforms; contraceptive security; community-based approaches; expanding access to voluntary long-acting and permanent contraceptive methods; promoting healthy birth spacing; and focusing on cross-cutting issues of gender, youth, and equity.

Nutrition ($101 million): More than 200 million children under age five and one in three women in the developing world suffer from undernutrition. Undernutrition contributes to 45 percent of child deaths and leads to irreversible losses to children's cognitive development, resulting in lower educational attainment and lower wages. Since 2008, 53 million infants, children, and women have been provided core nutrition interventions. Nutrition activities will be linked with the Feed the Future Initiative and evidence-based interventions that focus on the prevention of undernutrition through integrated services. These include nutrition education to improve maternal diets, nutrition during pregnancy, exclusive breastfeeding, and infant and young child feeding practices; diet quality and diversification through fortified or biofortified staple foods, specialized food products, and community gardens; and delivery of nutrition services such as micronutrient supplementation and community management of acute malnutrition.

Vulnerable Children ($14.5 million): Funding for the Displaced Children and Orphans Fund (DCOF) supports projects that strengthen the economic capacity of vulnerable families to protect and provide for the needs of their children, strengthen national child protection systems, and facilitate family reunification and social reintegration of children separated during armed conflict, including child soldiers, street children and institutionalized children. In addition to DCOF, funding is requested to implement the Action Plan for Children on Adversity, which is the first-ever whole-of-government strategic guidance on international assistance for children in adversity. Children in adversity include those affected by HIV/AIDS, in disasters, or who are orphans, trafficked, exploited for child labor, recruited as soldiers, neglected, or in other vulnerable conditions. This effort builds on the success of the Child Survival Call to Action, enhancing it by integrating models of assistance and measuring results to help ensure that children ages 0-18 not only survive, but also thrive.

Creating an AIDS-free Generation

The President's Emergency Plan for AIDS Relief (PEPFAR), the largest effort by any nation to combat a single disease, continues to work towards achieving ambitious prevention, care, and treatment goals while strengthening health systems and emphasizing country ownership in order to build a long-term sustainable response to the epidemic and to create an AIDS-free generation. PEPFAR represents U.S. leadership in meeting the shared responsibility of all global partners to make smart investments to save lives. Under this Administration, unprecedented progress has been made in the fight against AIDS.

By September 30, 2013, PEPFAR exceeded President Obama's 2011 World AIDS Day goal of putting 6 million people on treatment by directly supporting lifesaving treatment for 6.7 million men, women, and children worldwide. This is an almost four-fold increase since the start of this Administration, and an increase from 1.7 million persons on treatment in 2008. In FY 2013, PEPFAR provided care and support for a total of 17 million people, including more than 5 million orphans and vulnerable children (OVC). HIV testing and counseling is the starting point for strong HIV care and treatment programs as well as prevention of mother-to-child transmission (PMTCT) programs. In 2013, PEPFAR supported HIV counseling and testing for more than 57.7 million people, of whom more than12.8 million were pregnant women, contributing to 95 percent of these babies being born HIV-free (including 240,000 that would otherwise have been infected). In just the last two years, over 1.5 million HIV-positive pregnant women received antiretroviral (ARV) interventions to prevent mother-to-child transmission meeting another of the President's 2011 World AIDS Day goals. In addition to these strong FY 2013 results, PEPFAR programs performed a cumulative number of more than 4.2 million voluntary medical male circumcisions (VMMC) procedures since it began supporting VMMC programs in 2007, with 2.2 million performed in FY 2013 alone representing the largest annual result to date.

Scientific advances and their successful program implementation have brought the world to a point where it is possible to envision HIV epidemic control. Strong U.S. leadership along with a heightened commitment by other partners, landmark scientific advances, and success in implementing effective programs has put us on a path to an AIDS-free generation. In sub-Saharan Africa, where the epidemic has hit the hardest, new HIV infections are down by nearly 40 percent since 2001, and AIDS-related mortality has declined by nearly one-third since 2005. This progress is due, in large part, to the unique efforts of and partnership between PEPFAR, the Global Fund to Fight AIDS, Tuberculosis and Malaria (the "Global Fund"), and host country governments. PEPFAR will help countries reduce new HIV infections and decrease AIDS-related mortality, while simultaneously increasing the capacity of countries to sustain and support these efforts over time.

PEPFAR continues to focus efforts on the long-term goals of saving lives, making smart investments, fostering shared responsibility, and driving results with science. PEPFAR's strategy comprises a core set of interventions that, particularly when pursued in concert and with partners, provide the potential to end the epidemic: expanding PMTCT programs; increasing coverage of HIV treatment to both reduce AIDS-related mortality and to enhance HIV prevention; increasing the number of males who are circumcised for HIV prevention; and increasing access to, and uptake of, HIV testing and counseling, condoms and other evidence-based, appropriately-targeted prevention interventions. In addition, PEPFAR platforms are being utilized by other U.S. government global health programs under GHI to advance other priorities such as reducing maternal mortality rates, addressing co-infection of HIV and tuberculosis and curbing malaria.

The GHP account is the largest source of funding for PEPFAR and this account is overseen and coordinated by the Department of State's Office of the U.S. Global AIDS Coordinator. The request includes $5,700 million ($5,370 million GHP-State and $330 million GHP-USAID) for country-based HIV/AIDS activities; technical support, strategic information, and evaluation support for international partners; and oversight and management. PEPFAR implementation is a broad interagency effort that involves the Department of State, USAID, the Peace Corps, and the Departments of Health and Human Services, Defense, Commerce, and Labor as well as local and international non-governmental organizations, faith- and community-based organizations, private sector entities, and partner governments.

Highlights:

Integrated HIV/AIDS Prevention, Care, and Treatment and Other Health Systems Programs ($3,996 million, including $3,760 million in GHP-State and $236 million in GHP-USAID):

- $3,760 million requested in GHP-State will support ongoing implementation of current HIV/AIDS prevention, care, treatment and other health systems programs in high burden countries and among key populations together with prioritization of combination activities based on sound scientific evidence that can have the maximum impact on reducing the rate of new infections and save more lives. Antiretroviral treatment (ART) as prevention, voluntary medical male circumcision (VMMC), condom distribution, and PMTCT – including the option of continuous ART for HIV-positive pregnant women regardless of the degree of disease progression – will continue to be instrumental in further turning the trajectory of the global AIDS epidemic.   These efforts and other complementary interventions, such as HIV testing and counseling, prevention programs for persons living with HIV and populations at high risk for infection continue to be core interventions for stemming the course of the epidemic.

FY 2015 funds will continue to be used for priority programs that address gender issues, including gender-based violence, and health systems strengthening (HSS), especially in nations with a severe shortage of healthcare workers and poorly functioning supply chain systems.   PEPFAR's investments made in HSS are intended to develop the infrastructure, systems, and country capacity needed to achieve an AIDS-free generation, as well as to benefit the health of the population for years to come.   Investments in HSS also form the basis of a strong heath care delivery system – the backbone of sustainability and an investment in country ownership.

PEPFAR continues to move beyond an emergency response, expanding efforts in ways that are sustainable and focused on integrated health delivery programs.   This approach promotes deeper strategic engagement with host governments to strengthen country-owned systems and workforces that are structured to support long term HIV/AIDS programs.   In FY 2015, this country ownership framework focused on sustainability will continue to be an important part of country plans and the strategies for engaging with host governments and civil society, encouraging them to bring complementary resources to the table.

- $236 million requested in GHP-USAID contributes to PEPFAR's global fight against the HIV/AIDS epidemic by targeting funds to meet critical needs of USAID field programs and by providing technical leadership worldwide.   Funding supports centrally driven initiatives that catalyze new interventions at the field level, translate research findings into programs, and stimulate scale-up of proven interventions.   GHP-USAID field resources leverage larger contributions from multilateral, international, private, and partner country sources by providing essential technical assistance for health systems strengthening, sustainability, capacity building, and country ownership.   In addition to country programs, USAID also will continue to support the development of advanced product leads including Tenofovir gel.   USAID collaborates closely with the Office of the U.S. Global AIDS Coordinator and other U.S. government agencies to ensure that activities funded with these resources complement and enhance efforts funded through the GHP-State account.

International Partnerships ($1,489 million, including $1,395 million in GHP-State and $94 million in GHP-USAID):

- PEPFAR will continue to expand multilateral engagement with the goal of leveraging the work of multilateral partners to maximize the impact of country programs.   A total of $1,395 million is requested in GHP-State to support a $45 million contribution to UNAIDS and a $1,350 million contribution to the Global Fund, supporting President Obama's pledge to provide $1 for every $2 pledged by other donors to the Global Fund.

- In addition to this request for the Global Fund, the Administration's Opportunity, Growth, and Security Initiative, if enacted, will provide $300 million to encourage even more ambitious pledges from other donors.

- $94 million is requested in GHP-USAID to support the Commodity Fund, which is used to procure condoms, HIV vaccine development through the International AIDS Vaccine Initiative (IAVI), and major research with worldwide impact including microbicides research activities.

Oversight and Management ($135 million in GHP-State):   FY 2015 resources will support costs incurred by multiple U.S. government agency headquarters including: supporting administrative and institutional costs; management of staff at headquarters and in the field; management and processing of cooperative agreements and contracts; and the administrative costs of the Office of the U.S. Global AIDS Coordinator.

Technical Support, Strategic Information, and Evaluation ($80 million in GHP-State):   Funding will support central technical support and programmatic costs and strategic information systems that monitor program performance, track progress, and evaluate the effectiveness of interventions.   PEPFAR aims to support the expansion of the evidence base around HIV interventions and broader health systems strengthening in order to support sustainable, country-led programs.   While not a research organization, PEPFAR works with implementers, researchers, and academic organizations to help inform public health and clinical practice.   Technical leadership and direct technical assistance activities (including scientific quality assurance) are supported for a variety of program activities, including: antiretroviral treatment, prevention (including sexual transmission, mother-to-child transmission, medical transmission, and testing and counseling), and care (including programs for orphans and vulnerable children and people living with or affected by HIV/AIDS), as well as cross-cutting efforts such as human capacity development, training for health care workers, and supply chain management.

Protecting Communities from Infectious Diseases

While the GHI emphasizes two key areas where the U.S. government can make a marked difference – ending preventable child and maternal deaths and creating an AIDS-free generation – U.S. government efforts also will continue to combat other infectious diseases that threaten the lives of millions of people each year including tuberculosis, neglected tropical diseases, and pandemic influenza.   The FY 2015 request includes $328 million GHP-USAID for programs to fight these other infectious diseases.

Highlights:

Tuberculosis (TB) ($191 million):   Funding will support programs that address a disease which is the leading cause of death and debilitating illness for adults throughout much of the developing world. Globally, 1.3 million people die annually from TB, and there are 8.6 million new cases of TB each year. Annually, there are approximately 630,000 cases of multi-drug resistant (MDR) TB, which are difficult to cure and are often deadly.   USAID program efforts focus on early diagnosis and successful treatment of the disease to both cure individuals and prevent transmission to others.   Funding priority is given to those countries that have the greatest burden of TB and MDR-TB.   Country-level expansion and strengthening of the Stop TB Strategy will continue to be the focal point of USAID's TB program, including increasing and strengthening human resources to support the delivery of priority health services such as Directly Observed Treatment, Short Course (DOTS) implementation, preventing and treating TB/HIV co-infection, and partnering with the private sector in DOTS.   In particular, USAID will continue to accelerate activities to address MDR-TB and extensively drug resistant TB, including the expansion of diagnosis and treatment, and infection control measures.   USAID collaborates with PEPFAR, other U.S. government agencies, and the Global Fund to integrate health services and strengthen delivery platforms to expand coverage of TB/HIV co-infection interventions.

Neglected Tropical Diseases (NTDs) ($86.5 million):   More than one billion people worldwide suffer from one or more neglected tropical diseases (NTDs), which cause severe disability, including permanent blindness, and hinder growth, productivity, and cognitive development. USAID focuses the majority of its NTD support on scaling-up preventive drug treatments for seven of the most prevalent NTDs, including schistosomiasis, onchocerciasis, lymphatic filariasis, trachoma, and three soil-transmitted helminths. USAID programs will use an agency-tested and World Health Organization (WHO)-approved integrated mass drug administration delivery strategy that will target affected communities, using drugs that have been proven safe and effective and can be delivered by trained non-health personnel. Through USAID partnerships with pharmaceutical companies, the vast majority of drugs are donated, valued at close to one billion dollars each year. Expanding these programs to national scale will support acceleration of global efforts to eliminate lymphatic filariasis and blinding trachoma globally, and onchocerciasis in the Americas. USAID will continue to work closely with the WHO and global partners to create an international NTD training course and standardized monitoring and evaluation guidelines for NTD programs, and ensure the availability of quality pharmaceuticals.

Pandemic Influenza and Other Emerging Threats (PIOET) ($50 million): Funding will support programs that focus on mitigating the possibility that a highly virulent virus such as H5N1, H1N1, or another pathogen variant could develop into a pandemic. Nearly 75 percent of all new, emerging, or re-emerging diseases affecting humans at the beginning of the 21st century originated in animals (zoonotic diseases), underscoring the need for the development of comprehensive disease detection and response capacities that span the traditional domains of animal health, public health, ecology, and conservation. In particular, activities will expand surveillance to address the role of wildlife in the emergence and spread of new pathogens; enhance field epidemiological training of national partners; strengthen laboratory capability to address infectious disease threats; broaden ongoing efforts to prevent H5N1 transmission; and strengthen national capacities to prepare for the emergence and spread of a pandemic.

Development Assistance

($ in thousands)	FY 2013 Actual	FY 2014 Estimate	FY 2015 Request	Increase / Decrease
Development Assistance	2,717,671	2,507,001	2,619,984	112,983

The FY 2015 Development Assistance (DA) request of $2,620 million supports the development principles outlined in the Presidential Policy Directive on Global Development (PPD-6), a policy framework that elevates global development as a key pillar of American power alongside defense and diplomacy. DA contributes to ending extreme poverty and promoting the development of resilient, democratic societies that are able to realize their potential. Ending extreme poverty requires enabling inclusive, sustainable growth; promoting free, peaceful, and self-reliant societies with effective, legitimate governments; and building human capital and creating social safety nets that reach the poorest and most vulnerable.

The FY 2015 request is designed to achieve the goals outlined in PPD-6 by supporting programs focused on sustainable development, economic growth, democratic governance, game-changing development innovations, sustainable systems for meeting basic human needs, and building resilience. Almost half of the funding requested from this account supports the Presidential Initiatives for Global Climate Change and Feed the Future. The U.S. government's programs funded by DA play a crucial part in the effort, along with the work of our allies, to eradicate extreme poverty in the next two decades.

A key outcome of the PPD-6 is Partnerships for Growth (PfG), a coordinated whole-of-government approach to enhanced engagement with countries that have demonstrated a strong commitment to democratic governance and sustainable development. By supporting well-governed countries with potential for broad-based economic growth, U.S. programs will help to seed a new generation of emerging markets, which in turn are likely to become trade and investment partners with the United States. In FY 2015, the Department of State and the U.S. Agency for International Development (USAID) will continue working with the PfG counties - El Salvador, Ghana, Philippines, and Tanzania - to promote broad-based economic growth.

In FY 2015, the DA request will also fund programs in the areas of basic and higher education, economic growth, governing justly and democratically, as well as expanded efforts in the areas of innovation, science and technology, evaluation and empowering women. Funding in these areas respond to entrenched challenges to human and economic security and support the rise of capable new players who can help solve regional and global problems and help protect U.S. national security. The request also includes funding in support of the Administration's strategic rebalance to Asia, which will intensify and expand USAID's environment, food security, governance, economic growth, and health programs in the region. It will enhance regional cooperation and build synergies among bilateral programs to address pressing transnational challenges vital to regional stability.

DA-funded programs are coordinated with programs managed by the Millennium Challenge Corporation and other international agencies. As mutually reinforcing foreign assistance activities, these programs advance and sustain overall U.S. development goals in targeted countries. Programs funded through this account contribute to international efforts working to achieve the Millennium Development Goals. In addition, programs support the efforts of host governments and their private sector and non-governmental partners to implement the systemic political and economic changes needed for sustainable development progress.

Highlights:

The Administration's principal priorities for DA funding in FY 2015 include:

- **Feed the Future (FTF) ($924 million):** Nearly 842 million people around the world suffer from chronic hunger and more than 3.5 million children die from undernutrition every year. By 2050, the world's population is projected to increase to more than nine billion requiring up to a 60 percent increase in agricultural production. The President's Feed the Future initiative, a USAID-led, whole-of-government effort, is the primary vehicle through which the U.S. government is pursuing its global food security objectives. With a focus on smallholder farmers, particularly women, FTF supports countries in developing their own agriculture sectors to produce more and more nutritious food and generate opportunities for economic growth and trade, helping to reduce poverty, hunger, and stunting. Agricultural growth is a highly effective way to fight poverty. Seventy-five percent of the world's poor live in rural areas in developing countries, where their livelihoods rely directly on agriculture. FTF is also focused on helping to prevent food crises by building the resilience of vulnerable populations. The FY 2015 request for FTF will fund the sixth year of this Presidential initiative.

  The FY 2015 FTF request allocates resources to countries based on clear criteria that measure need and opportunity. FTF investments address key constraints along the entire value chain – from bringing to scale innovative technologies that sustainably intensify on-farm productivity to improving crop storage and handling to increasing market access. FTF also fosters improvements in government policies that favor market-based agriculture-led economic growth. Programs are integrated in order to capitalize on the synergies between agriculture, health, nutrition, water, and climate change. In crisis, conflict, and post-conflict stabilization settings, programs contribute to sustainably reducing hunger, improving nutrition, and building resilience among vulnerable populations. Funding promotes greater private sector investment in agriculture, connects smallholders to markets, and builds the capacity of vulnerable and chronically food insecure households to participate in these economic activities. Funding also aims to reduce long-term vulnerability to food insecurity, especially in the Horn of Africa and the Sahel.

  The FY 2015 FTF request will also support programs that promote nutrition-sensitive agriculture. This includes promoting dietary diversity and quality by increasing access to nutritious foods across the value chain through both commercial and home-based efforts as well as enabling small- to medium-scale producers to access markets for nutritious foods. FTF nutrition activities will improve nutrient quality and food supply safety across value chain programs, including by reducing mold and improving post-harvest processing and storage. Activities aim to improve nutrition outcomes for all, but will especially target vulnerable populations during the 1,000 day window of opportunity between a woman's pregnancy and her child's second birthday. Additionally, FTF nutrition funding will foster global leadership, including supporting greater learning and exchange of evidence on nutrition, and support development and implementation of country-owned nutrition plans.

  This request continues to support the U.S. commitments to the New Alliance for Food Security and Nutrition, which joins donors to supports the commitments of Africa's leadership to drive effective policies; encourages greater local and international private sector investment in agricultural development; and acts to bring agricultural innovations to scale to support effective finance, mitigate risk, and improve nutrition. Specifically, funding supports the adoption and scale up of key technologies, such as improved seeds, and encourages principals for responsible land use, labor practices, and agricultural investment.

In addition to this request for the FTF initiative, the Administration's Opportunity, Growth, and Security Initiative, if enacted, would provide additional funding for bilateral food security in order to deepen and intensify the impact of the initiative as well as additional funding for multilateral food security funding.

- **Global Climate Change (GCC) ($316.9 million):** Global climate change threatens the livelihoods of millions in developing countries, and, if not addressed, will stall or even reverse the gains of many development efforts. The poor in developing countries are often the earliest and hardest hit by climate change, as they are heavily dependent on climate sensitive economic activities such as agriculture, fisheries, forestry, and tourism, and they lack the capacity to cope with economic or environmental shocks.

  The GCC Initiative invests in climate change adaptation as well as clean sustainable economic development. Globally, projected climate change impacts will reduce agricultural productivity, threaten vital infrastructure, negatively impact fisheries, and undermine public health. Additionally, climate change poses national security challenges, especially from the destabilizing impact it can have on economies and governance. Strategic investments will build more resilient and sustainable economies by helping vulnerable populations adapt to the impacts of climate change, and spurring economic growth while reducing net greenhouse gas (GHG) emissions.

  GCC Initiative funding will support programs in three pillar areas: clean energy, sustainable landscapes, and adaptation.

  Clean energy programs will reduce long-term emissions trends while supporting: sustainable economic growth and helping economies to leap frog emissions-intensive energy technologies with support for renewable energy and energy efficiency; emissions inventories; modernization of policy, planning and regulatory systems; improved grids; access to finance; and actions to reduce emissions in energy, industry, transportation, and buildings. Clean energy programs will focus on major emerging economies and potentially large emitters through Enhancing Capacity for Low Emission Development Strategies (EC-LEDS) programs in selected countries, including major emitters in Asia and countries participating in the Power Africa initiative.

  Sustainable landscapes programs, focused primarily in countries with globally important forests, will reduce GHG emissions while promoting economic opportunity by helping countries to address the drivers of deforestation and degraded lands. Sustainable landscapes programming will launch public-private partnerships to reduce tropical deforestation associated with key value chains through the Tropical Forest Alliance 2020. Sustainable landscapes programs will also develop and implement actions to address reducing emissions from land use under the EC-LEDS program, and build capacity to measure and monitor GHG emissions from forests, wetlands, and other carbon-rich landscapes. Programs in this pillar area will also promote policies and incentives that reward sustainable land use practices, build forest management capacity, and enhance property rights of local communities to help ensure better stewardship and management.

  Adaptation programs will assist countries to develop and implement effective strategies for reducing the impact of global climate change on vulnerable populations and for increasing those populations' resilience. Adaptation activities will support public-private partnerships, and also focus on least-developed countries, glacier-dependent nations, countries prone to climate related disasters, and small-island developing nations.

- **Education:** Education is foundational to human development. It is critical to promoting long-term, broad-based economic growth, reducing poverty and inequality, improving health, and promoting participatory democracy. However, around 57 million children of primary school age are still out of school without access to basic educational opportunities. Over half of these out-of-school children live in conflict-affected and crisis contexts. To compound matters, recent studies show that for many students in low-income countries, very little learning actually occurs in the classroom. Recent reports estimate that nearly 250 million primary school age children are not learning basic skills such as reading --whether they have been to school or not. If these children do not learn to read, they will have fewer opportunities and struggle with learning for the rest of their lives.

As they grow older, an increasing number of young people in developing countries find themselves without relevant knowledge and skills and are unable to fully participate in and contribute to economic development. The current scale of youth underemployment and unemployment is a matter of worldwide concern. Around 40 percent of the world's unemployed are youth, with young people out of work at up to four times the rate of adults. This brings major costs to both young people and society at large. Yet job creation requires a population that is educated, informed, and skilled.

To overcome all of these challenges, USAID's Education Strategy addresses learning across the education spectrum, including basic education, higher education, and workforce development. The majority of education funding is for basic education, with a primary focus on reading acquisition in primary grades to achieve the goal of improving reading skills for 100 million children by 2015. The Strategy also prioritizes increased equitable access to basic educational services for 15 million learners by 2015 in conflict or crisis contexts. Investments in workforce development and tertiary education that increase national capacity to support country development goals by 2015 are also critical.

FY 2015 resources support the implementation of education programs under the current Education Strategy. These programs are based on interventions that aim to measurably improve student learning outcomes, and that promote access and equity, relevance to national development, systemic reform, and accountability for results. This will be a critical time to support strong pushes to take effective interventions to greater scale.

- **Economic Growth:** Economic growth is essential to ending extreme poverty, promoting the development of resilient, democratic societies, and enabling governments to effectively provide basic public services. The quality of economic growth matters as much as how it is generated. To be sustainable, growth must be widely shared; inclusive of all ethnic groups, women, and other marginalized groups; and compatible with the need to both reduce climate change impacts and manage natural and environmental resources responsibly. Economic growth programs will help countries develop the policies and practices they need to support rapid and sustainable economic growth. Economic policies, regulations, and approaches also affect countries' ability to meet other development objectives. Funding will support programs that work with countries to improve the enabling environment for private investment, entrepreneurship, and broad-based economic growth by addressing issues such as property rights, business registration, administrative red tape, well-regulated competition, trade policies and capacity, and access to credit.

- **Governing Justly and Democratically:** Democracy, human rights, and governance are inseparable from other development goals. Without capable, transparent, accessible, and accountable public institutions, economic growth, broad-based opportunity, and key public services cannot be sustained. At the same time, citizens who enjoy access to services but do not live in a democratic society cannot realize the freedom and opportunity. U.S. assistance will support democracy, human rights, and governance to consolidate democratic institutions, make governments more effective and responsive to their populations, and expand the number of countries that respect human rights and act responsibly in the international system. The focus of DA interventions in this area will be on new and fragile democracies, as well as on those that have committed, through sound policies and practice, to build effective, transparent, and accountable governments, particularly in sub-Saharan Africa, Asia, and Latin America, to help ensure that they are able to deliver both political and socioeconomic benefits to their citizens. Programs will include efforts to increase political competition; strengthen civil society's role in political, economic, and social life; support the free flow of information; promote government that is effective and legitimate; strengthen the rule of law; and advance anti-corruption measures. Programming will pursue specific goals, including (1) increasing the ability of government officials, law professionals, non-governmental organization affiliates, journalists, election observers, and citizens to strengthen the effectiveness, accountability, and participatory nature of democratic institutions within new and fragile democracies; (2) strengthening domestic human rights organizations, supporting public advocacy campaigns on human rights, and training domestic election observers in order to foster respect for human rights, increase citizens' political participation, and expand political competition in closed societies; and (3) promoting stability, reform, and recovery to lay the foundations for democratic governance in conflict and failed states.

- **New Model of Development: Global Development Lab ($146.3 million):** USAID is accelerating development and using science, technology, innovation and partnerships to advance our goals through The U.S. Global Development Lab. The Lab scales major development breakthroughs and supports a set of initiatives and reforms aimed at transforming USAID into a fully modern development enterprise, as called for in the PPD-6 and the Quadrennial Diplomacy and Development Review (QDDR). The Lab will tap the expertise of Cornerstone partners from corporations, universities, foundations, and NGOs to jointly sponsor initiatives on innovation, science and technology, and evaluation. For example, the Development Innovation Ventures (DIV) program borrows from the private venture-capital model to invest resources in innovative development projects. DIV has proven a highly attractive model to attract resources from other development agencies and developing countries of the world to produce development breakthroughs. To leverage the power of research and development as envisioned in the PPD-6, the Lab will engage universities and mobilize the global science and technology community for development results, including in developing countries, and sponsor revolutionary, multi-disciplinary applied research in order to increase global understanding of complex development issues and accelerate science and technology-based solutions. DA funds will also expand access to mobile banking technology, which has the potential to bring low-cost financial services and cashless transactions to millions of people, small businesses, and microenterprises. Funding will support Private Sector Alliances and Global Development Alliances, which can leverage additional outside resources and improve the sustainability of development interventions by attracting private-sector, market-driven resources for the long term. Science and technology funding supports a series of Grand Challenges for Development, as well as partnerships between American scientists and those in developing countries, and other efforts to bring the power of science to bear on major development problems.

  In addition to this request, the Administration's Opportunity, Growth, and Security Initiative, if enacted, would include additional funding for science, technology, innovation, and partnerships to scale up innovative solutions and fund new programs focused on achieving transformational development results and accelerating progress toward development goals.

- **Gender:** To optimize outcomes for U.S. foreign policy objectives, including stability, peace, and development, the FY 2015 foreign assistance budget request supports U.S. promotion of gender equality and advancement of the political, economic, social, and cultural status of women and girls. USAID, through its 2012 Gender Equality and Female Empowerment Policy, and the Department of State are systematically addressing gender inequality in all foreign assistance programming and implementing commitments under the Women Peace and Security (WPS) National Action Plan and the U.S. Strategy to Prevent and Respond to Gender-Based Violence (GBV) Globally. USAID is programming DA funds for activities that promote women's leadership and empowerment, prevent and respond to GBV, and pursue specific objectives related to WPS and women's inclusion in peace-building. Funding will also be used to aid operating units in integrating gender equality into their strategies, project design, and monitoring and evaluation activities.

International Disaster Assistance

($ in thousands)	FY 2013 Actual	FY 2014 Estimate	FY 2015 Request	Increase / Decrease
International Disaster Assistance	1,550,395	1,801,000	1,300,000	-501,000
Enduring	799,468	876,828	665,000	-211,828
Overseas Contingency Operations	750,927	924,172	635,000	-289,172

The FY 2015 International Disaster Assistance (IDA) enduring request of $665 million will provide funds to save lives, reduce suffering, and mitigate and prepare for natural and complex emergencies overseas through food assistance, disaster relief, rehabilitation, and reconstruction assistance, including activities that transition to development assistance programs and disaster preparedness/risk reduction activities. This amount includes $166 million for emergency food assistance. The IDA request will enable the U.S. government to meet humanitarian needs quickly and support mitigation and preparedness programs.

The U.S. Agency for International Development's (USAID) Office of U.S. Foreign Disaster Assistance will administer $499 million to respond to natural disasters, civil strife, global economic downturns, food insecurity, and prolonged displacement of populations that continue to hinder the advancement of development and stability. IDA funds benefit the most vulnerable populations affected by natural disasters and complex emergencies, including internally displaced persons. These programs alleviate suffering, save lives, and reduce the impact of disasters. This funding level will allow the United States to maintain a reasonable level of resources to address continuing complex emergencies and invest in disaster risk reduction, while also maintaining sufficient resources to respond to new disasters.

USAID's Office of Food for Peace will administer $166 million for emergency food response. The IDA request ensures that the U.S. government can respond effectively and efficiently by using the right tool at the right time to respond to emergency situations and food insecurity with a range of interventions, including local and regional purchase of agricultural commodities, food vouchers, cash transfers, and cash for work programs. This funding level will allow the United States to continue providing life-saving food assistance in countries where in-kind food aid is not feasible while responding to new food crises.

In addition, approximately $1 million in IDA will be used to meet USAID's responsibility to cover certain necessary recurring and non-recurring costs for providing U.S. disaster assistance under the Compact of Free Association between the United States and the Republic of the Marshall Islands (RMI) and the Federated States of Micronesia (FSM). These funds are in addition to the $1 million in Development Assistance provided through USAID's Asia Bureau.

Details of the FY 2015 OCO Request for IDA are addressed in the OCO chapter.

Transition Initiatives

($ in thousands)	FY 2013 Actual[1]	FY 2014 Estimate	FY 2015 Request	Increase / Decrease
Transition Initiatives	68,828	57,600	67,600	10,000
Enduring	47,604	48,177	67,600	19,423
Overseas Contingency Operations	21,224	9,423	-	-9,423

1/ The FY 2013 OCO Actual level reflects the transfer of $15 million from the Foreign Military Financing account to the Transition Initiatives account.

The FY 2015 request of $67.6 million for the Transition Initiatives (TI) enduring account will address opportunities and challenges facing conflict-prone countries and those countries making the transition from the initial crisis stage of a complex emergency to sustainable development and democracy.

TI funds will support fast, flexible, short-term assistance to advance peace and democracy in countries that are important to U.S. foreign policy.   Examples of assistance include promoting responsiveness of central governments to local needs, civic participation programs, media programs raising awareness of national issues, addressing underlying causes of instability, and conflict resolution measures.

The request for TI also includes $20 million to address emerging needs and opportunities in the Middle East and North Africa (MENA) region.   Since 2011, the Department of State and USAID have used contingency funds to support shorter-term, high-impact programs that help countries transition toward sustainable development and democracy.   These programs focus on strategic priorities such as strengthening government institutions, building civil society, promoting conflict resolution, developing strong, independent media, improving service delivery, and expanding economic growth.   The MENA-related amounts requested in TI for FY 2015 will ensure transition-related funding for the region is prioritized and that there are sufficient funds remaining for other global needs.   TI-funded programs will meet policy objectives and be coordinated with existing assistance programs.

Complex Crises Fund

($ in thousands)	FY 2013 Actual[1]	FY 2014 Estimate	FY 2015 Request	Increase / Decrease
Complex Crises Fund	52,994	40,000	30,000	-10,000
Enduring	9,496	20,000	30,000	10,000
Overseas Contingency Operations	43,498	20,000	-	-20,000

1/   The FY 2013 OCO Actual level reflects the transfer of $15 million from the International Narcotics Control and Law Enforcement account to the Complex Crises Fund account.

The FY 2015 enduring request of $30 million for the Complex Crises Fund (CCF) will support the ability of the U.S. Agency for International Development (USAID) and the Department of State to rapidly respond during critical windows of opportunity by providing resources to address unforeseen political, social, or economic challenges that threaten stability, and support sustainable programs to foster long-term development.   The overarching goal is to seize opportunities to prevent or respond to emerging or unforeseen complex challenges and crises overseas, such as advancing peaceful transitions, democratic governance, and development progress.   The funds often target countries or regions that demonstrate a high or escalating risk of conflict or instability, but also can support an unanticipated opportunity for progress in a newly-emerging or fragile democracy.   Projects aim to address and prevent root causes of conflict and instability through a whole-of-government approach, but they can also work to support atrocity prevention and conflict mitigation so that development gains are not hindered due to conflict.

The request for CCF also includes $10 million designated to address emerging opportunities in the Middle East and North Africa (MENA) region.   Since 2011, the Department of State and USAID have used contingency funds to support shorter-term, high-impact programs that focus on strategic priorities in this region by supporting democratic transitions, strengthening civil society, improving service delivery, and expanding economic growth.   The MENA-related amounts requested in CCF for FY 2015 will ensure that funding for the region is prioritized and that there are sufficient funds remaining for other global needs.   CCF-funded programs will meet policy objectives and be coordinated with existing assistance programs.

Development Credit Authority

($ in thousands)	FY 2013 Actual	FY 2014 Estimate	FY 2015 Request	Increase / Decrease
Development Credit Authority - Subsidy	[40,000]	[40,000]	[40,000]	[0]
Development Credit Authority - Administrative Expenses	7,880	8,041	8,200	159

The FY 2015 request includes $40 million in Development Credit Authority (DCA) transfer authority to provide loan guarantees in all regions and sectors targeted by the U.S. Agency for International Development (USAID), and $8.2 million for DCA administrative expenses. DCA transfer authority allows field missions to transfer funds from USAID appropriation accounts to the DCA program account to finance the subsidy cost of DCA partial credit guarantees. These projects allow credit to be used as a flexible tool for a wide range of development purposes, and can help to promote broad-based economic growth in developing and transitional economies. DCA guarantees augment grant assistance by mobilizing private capital for sustainable development projects. In coordination with related technical assistance, DCA supports host countries in the financing of their own development.

In a little more than a decade, DCA has been used to mobilize in excess of $3.1 billion in local private financing at a budget cost of $129 million. DCA transfer authority has enabled 72 USAID missions to enter into over 300 guarantee agreements in virtually every development sector. USAID has incurred only $10.9 million in default claims to-date for all of the guarantees made under DCA, which represents an overall default rate of 1.75 percent. DCA projects have proven to be very effective in channeling resources to microenterprises, small-and medium-scale businesses, farmers, healthcare providers, and certain infrastructure sectors. In FY 2013, working directly with our partners and USAID missions, DCA completed 26 transactions in 19 countries that will leverage up to $495 million in private capital for critical investments in agriculture, health, education, municipal infrastructure, water, energy and other sectors. In FY 2013, DCA implemented several innovative guarantees: in Tanzania, it was used to implement the first-ever guarantee in support of Power Africa; in India, it was used to support $100 million in investment in small- and medium-scale clean energy power projects; in Mexico, it was used in collaboration with Credit Suisse and other private institutions to support $60 million in small- and medium-enterprise financing. In support of USAID Forward and other agency-wide priorities, the DCA portfolio in sub-Saharan Africa continues to grow. In FY 2014, the Africa portfolio will represent at least 50% of the value of all DCA transactions.

In FY 2015, DCA will continue to use guarantees to help banks and microfinance institutions access affordable long term capital for small- and medium-enterprise lending at longer tenors, particularly in sub-Saharan Africa. DCA will also continue to take advantage of more developed municipal capacity and capital markets to expand successful sub-sovereign financing models developed in Asia and Eastern Europe. In addition, DCA will test new applications of credit guarantees and develop new partnerships with diaspora groups, leasing companies, pension funds, and other guarantors, both public and private. Lastly, DCA guarantees will be used to increase investments in climate change activities including sustainable forestry, adaptation, and mitigation.

In accordance with the Federal Credit Reform Act of 1990, the request for credit administrative expenses will fund the total cost of development, implementation, and financial management of the DCA program, as well as the continued administration of USAID's legacy credit portfolios, which amount to more than $17 billion.

Economic Support Fund

($ in thousands)	FY 2013 Actual[1/]	FY 2014 Estimate	FY 2015 Request	Increase / Decrease
Economic Support Fund	5,867,473	4,589,182	5,077,094	487,912
Enduring	2,573,587	2,932,967	3,398,694	465,727
Overseas Contingency Operations	3,293,886	1,656,215	1,678,400	22,185

1/ The FY 2013 OCO Actual level reflects the following transfers: $223.667 million from the Foreign Military Financing account; $35.5 million from the Migration and Refugee Assistance account; and $25.78 million from the International Narcotics Control and Law Enforcement account to the Economic Support Fund account.

The FY 2015 Economic Support Fund (ESF) enduring request of $3,398.7 million advances U.S. interests by helping countries meet short- and long-term political, economic, and security needs.   These needs are addressed through a range of activities, including countering terrorism and extremist ideology; increasing the role of the private sector in the economy; assisting in the development of effective, accessible, independent legal systems; supporting transparent and accountable governance; and empowering citizens. Programs funded through this account are critical to U.S. national security because they help to prevent wars and contain conflicts, and foster economic prosperity at home by opening markets overseas, promoting U.S. exports, and helping countries transition to developed economies.

Highlights:

Sub-Saharan Africa ($521.1 million):   The FY 2015 request includes funding for programs that strengthen democratic institutions and support conflict mitigation and reconciliation, basic education, and economic growth in key African countries, including:

- **Democratic Republic of the Congo ($71.4 million):**   The FY 2015 request will support conflict mitigation to avert violence and human rights violations, the prevention and treatment of victims of sexual and gender-based violence, basic education, agriculture, and capacity building for the legislature, justice, and media sectors.   Funds will also be used for rule of law programs to support the development of democratic institutions that provide basic needs and services for citizens.

- **Liberia ($82.6 million):**   The FY 2015 request will support Liberia's efforts to consolidate progress made over the past few years and move more clearly from post-crisis activities into sustainable assistance programs as the United Nations Mission in Liberia draws down and the Liberian government takes on greater responsibilities to solidify confidence in public governance.   Funding will also be used to sustain health, water, governance, education, and agriculture programs, and expand infrastructure programs, especially in the energy sector.

- **Somalia ($79.2 million):**   The FY 2015 request will continue to support the formation of legitimate, durable governing institutions that are essential to alleviating humanitarian suffering in the broader Horn of Africa.   Increased resources will focus on stabilization and reconciliation efforts; nascent political party development; civil society efforts to promote peace, good governance, and consensus-building; and programs in education, livelihoods, and economic growth.

- **South Sudan ($225.4 million):**   Although South Sudan has been experiencing internal violence, this continued robust funding request enables the United States to support an inclusive peace process and be poised to respond to opportunities in this new nation as conditions permit. South Sudan will continue to need significant multi-donor assistance in developing governmental and civil society capacity and economic infrastructure to advance towards a lasting peace and democratic future. U.S. assistance will be positioned to support progress in governance, rule of law, conflict mitigation, civil society building, agriculture, infrastructure, health, and basic education.

- **Sudan ($9.5 million):** Peace and stability in Sudan remain critical objectives of the United States, both in the context of resolving outstanding and post-Comprehensive Peace Agreement (CPA) issues, as well as improving conditions in Darfur and seeking an end to the conflict there. In the Three Areas, Darfur, and other marginalized areas, efforts will focus on peacebuilding and conflict mitigation.

- **Zimbabwe ($19 million):** The FY 2015 request will expand efforts to improve governance in Zimbabwe by placing greater emphasis on strengthening Parliament, local governments, and executive branch structures and supporting civil society efforts to give voice to the people and hold government accountable. Efforts will also focus on improving food security.

- **State Africa Regional ($26.1 million):** These funds will support cross-cutting programs that prevent, mitigate, and resolve armed conflict and address regional transnational threats; strengthen democratic institutions; support social services for vulnerable populations; and foster economic growth (Africa Regional Democracy, Ambassadors' Special Self Help, Anti-Piracy Incentive, Conflict Minerals, Kimberley Process, Partnership for Regional East African Counter Terrorism, Safe Skies for Africa, Trafficking in Persons, Trans-Sahara Counter-terrorism Partnership, and Africa-Women, Peace and Security).

East Asia and the Pacific ($99.2 million): The FY 2015 request funds the Administration's strategic rebalance to the Asia-Pacific to strengthen regional economic integration and trade that advance democratic and economic development in the region, while supporting economic growth in the United States. Highlights include:

- **Burma ($58.7 million):** The FY 2015 request supports a forward-leaning U.S. policy that builds on Burma's political and economic reform agenda to promote national reconciliation, democracy, human rights, and the rule of law; foster economic opportunity; increase food security; and meet other basic human needs to enable Burma's population to contribute to and sustain reforms. By focusing on inclusivity, transparency, accountability, and local empowerment, programs strengthen civil society and promote democratic culture and practices. ESF-funded programs also provide crisis assistance and recovery programs to Burmese refugees and internally displaced persons.

- **East Asia and Pacific Regional ($26 million):** The FY 2015 request supports Asia's remarkable economic growth while advancing trade and investment opportunities for the United States. The Department of State leverages partnerships with key regional multilateral fora such as the Asia-Pacific Economic Cooperation Forum (APEC), the Association of Southeast Asian Nations (ASEAN), the ASEAN Regional Forum (ARF), the Pacific Islands Forum (PIF), and the Lower Mekong Initiative (LMI) to strengthen U.S. engagement at the annual East Asia Summit, the region's preeminent forum to discuss political and strategic issues. EAP Regional programs support these important multilateral institutions to help maintain momentum for key economic priorities, pursue broad improvements in good governance, encourage regional standards that more closely align governments with the Unites States, and support regional connectivity and integration. These programs will also fulfill the President's commitments to the Enhanced Economic Engagement

Initiative (E3) and the U.S.-Asia Pacific Comprehensive Partnership for a Sustainable Energy Future, announced by President Obama in November 2012 at the East Asia Summit.

- **Regional Development Mission for Asia ($5 million):**   The FY 2015 request builds the capacity of LMI countries to sustainably manage their natural resources, including management of increasingly variable shared water resources.   These efforts will increase the capacity of environmental civil society organizations to advocate for sound natural resource management, advance regional multi-stakeholder dialogues, and increase access to information on the environmental and social risks of large-scale infrastructure investments.

Europe and Eurasia ($316.1 million):   The FY 2015 ESF request for Europe and Eurasia is focused on supporting U.S. efforts to stabilize and transition Southeastern Europe and the independent states of the former Soviet Union towards becoming more secure, pluralistic, and prosperous countries.   Highlights include:

- **Bosnia and Herzegovina ($23.3 million):**   Funding will help Bosnia and Herzegovina regain momentum toward Euro-Atlantic integration and improve its uneven progress on reform. U.S. assistance will also support the development of state-level institutions; strengthen the rule of law; foster a sound financial and regulatory environment to promote investment; increase the competitiveness of small and medium enterprises in targeted sectors; improve governance at the sub-state level; build the capacity of local government and civil society; and address ethnic tensions.

- **Georgia ($38.3 million):**   The funding requested in FY 2015 will support Georgia's democratization, development of its economy, and Euro-Atlantic integration.   U.S. programs will help strengthen institutional checks and balances and the rule of law; develop a more vibrant civil society; promote political pluralism; bolster independent media and public access to information; increase energy security and clean energy investment; promote reforms necessary to foster economic development and attract foreign investment; and reinforce the use of science, technology, and innovation.

- **Kosovo ($35.5 million):**   Funding will help still nascent institutions in Kosovo adjust to the challenges of effective governance; further the development of the justice sector; drive private sector-led economic growth through policy reform and support to key sectors; strengthen democratic institutions; develop future leaders; build the capacity of civil society and independent media to address corruption and promote government accountability; as well as mitigate conflict by building tolerance among Kosovo's diverse communities.

- **Moldova ($15.1 million):**   Funding will support reforms necessary for Moldova's Euro-Atlantic integration by improving governance; increasing transparency and accountability; strengthening the rule of law; addressing corruption; supporting civil society and civic activism; improving the investment climate; and strengthening the productivity and competitiveness of entrepreneurs.

- **Ukraine ($57 million):**   U.S. assistance will promote democratic and economic reforms to support Ukraine and the aspirations of its people for Euro-Atlantic integration.   Funding will also help to strengthen democratic institutions and processes; enhance government accountability; support civil society, independent media, judicial reform, and anti-corruption efforts; improve conditions for investment, economic growth and competiveness; improve energy security and clean energy investment; and help bring the damaged Chornobyl nuclear facility to an environmentally safe and stable condition and properly store its nuclear waste.   Since the situation in Ukraine is currently in flux, the longer-term specifics of the program will be reviewed in light of changing circumstances.

- **Europe and Eurasia Regional ($61.8 million):** Resources will support initiatives to advance economic and democratic transition in the region by promoting cross-border energy linkages; advancing economic integration across the western Balkans; supporting lower emissions development pathways for the region; promoting civil society development and networks; sharing best practices related to democratic political processes; fostering professional investigative journalism; and leveraging transition experience and resources from emerging donors.

Near East ($1,492.8 million): The FY 2015 request includes funding to support democratic reform and political institution building in the Middle East and North Africa and to help create economic opportunities for youth in the region. Funding will continue for programs that advance U.S. national security interests.

- **MENA Initiative Reforms ($225 million):** These funds are requested for targeted programs that will advance the transitions under way across the region. Programs will focus on jobs, democratic governance, rule of law, and human rights. They will specifically target reformers at all levels of society and across national lines — entrepreneurs, community leaders, media influencers, and reform-minded ministers/ministries. They will also target women and young people, who are the principal drivers of reforms. The programs will also seek to empower citizens to work with governments on transition challenges and will support those governments undertaking reforms. Supporting locally-led change and emerging reformists will help form a new relationship between the United States and the people of the region. Funds are requested against several specific program areas that are critical to sustainable democratic transition and economic growth and where we have a comparative advantage. Key program areas may include: private sector financing and technical assistance, water, science and technology exchange, education, trade, and transitional justice. Funding will also support programs that promote minority and women's rights and support vulnerable populations.

- **Egypt ($200 million):** The FY 2015 request will encourage broad-based private-sector growth and job creation through a focus on micro, small and medium enterprises (including continued funding for the Egyptian American Enterprise Fund), trade promotion, and the development of the high-employing tourism and agricultural sectors; to promote a sustainable, inclusive, and nonviolent transition to democracy that includes protecting the rights of all Egyptians; support improvements in education, including through scholarships to underserved communities; and help improve the quality of health services and health outcomes.

- **Iraq ($22.5 million):** The requested funds continue the enduring programs of our reduced U.S. government footprint in Iraq. Programs focus on U.S. priorities such as programs for vulnerable populations, democracy and governance, and commercial development, especially in the energy sector.

- **Jordan ($360 million):** The FY 2015 request supports the Government of Jordan's capacity to advance its political, economic, and social reform agendas. Programs will support these reforms as well as encourage competitiveness and job creation, combat poverty, support workforce development, enhance government accountability, bolster civil society, and increase public participation in political processes. Assistance will also support improvements in basic education and healthcare. Funds will also provide balance of payments support to the Government of Jordan to enhance economic stability.

- **Lebanon ($58 million):** The FY 2015 request supports Lebanese institutions that advance internal and regional stability, combat the influence of extremists, and promote transparency and economic growth. Stability and good governance in Lebanon contribute to a peaceful Middle East and a direct enhancement of U.S. national security. The request includes assistance to promote Lebanon's sovereignty and stability by strengthening credible and capable public institutions, improving the quality of life for ordinary Lebanese, and promoting economic prosperity across sectarian lines. The United States monitors developments in Lebanon, in particular the Government of Lebanon's adherence to international obligations and the rule of law, and uses its assistance programs to advance those objectives. The program continues to emphasize the funding of non-governmental organizations.

- **Tunisia ($30 million):** U.S. support for Tunisia's democratic and economic evolution directly advances U.S. interests in a number of ways by helping to build a locally legitimate example of responsive and accountable governance, economic prosperity, and regional stability. The FY 2015 request funds activities that bolster governance and civic engagement; develop Tunisia's information and communications technology sector; expand access to capital for Tunisian small and medium enterprises; and provide technical assistance on financial regulation reform activities. The FY 2015 request also includes $20 million in support of the Tunisian-American Enterprise Fund.

- **West Bank and Gaza ($370 million):** U.S. government assistance creates an atmosphere that supports negotiations, encourages broad-based economic growth, promotes democratic governance, and improves the everyday lives of Palestinians, thereby creating an environment supportive of a peace agreement and contributing to the overall stability and security of the region. The FY 2015 request will help advance a negotiated, two-state solution to the Israeli-Palestinian conflict by working with the Palestinian Authority (PA) to build the institutions of a future Palestinian state and deliver services to the Palestinian people. FY 2015 ESF will be used to provide direct budget support to the PA to leverage additional financial support from other donors and to help the PA meet recurrent commitments. It will also provide much needed humanitarian relief to Palestinians living in Gaza by providing assistance through the UN and non-governmental organizations as a counterweight to Hamas.

- **Yemen ($64.5 million):** The FY 2015 request will support Yemen's ongoing political transition and reform efforts, with a focus on cementing gains already made in the transition, advancing U.S. interests by promoting good governance, democratic reform, and regional stability, and ensuring that women and young people retain a voice in the country's future. The request will also continue to support Yemen's critical humanitarian and economic development needs, including through community livelihood programs, particularly for at-risk populations; funding for key agriculture programs in a sector that historically accounts for roughly one half of Yemen's employment; as well as training and supporting youth entrepreneurs and equipping them with the tools they need to launch viable businesses that create jobs.

- **Near East Regional Democracy ($30 million):** The FY 2015 request will continue to support programmatic initiatives that strengthen democratic organizations and institutions, increase respect for human rights, as well as further integrate people in the region with the global community. The request includes $7 million to support cutting edge tools and requisite training that promote Internet Freedom and enhance the safe, effective use of communication technologies. As specific opportunities arise or new openings occur, additional focus areas may emerge that are in line with U.S. government policy in the region.

South and Central Asia ($317.2 million): The FY 2015 base request for South and Central Asia includes funding to support greater regional integration, increase economic reconstruction and development, promote democracy and good governance, and continue stabilization initiatives throughout the region.

- **Afghanistan ($117.6 million):** In FY 2015, Afghanistan will be entering into a new era with the complete transition of security responsibility, U.S. military operations shifting to a train and assist mission, and the election of a new Afghan president. FY 2015 funds will ensure critical support for the government that will be elected in 2014. Supporting the incoming government and assisting with the transition are key foreign policy priorities as the government will be tested in 2015 and 2016 by economic and governance challenges as well as threats to stability posed by violent extremism. These resources, in concert with OCO funding, will sustain the gains made over the past decade, particularly in health and education, and will prioritize economic self-sufficiency, good governance, rule of law, and women's rights as laid out in the Strategic Partnership Agreement. Investments will promote a more sustainable and resilient economy with a revenue structure built upon private sector-led investment and growth, and stronger regional market linkages. To foster sustained growth, FY 2015 funds will also support investments in high-growth potential sectors such as agriculture and extractive industries. U.S. assistance will be allocated in accordance with the Tokyo Mutual Accountability Framework, which prioritizes and incentivizes Afghan reforms in areas including respect for the rights of women and minorities, improved governance, anti-corruption efforts, and improved legislation to support private investment.

- **Kyrgyz Republic ($33.1 million):** U.S. assistance is focused on supporting newly formed democratic institutions and addressing the Kyrgyz Republic's broad, underlying development challenges and chronic instability, which were exacerbated by the effects of the 2010 political upheaval and ethnic violence. Programs will work to bolster civil society and democratic institutions, support the rule of law and human rights, empower the private sector, and address key social issues such as education.

- **Nepal ($12.5 million):** Funding will help increase food security; combat the effects of global climate change; and support community mediation to address local disputes before they escalate to conflict and violence. Programs will also build the capacity of governmental and non-governmental organizations to combat human trafficking; support the integration of former Maoist combatants into a post-conflict society; and assist the Government of Nepal with its democratic transition and economic reform efforts. Disaster risk reduction will be integrated across foreign assistance activities.

- **Pakistan ($100 million):** Pakistan will remain a key player in U.S. counterterrorism and nuclear nonproliferation efforts in FY 2015, as well as in our long-term objectives of economic development and stability in the region. Developing an enduring and collaborative relationship with an increasingly stable and prosperous Pakistan that plays a constructive role in the region will therefore continue to be a priority for the United States. FY 2015 base funds will support the new Government of Pakistan in its reform, economic growth, and long-term stabilization efforts and demonstrate that the U.S. will remain engaged in the region following the transition in Afghanistan. These funds will continue our long-term engagement policy that is designed to strengthen Pakistan's civilian government and enhance its ability to respond to the economic, social, and security needs of its people. These resources will sustain the five-pillar strategy that includes supporting the government's efforts to build a commercially viable energy sector, including both reforms and expanding power generation; fostering economic growth and employment; increasing long-term stability in volatile areas threatened by extremism, particularly those along the border with Afghanistan; and improving Pakistan's ability to provide education and health care to its population, long-term.

- **Tajikistan ($15.9 million):**   Assistance is focused on ensuring the stability of Tajikistan, particularly in light of the military drawdown in Afghanistan.   Programs will seek to strengthen local governance and improve education.   Funding will also be used to increase food security by seeking to solve systemic problems that contribute to food shortages such as inequitable access to water, inadequate supplies of seeds and fertilizer, a lack of modern technologies, and poor farm practices.

- **Central Asia Regional ($16.9 million):**   In FY 2015, U.S. assistance will continue to support regional cross-border activities under the New Silk Road initiative, which aims to further Afghanistan's economic integration into the broader region.   Specifically, these resources will fund projects that increase trade and improve the transit of legal goods and services across borders, increase regional cooperation on the use of energy resources, increase cooperation and rational use of water and other natural resources, and improve governance along trade and transit corridors.

Western Hemisphere ($392.9 million):   The FY 2015 ESF request for the Western Hemisphere promotes four interconnected and broadly shared goals: expanded economic and social opportunity, citizen safety for all peoples, effective democratic governance and institutions, and a clean energy future. The investments in the regions are critical to deterring the reach of transnational criminal organizations and violence throughout the region.   Funding will be targeted strategically at development needs that help support regional security.   Social prevention programs will strengthen the resiliency of at-risk communities against criminal activity.

- **Colombia ($132.9 million):**   The requested ESF will strengthen Colombia's capacity to implement a sustainable and inclusive peace, including improved presence of democratic institutions and processes in targeted areas; reconciliation among victims, ex-combatants, and other citizens; increased rural economic growth; and strengthened environmental resiliency.   Programs will build on the security gains achieved, support alternative development, strengthen the criminal justice system, support internally displaced persons and vulnerable populations, and expand economic opportunity. U.S. assistance will continue to target areas with a high concentration of vulnerable populations most affected by conflict, with particular focus on Afro-Colombians, indigenous groups, and former child soldiers, as well as strategic geographic zones in which violence, illicit crop cultivation, and drug trafficking converge.   U.S. assistance will need to remain flexible as a peace agreement may have implications for the scale and focus of assistance.

- **Cuba ($20 million):**   The FY 2015 request will support fundamental freedoms and respect for human rights.   Programs will support humanitarian assistance to victims of political repression and their families, strengthen independent Cuban civil society, and freedom of expression.

- **Haiti ($110 million):**   Funding in the FY 2015 request will continue supporting the U.S. commitment to help build a stable and more prosperous Haiti by engaging in partnership with the Government of Haiti, and other donors, local organizations, and private sector partners.   The request supports long-term development in the four strategic pillars of the Post-Earthquake U.S. Government Haiti Strategy and will focus on these key sectors: infrastructure and energy; food and economic security; health and other basic services; and governance and rule of law.   The request provides support in these areas to help Haiti continue to rebuild and transform itself into a secure, prosperous, democratic nation that meets the needs of its people and contributes to regional stability.

- **Mexico ($35 million):**   The FY 2015 request will support the United States' continued partnership with Mexico and expand mutual cooperation under the Merida Initiative to address security risks from drug trafficking, violent crime, and rule of law capacity in Mexico.   Specifically, ESF funding will focus on strengthening and building reforms to improve the rule of law and respect for human rights and building strong and resilient communities able to prevent and reduce crime and violence. A more stable Mexico will increase the U.S. national security, enhance economic growth potential, and protect U.S. citizens along our shared border.

- **Venezuela ($5 million):**   The FY 2015 request will help defend and strengthen democratic practices, institutions and values that support human rights and Venezuelan civic engagement.   FY 2015 activities will help civil society to promote institutional transparency, engage diverse constituencies in the democratic process, and defend human rights.

- **Western Hemisphere Regional ($90 million):**   The FY 2015 request will support critical and multi-account efforts under the Central America Regional Security Initiative (CARSI) ($60.0 million) and the Caribbean Basin Security Initiative (CBSI) ($28.0 million), as well as smaller investments in Western Hemisphere economic growth and Summit of the Americas-related initiatives ($2.0 million). CARSI and CBSI focus on reinforcing and creating accountable, democratic rule of law institutions, and address the underlying causes of violence tied to illicit trafficking, transnational crime, and organized gangs.   Violence from Central America and the Caribbean directly impacts U.S. security. U.S. assistance addresses these threats and supports the U.S. national interest.

    CARSI funding prioritizes the Northern Tier countries of Honduras, El Salvador, Belize, and Guatemala by strengthening rule of law institutions and empowering distressed communities to address the underlying risk factors that lead to crime and violence.   Funding will strengthen rule of law institutions to better administer justice, ensure due process, and protect human rights.

    In the Caribbean, CBSI builds and strengthens the rule of law, supports anti-corruption, and provides vocational training to at-risk youth and other vulnerable populations to increase their licit employment opportunities.

    In addition to CARSI and CBSI, funding will support trade capacity, as well as support other outcomes established through the 2015 Summit of the Americas process.

Global Programs ($259.4 million):   The FY 2015 ESF request also funds programs that are implemented worldwide.   Highlights include:

- **Democracy, Human Rights and Labor ($60 million):**   Through the implementation of innovative programs and use of new technologies, the FY 2015 request for the Human Rights and Democracy Fund will address human rights abuses globally, wherever fundamental rights are threatened; open political space in struggling or nascent democracies and authoritarian regimes; support civil society activists worldwide; and protect populations that are at risk, including women, religious and ethnic minorities, indigenous populations, and lesbian, gay, bisexual, and transgender peoples. Governments that protect human rights and fundamental freedoms are ultimately more stable, successful, and secure than those that do not.   The United States finds more willing, reliable, and lasting partners in those governments that reflect and act in the broad interests of their own people, rather than the narrow interests of the few.   Additionally, American workers are better off when their counterparts abroad can stand up for their basic rights

- **Energy Resources ($11.8 million):**   The FY 2015 request will promote improved energy sector governance and transparency, foster technical engagement to build the capacity of governmental partners to address the challenges involved in developing unconventional resources, and encourage power sector reform and development to support the expansion of access to electricity for the 1.3

billion people currently lacking access. These programs complement and support global diplomatic engagement on energy security issues and the Administration's energy initiatives, including Power Africa, Connecting the Americas 2022, and the U.S.-Asia Pacific Comprehensive Energy Partnership.

- **Oceans and International Environmental and Scientific Affairs (OES) ($149 million):** As part of the President's Global Climate Change Initiative (GCCI), OES programming constitutes an integral element of U.S. efforts on climate change. These funds include support for programs that forge new paths forward on clean energy and emissions reductions in connection with activities such as the Clean Energy Ministerial, the Major Economies Forum on Energy and Climate, and the Climate and Clean Air Coalition, all of which were established as a result of U.S. diplomacy. Adaptation funds will provide for U.S. contributions to the Least Developed Countries Fund and the Special Climate Change Fund as well as other programs that assist least developed and vulnerable countries in adapting to climate change. Funding for sustainable landscapes will support programs such as the Initiative for Sustainable Forest Landscapes, a multi-donor public-private initiative to implement strategies for reducing emissions from deforestation and forest degradation (REDD+) in developing countries, which protects forests and landscapes while improving the enabling environments for sustainable commodity production. OES funding will also fulfill U.S. obligations under the South Pacific Tuna Treaty, which promotes American jobs and economic development in the Pacific region. In addition, OES Partnerships funds will strengthen regional cooperation and build global capacity in science technology and innovation as well as for sound stewardship of environmental and natural resources in concert with global economic growth and social development.

Details of the FY 2015 OCO Request for ESF are addressed in the OCO chapter.

Migration and Refugee Assistance

($ in thousands)	FY 2013 Actual[1]	FY 2014 Estimate	FY 2015 Request	Increase / Decrease
Migration and Refugee Assistance	2,668,665	3,059,000	2,047,374	-1,011,626
Enduring	1,590,146	1,774,645	1,582,374	-192,271
Overseas Contingency Operations	1,078,519	1,284,355	465,000	-819,355

1/ The FY 2013 OCO Actual level reflects the transfer of $35.5 million from the Migration and Refugee Assistance account to the Economic Support Fund account.

The international humanitarian programs of the U.S. government provide critical protection and assistance to some of the world's most vulnerable people: refugees, internally displaced persons (IDPs), stateless persons, vulnerable migrants, and victims of conflict.   Reflecting the American people's dedication to assisting those in need, programs funded through the Migration and Refugee Assistance (MRA) account save lives and ease suffering while upholding human dignity.   They help stabilize volatile situations and prevent or mitigate conditions that breed extremism and violence, and are an essential component of U.S. foreign policy.   The FY 2015 MRA enduring request of $1,582.4 million will fund contributions to key international humanitarian organizations, including the UN High Commissioner for Refugees and the International Committee of the Red Cross, as well as contributions to non-governmental organization partners to address pressing humanitarian needs overseas and to resettle refugees in the United States.   These funds support programs that meet basic needs to sustain life; provide protection and assistance to the most vulnerable, particularly women, children and the elderly; assist refugees with voluntary repatriation, local integration, or permanent resettlement in a third country; and foster the humane and effective management of international migration policies.

Highlights:

- **Overseas Assistance ($1,177.4 million):**   In both emergencies and protracted situations overseas, humanitarian assistance helps refugees, IDPs, stateless persons, conflict victims, and other vulnerable migrants to meet their basic needs and enables them to begin rebuilding their lives.   Such support will include the provision of life-sustaining services, including water and sanitation, shelter, and healthcare, as well as programs that provide physical and legal protection to vulnerable beneficiaries and assist refugees to voluntarily return to their homes in safety or, when that is not an option, integrate into their host communities as appropriate.

- **Refugee Admissions ($360 million):**   Resettlement is a key element of refugee protection and efforts to find solutions to refugee displacement when repatriation and local integration are not viable solutions.   As the country with the largest resettlement program in the world, the United States welcomes the most vulnerable refugees from a diverse array of backgrounds.   Through non-governmental organization partners, these funds will help refugees and certain other categories of special immigrants to resettle in communities across the United States.

- **Humanitarian Migrants to Israel ($10 million):**   This funding will continue U.S. government support for relocation and integration of Jewish migrants, including those from the former Soviet Union, Eastern Europe, and Africa to Israel.

- **Administrative Expenses ($35 million):** The Bureau of Population, Refugees, and Migration is responsible for the oversight of all programs funded through MRA enduring and OCO appropriations as well as funding drawn from the U.S. Emergency Refugee and Migration Assistance (ERMA) for implementation by PRM. Funds requested for FY 2015 will be used to ensure sound stewardship of resources and maximum impact for beneficiary populations and American taxpayers by stressing accountability and transparency in its management and monitoring of these critical humanitarian programs. The largest portion of administrative expenses will cover the salary, benefits, and travel costs of U.S. direct hire staff, including regional refugee coordinators posted in U.S. embassies around the world.

Details of the FY 2015 OCO Request for MRA are addressed in the OCO chapter.

U.S. Emergency Refugee and Migration Assistance

($ in thousands)	FY 2013 Actual	FY 2014 Estimate	FY 2015 Request	Increase / Decrease
U.S. Emergency Refugee and Migration Assistance	25,823	50,000	50,000	-

The Emergency Refugee and Migration Assistance Fund enables the President to provide humanitarian assistance for unexpected and urgent refugee and migration needs worldwide. The FY 2015 request of $50 million will allow the United States to respond quickly to urgent and unexpected needs of refugees and other populations of concern.

In FY 2013, the President provided $15 million from ERMA to address emergency humanitarian needs related to the crisis in Syria.

Peace Corps

($ in thousands)	FY 2013 Actual	FY 2014 Estimate	FY 2015 Request	Increase / Decrease
Peace Corps	356,015	379,000	380,000	1,000

The FY 2015 budget request for the Peace Corps of $380 million, of which $5 million is for the Office of Inspector General, will allow the Peace Corps to continue to meet its core goals: to help countries meet their development needs by spearheading progress in those countries and to promote a better understanding of the American people by building bridges between American Volunteers and the peoples of the countries in which they live and work. This funding will also allow the agency to continue the sweeping reforms that have been put in place over the past few years.

The Peace Corps takes a unique approach to meeting its development and outreach goals. The agency selects, trains, and supports American Volunteers who spend 27 months living and working in areas that other programs are often unable to reach. Volunteers' activities are designed to build capacity at the community level so that communities are empowered to solve their development challenges long after the Volunteers have returned home. Peace Corps Volunteers help promote a better understanding of the United States and its values by serving as grassroots ambassadors around the world. By building person-to-person connections, they help to provide a positive image of the United States in areas of the world that may have little direct exposure to Americans. The Peace Corps' FY 2015 request will fund approximately 7,140 Peace Corps Volunteers in approximately 65 countries, ranging from the Caribbean to Central Asia; and from Africa to the Pacific islands.

In FY 2015, the Peace Corps will continue recent reforms to improve the Volunteer experience and impact. The health, safety, and security of Volunteers remain the agency's highest priorities. The Peace Corps launched the final stages of the Sexual Assault Risk Reduction and Response Program (SARRR), a comprehensive strategy for reducing risks and strengthening the response to Volunteers who have been the victims of sexual assault and other violent crimes. This program reflects the agency's steadfast commitment to the physical and emotional well-being of every single Volunteer. Another reform includes the annual Country Portfolio Review process, which is an objective, data-driven method for reviewing and making decisions about where and how the agency operates globally. Moreover, the Peace Corps is partnering with host governments, universities, nongovernmental organizations, and donors to ensure that Volunteers focus on projects that are, first and foremost, wanted by their communities and are evidence-proven to be most effective at achieving development results.

The Peace Corps works as a force multiplier by partnering with other government agencies to dramatically increase the impact and sustainability of U.S. international development programs. With its unique ability to bring about lasting change in hard-to-reach communities, the Peace Corps is an important partner in a number of whole-of-government and interagency development initiatives, including the President's Emergency Plan for AIDS Relief (PEPFAR), the President's Malaria Initiative, and Feed the Future. In FY 2015, the Peace Corps will continue, as well as expand, these partnerships, while seeking further strategic partnerships to leverage the Peace Corps' training and programmatic resources without compromising the agency's independence or mission.

This year, the Peace Corps will undertake a revitalization of its recruitment efforts with a focus on building a high-quality Volunteer force that represents the excellence and rich diversity that is the American people.

Volunteers' service to the United States continues long after they have left the Peace Corps by helping Americans learn about other cultures and peoples. When Volunteers return to the U.S., they are deeply changed by their experience and bring their knowledge, skills, and expertise with them wherever they go. The skills they acquire while serving—whether it be professional growth in cross-cultural settings, a new language, or technical development expertise—are invaluable to the United States, as is the commitment to public service that the Peace Corps instills. Ultimately, the investment made in Volunteers is repaid many times over, at home and abroad.

Millennium Challenge Corporation

($ in thousands)	FY 2013 Actual	FY 2014 Estimate	FY 2015 Request	Increase / Decrease
Millennium Challenge Corporation	852,728	898,200	1,000,000	101,800

The Millennium Challenge Corporation (MCC) is requesting $1,000 million for FY 2015. The increase in funding is based on the opportunity to advance U.S. global development priorities in a limited number of countries that are already demonstrating their commitment to good governance and democratic values, increasing the potential for economic growth and poverty reduction. MCC contributes to country-led and results-focused development through five-year compact assistance programs. MCC also supports smaller two-to-three year threshold programs that help countries to become compact eligible.

Highlights:

Of the FY 2015 request, MCC plans to use $766.0 million for compact assistance. The requested funding will enable MCC to enter into new compacts with Liberia, Morocco, Niger, and Tanzania, once the countries have successfully developed compact proposals and upon approval by MCC's Board of Directors. These countries, home to nearly 100 million people combined, are among the world's poorest, but each has taken significant steps to improve governance and achieve eligibility for MCC compact assistance. The increase in funding will support significant compact investments in these countries to unlock key constraints to economic growth, incentivize policy and institutional reforms necessary for private investment, and improve the well-being of some of the world's poorest people.

When MCC was established in 2004, it was understood that the agency would require enough annual funding to incentivize reform, promote economic growth, and fight poverty. Achieving those goals will be difficult if the recent trend toward smaller compacts continues. MCC will require the requested funding increase to achieve a more strategic and lasting impact on the economic development and public policies of countries the United States will look to as the emerging economic, political, and security partners of the 21st century.

Through these investments, MCC will advance U.S. global development priorities in coordination with broader U.S. Government initiatives. For example, through the President's Power Africa Initiative, MCC will play a key role in expanding access to electrical power in sub-Saharan Africa. Through institutional and regulatory reforms in partner countries, MCC will create an enabling environment for private sector investment in the energy sector. MCC will also make substantial infrastructure investments itself and has identified lack of access to affordable and reliable power as a binding constraint to growth in three African countries with compacts in development: Ghana, Liberia, and Tanzania.

In addition, MCC employs an evidence-based decision making process and has made efforts to publish its data in a manner that achieved a first place ranking in the 2013 Aid Transparency Index. The number one ranking reflects MCC's commitment to and investment in making data and information across its portfolio—on country selection, investment decisions, program monitoring, and independent evaluations—publicly available, so that the U.S. Congress and other stakeholders can hold the agency accountable and learn from its investments. The requested funding will continue that commitment and investment.

MCC also plans to explore creative financing mechanisms in new MCC compacts to link payments more directly to development results. Such mechanisms could include pay-for- performance, cash-on-delivery or other outcome-based payment approaches that fit within MCC's operational model.

Opportunity, Growth, and Security Initiative:

In addition to the base request of $1.0 billion, the Administration is proposing $350.0 million in resources for MCC as part of the $56 billion Opportunity, Growth, and Security Initiative included in the President's FY 2015 Budget. The initiative includes additional resources for MCC because of the agency's strong commitment to evidence and evaluation and impact-based budgeting. These supplemental funds will focus on bolstering MCC's key role in establishing enabling environments overseas where US and other businesses can compete and win. MCC works with partner countries to reform laws, policies, and institutions so as to create a pro-business climate, while investing in projects such as transportation infrastructure and vocational training to enhance workforce skills that will have the greatest impact on economic development and poverty reduction. In addition, MCC's compact procurements are fair and open, without geographic preferences, thus ensuring a level playing field for U.S. companies seeking a foothold in fast-growing markets overseas.

The resources in the initiative will enable MCC to increase support for the President's Power Africa Initiative through additional compact investment opportunities in Ghana, Liberia, and Tanzania. The Liberia Compact may focus on two critical constraints to growth, including inadequate power. The Ghana Compact is anticipated to focus solely on reform of and catalytic investment in the power sector, identified as one of the key constraints to private-sector-led growth. And in Tanzania, the country has identified the lack of reliable, inexpensive electric power as one of the most critical constraints to long-term economic growth.

MCC's Data-Led Country Selection Process:

Across its portfolio, MCC emphasizes results and transparency. For all major compact investments, MCC estimates economic rates of return to assess the economic viability and return on the proposed investments, and posts the results on its website (www.mcc.gov). MCC also works with partner countries to develop detailed monitoring and evaluation plans for compacts and tracks the progress of its compacts and projects against defined benchmarks and outcomes, which are also available on MCC's website.

The first step in MCC's grant-making process is for MCC's Board of Directors to determine which countries should be eligible for MCC assistance. When making compact eligibility determinations, the Board starts with a list of countries that are candidates for MCC funding on the basis of per capita income and assesses the countries' performance on twenty indicators that measure policy performance in three categories: ruling justly, investing in people, and encouraging economic freedom. In addition to the policy performance indicators, the Board factors in the availability of funds to MCC and a compact's ability to reduce poverty and improve economic growth. After the Board selects countries as compact eligible, MCC works with countries to develop a compact. Countries are responsible for identifying and prioritizing their own barriers to poverty reduction and economic growth, and conducting consultations across the private sector and civil society to ensure that there is widespread public support for compact investments. Throughout the process, MCC works to ensure there is transparency and country ownership of compact programs.

Since 2004, MCC has signed 27 compacts and 24 threshold program agreements, committing nearly $10.0 billion to worldwide poverty reduction through results-driven programs built on measurable and transparent objectives.

Inter-American Foundation

($ in thousands)	FY 2013 Actual	FY 2014 Estimate	FY 2015 Request	Increase / Decrease
Inter-American Foundation	21,361	22,500	18,100	-4,400

The FY 2015 request of $18.1 million for the Inter-American Foundation (IAF) will enable targeted investments in citizen-led development initiatives in marginalized communities throughout Latin America and the Caribbean. In FY 2015, the IAF will serve U.S. interests by creating economic opportunities, strengthening the practice of democracy, furthering social inclusion and fostering secure communities.

The IAF will provide grants to support projects that create jobs, increase incomes, improve nutrition, encourage civic engagement, advance education and training, conserve the environment, and improve access to basic needs and services in communities that are the foundation for democratic U.S. allies. The IAF has developed the specialized expertise to identify and invest in poor and marginalized groups with the capacity to advance their own communities.

The IAF has 40 years of experience of leveraging resources from others. It requires that grantee partners contribute and mobilize their own resources toward their projects. Over the last five years, each dollar invested by the IAF leveraged another $1.30 from grantee partners and others.

The IAF also collaborates with private and community foundations, private companies and diaspora groups in joint funding initiatives. Through the IAF-initiated business sector network, RedEAmérica, Latin American corporate foundations direct an additional three dollars for every dollar invested by the IAF in grassroots organizations. This initiative has helped corporate partners move beyond philanthropic giving to more strategic investments that benefit the communities and businesses in the long-term.

Due to budgetary constraints, the FY 2015 budget cuts the IAF's funding by nearly 20 percent. Despite these cuts, the IAF will seek to maintain its current program level by pursuing partnership opportunities with other U.S. Government agencies, the private sector and by further reducing overhead costs.

The IAF will complement and enhance the value of investments made by other U.S. foreign assistance agencies by helping grassroots groups access and take advantage of large-scale investments, new markets and trade opportunities.

U.S. African Development Foundation

($ in thousands)	FY 2013 Actual	FY 2014 Estimate	FY 2015 Request	Increase / Decrease
U.S. African Development Foundation	28,481	30,000	24,000	-6,000

The FY 2015 request of $24 million for the U.S. African Development Foundation (USADF) programs will provide resources to establish new grants in 15 African countries and to support an active portfolio of 400 grants to producer groups engaged in community-based enterprises. USADF is a Federally-funded, public corporation promoting economic development among marginalized populations in Sub-Saharan Africa. USADF impacts 1,500,000 people each year in underserved communities across Africa. Its innovative small grants program (less than $250,000 per grant) supports sustainable African-originated business solutions that improve food security, generate jobs, and increase family incomes. In addition to economic impacts to rural populations, USADF programs are at the forefront of creating a network of in-country technical service providers with expertise critical to advancing Africa's long term development needs.

USADF furthers U.S. priorities by directing small amounts of development resources to disenfranchised groups in hard to reach, sensitive regions across Africa. USADF ensures that critical U.S. development initiatives such as Ending Extreme Poverty, Feed the Future, Power Africa, and the Young African Leaders Initiative reach beyond urban areas to Africa's underserved rural populations. USADF operates in Africa using a cost- effective African led and managed development model that "right sizes" efforts, directing development resources to rural areas of greatest need and potential for impact. USADF programs also leverage funds from other donors. By matching U.S. Government funds with those from host African governments and/or other private sector foundations, USADF increases the development impact of each tax dollar appropriated. USADF's size and lower-cost operating model makes it a highly flexible, innovative, and effective foreign assistance provider to Africa.

Department of Treasury

($ in thousands)	FY 2013 Actual	FY 2014 Estimate	FY 2015 Request	Increase / Decrease
Department of Treasury	37,026	23,500	23,500	-
International Affairs Technical Assistance	25,634	23,500	23,500	-
Technical Assistance - Enduring	24,160	23,500	23,500	-
Technical Assistance - Overseas Contingency Operations	1,474	-	-	-
Debt Restructuring - Enduring	11,392	-	-	-

Treasury Technical Assistance

The FY 2015 request includes $23.5 million for Treasury's Office of Technical Assistance (OTA). This small program achieves big objectives as it fosters economic growth by enabling governments in fragile and developing countries to provide better services for their citizens and reduce dependency on foreign aid. For over 20 years, OTA has helped developing countries build effective financial management systems—a core element of a well-functioning state. These financial management systems include efficient revenue collection, well-planned and executed budgets, judicious debt management, sound banking systems, and strong controls to combat corruption and other economic crimes. The program provides significant, cost-effective value for U.S. development, foreign policy, and national security objectives.

Debt Restructuring

No funding is requested for the Debt Restructuring account in FY 2015, though the request includes transfer authority to allocate funding for bilateral debt relief under the Heavily Indebted Poor Countries (HIPC) Initiative for Sudan, should they meet the requirements to qualify.

International Narcotics Control and Law Enforcement

($ in thousands)	FY 2013 Actual[1/]	FY 2014 Estimate	FY 2015 Request	Increase / Decrease
International Narcotics Control and Law Enforcement	1,858,678	1,350,000	1,117,911	-232,089
Enduring	1,005,611	1,005,610	721,911	-283,699
Overseas Contingency Operations	853,067	344,390	396,000	51,610

1/ The FY 2013 OCO Actual level reflects the following transfers: $15 million to the Complex Crises Fund account; $25.78 million to the Economic Support Fund account; and $38.62 million to the Peacekeeping Operations account.

The FY 2015 International Narcotics Control and Law Enforcement (INCLE) enduring request of $721.9 million will support country and global programs critical to combat transnational crime, disrupt illicit trafficking, and assist partner nations to build their capacities to extend their reach of justice under the rule of law. INCLE-funded programs seek to close the gaps between law enforcement jurisdictions and strengthen weak or corrupt law enforcement institutions. FY 2015 INCLE funds are focused where civilian security institutions are weak and are used in tandem with host country government resources in order to maximize impact.

The INCLE request for FY 2015 recognizes that criminal networks disrupt U.S. trade, licit productivity, and economic opportunities, while creating security vulnerabilities for U.S. citizens around the world. The resources requested will continue to address national and personal security concerns in strategically important geographic regions such as the Western Hemisphere, South Central Asia, and the Near East. The request also focuses on emerging threats to stability and regional security in Central Asia and Africa.

Highlights:

Africa

- **Liberia ($11.5 million):** As the United Nations Mission in Liberia (UNMIL) further draws down its military forces, INCLE assistance will support the gradual transition of security responsibilities to the Government of Liberia.   Assistance will continue to provide a U.S. civilian police contribution to UNMIL as well as bilateral support to the Liberia National Police, other civilian law enforcement agencies (including both drug demand and supply reduction efforts), the justice sector, and the judiciary.

- **South Sudan ($20 million):** Funding will be used to develop the Republic of South Sudan's capacity to provide civilian security and basic justice services. Funds will support technical assistance and training for South Sudan's criminal justice sector officials, both through bilateral programs and through support to the UN Mission in South Sudan. INCLE programs will enhance short and long-term stability as South Sudan transitions domestic security responsibility away from the military to the South Sudan National Police Service and develops its justice and correctional institutions.

- **State Africa Regional ($17 million):** The request includes funding for four programs that focus on countering terrorism and reducing transnational criminal threats: the Trans-Sahara Counter-terrorism Partnership (TSCTP), the Partnership for Regional East African Counter Terrorism (PREACT), the

West Africa Regional Initiative (WARSI), and Regional Wildlife Trafficking. Both TSCTP and PREACT focus on enhancing the capabilities of partner nations to prevent and respond to terrorism in their respective regions. WARSI focuses on enhancing rule of law, promoting security sector reform, and building partner nations' capacity to counter transnational threats, including narcotics trafficking. Within the Regional Wildlife Trafficking program, INCLE funding supports the Presidential Executive Order on combating wildlife crime– the poaching and illegal trade in wild animals and animal parts. Funds will assist rangers, police, customs officials, prosecutors, investigators, and judiciaries in addressing this growing threat. Resources will also seek to build institutional capacity in the justice and security sectors in the Sahel, in support of cross-regional programs to address emerging security challenges facing the Sahel region of sub-Saharan Africa and the Maghreb region of North Africa.

East Asia and the Pacific

- **Burma ($3 million):**   Funding will be used to continue to assist the Government of Burma in its democratic transition by providing targeted and specialized programming in the areas of counternarcotics and law enforcement. Programs will address the continued rise of poppy cultivation and opium production, drug trafficking, and drug use within Burma. Funds will support the creative expansion of counternarcotics efforts in the areas of supply reduction, interdiction, and demand reduction. In addition, funding will support expanded training opportunities to build the capacities of Burmese law enforcement institutions to address and combat crime within and across its borders.

- **Indonesia ($10 million):**   Assistance programs in Indonesia will strengthen and professionalize criminal justice sector institutions, including police, prosecutors, and judges. In addition to broad reform and institution-building efforts, the programs will support specialized capacity to investigate, interdict, and prosecute money laundering, terrorism, and other transnational crimes. INCLE funding will also support the Indonesian government's counternarcotics efforts.

- **Philippines ($9 million):**   Funding for the Philippines will build on previous years' achievements by broadening and deepening Philippine criminal justice sector institutional capacity. Funds will support police training and infrastructure development in the southern Philippines to shore up internal stability and build police investigative capacity in the wake of the transition of law enforcement functions from the military to civilian authorities in the south. Programs will support police specialization and training institutionalization at police academies. In the justice sector, funds will support leadership development in the judiciary and prosecutors' offices and add a greater focus on anti-corruption assistance. Further, funds will be used to support training and assist Philippine law enforcement to combat transnational criminal networks.

Europe and Eurasia

- **Bosnia and Herzegovina ($3.8 million):**   Funding for Bosnia and Herzegovina will support programs designed to strengthen and professionalize the law enforcement and justice sector institutions. Specifically, funds will support efforts to increase the use of advanced investigative skills for police and prosecutors, improve the trial advocacy capacity of state and sub-state level prosecutors, and strengthen the judge's role as a neutral arbiter. Funding will also support victim/witness support offices at the sub-state level, and enhance police-prosecutor cooperation, with special emphasis on organized crime, corruption, and war crimes cases.

- **Kosovo ($6.8 million):**   U.S. assistance in Kosovo will support efforts to increase the capacity, professionalism, and accountability of law enforcement and justice sector institutions. Funds will be used to support the U.S. contribution to the European Union's rule of law mission; continue efforts to create and institutionalize democratic legal structures that meet international standards; and improve Kosovo's ability to investigate and prosecute complex criminal cases, such as war crimes, organized crime, and corruption.

Near East

- **Iraq ($11 million):** Programs in FY 2015 will continue to build on progress in combating corruption, promoting civilian security, and strengthening the Iraqi government's capacity to investigate, prosecute, and resolve criminal activity in a fair and transparent manner.

- **Lebanon ($10 million):** Support for Lebanon's security forces is a key component of U.S. efforts to strengthen the institutions of the Lebanese state, promoting stability and security in both Lebanon and the region. Funding will continue to improve the capacity of the Internal Security Forces (ISF) to exert sovereign authority throughout Lebanese territory, which is critical to the successful implementation of UNSCRs 1559 and 1701. FY 2015 funding will be used to provide technical assistance to the ISF to increase their professionalism and continue their shift in orientation toward the protection of, and service to the Lebanese population, while improving country-wide perceptions of the ISF as a professional, non-sectarian institution. Additionally, funding will continue to support corrections reform efforts to improve the capacity of prison and judicial authorities to effectively manage and operate a prison and detention system.

- **Tunisia ($7 million):** INCLE funding support will sustain and build on security sector reforms accomplished during Tunisia's transition period. Programming will continue to support the transition of Tunisia's civilian law enforcement institutions to be more accountable and transparent to the public; enhance the professionalism, independence, and accountability of the judiciary; enhance the capacity of the Tunisian correctional system to manage prisons and detention centers in a safe, secure, humane, and transparent fashion; and enhance the capabilities of law enforcement officials to engage with U.S. law enforcement and respond to terrorism and other types of international organized crimes.

- **West Bank and Gaza ($70 million):** Assistance will continue to focus on reforming the Palestinian Authority (PA) security sector, and sustaining and maintaining the capabilities that the security forces have developed. Security in the West Bank remains a key component of the Middle East peace negotiations. Greater emphasis on technical assistance, including the continuation of infrastructure support and initial, basic, refresher and specialized training to the security forces, will encourage PA Security Forces to be more self-sufficient. Funding also will be used to replenish worn security force equipment. Technical assistance and project support will be provided to the PA Ministry of Interior to improve its ability to manage and provide oversight over the security forces. Additional training, equipment, infrastructure support, and technical assistance will be provided for the justice and corrections sectors to ensure their development keeps pace with the rising performance of the security forces.

South and Central Asia

- **Central Asia Counternarcotics Initiative (CACI) ($4 million):** This initiative focuses on improving the ability of Central Asian countries to disrupt drug trafficking originating from Afghanistan and dismantle related criminal organizations through effective investigation, prosecution and conviction of mid- to high-level traffickers. CACI provides specialized training and mentoring through the Drug Enforcement Administration (DEA) and equipment to enhance the counternarcotics capacities of law enforcement agencies in the region.   Promotion of regional cooperation between Afghan counternarcotics units and their Central Asian counterparts is an important goal of this initiative, in line with the U.S. Counternarcotics Strategy for Afghanistan.

- **Tajikistan ($4 million):**   Assistance to Tajikistan focuses on promoting security sector reform and the development of democratic institutions through police reform, counternarcotics, border security, and justice reform programming.   These resources will build the capacity of Tajikistan's law enforcement agencies to address transnational threats including from Afghanistan.

Western Hemisphere

- **Colombia ($117 million):**   Funding will continue U.S. government support for Colombian-led consolidation efforts to expand security, reduce drug trafficking and the cultivation of illicit crops, promote economic development, and increase access to government services through a comprehensive, whole-of-government approach in conflict zones and priority rural areas.   INCLE resources will build the capacity of the Colombian National Police (CNP) to assume additional security responsibilities – especially in rural areas – as well as to combat illegally-armed groups and criminal organizations.   Funds will also build the capacity of the Colombian government to export its security-expertise and training to third countries, primarily in Central America and the Caribbean. Resources in FY 2015 will support the aerial and manual eradication of illicit crops, primarily coca, as well as environmental monitoring and outreach programs.   Support for interdiction efforts with the CNP and Colombian Navy and Coast Guard will continue to prevent the trafficking of multiple metric tons of drugs to the United States and weaken drug trafficking organizations.   FY 2015 resources will also support Colombia's judicial institutions, enhancing the protection of human rights and developing local capacity to investigate, prosecute, and adjudicate complex criminal cases.

- **Mexico ($80 million):**   With the FY 2015 INCLE request, the U.S. and Mexican governments will continue to focus on institutionalizing the rule of law, disrupting and dismantling criminal organizations, creating a 21st century border, and building strong and resilient communities through the Merida Initiative.   INCLE-funded programs will focus on developing Mexico's rule of law institutions through training, technical assistance, and limited equipment purchases.   Programs will continue to provide assistance to federal and state criminal justice institutions, including law enforcement, prosecutorial, judicial, and corrections institutions.

- **Peru ($37 million):**   The FY 2015 request will support efforts by the Government of Peru to combat the illicit drug industry, including efforts to extend state presence in the Monzon region as well as the Apurimac and Ene River Valleys in order to oppose drug traffickers aligned with the Shining Path terrorist group.   Coordinating closely with a supportive Government of Peru, FY 2015 INCLE funds will support drug interdiction and coca eradication operations as well as precursor chemical seizures, improved controls at ports and airports, judicial reform, police academies, training on community policing, and capacity building for rule of law actors.

- **State Western Hemisphere Regional ($92 million):**   INCLE funding will support the Central America Regional Security Initiative (CARSI) ($70 million) and the Caribbean Basin Regional Security Initiative (CBSI) ($22 million).   CARSI funds will support training and build capacity of law enforcement and rule of law institutions throughout Central America.   Among other efforts, activities will address border and port security; support for vetted units and maritime and land interdiction; law enforcement capacity to address transnational crime, including anti-gang training; regional aviation; and efforts to combat impunity.   In support of CBSI, INCLE funding will continue efforts to combat illicit trafficking and organized crime, increase port and border security, and strengthen the rule of law through training and technical assistance. Funding will support efforts to promote information sharing and collaboration among CBSI partner nations, while enhancing the capacity of criminal justice and security institutions.

Global Programs

These programs support transnational crime and counternarcotics efforts as well as policing in peacekeeping and crisis response operations worldwide. Key components include:

- **Inter-regional Aviation Support ($38.5 million):** Funding will provide centralized core services for counternarcotics and border security aviation programs. These programs involve fixed- and rotary-wing aircraft deployed worldwide.

- **Program Development and Support ($30 million):** Funding will provide for annual costs of direct hires, travel, equipment, communications and utilities, and other support services to design, implement, monitor, evaluate, and oversee INCLE programs.

- **International Law Enforcement Academy (ILEA) ($24 million):** Funds will support existing ILEAs in Bangkok, Budapest, Gaborone, Roswell, San Salvador, and Regional Training Centers (RTC) in Accra and Lima. Additionally, funds made available to support the Shared Security Partnership initiative will be used to support emerging regional security priorities in West Africa to enhance regional and local-level criminal justice institutions. The focus of this programming will be on facilitating regional cooperation and capacity building by providing strategic training at the West Africa RTC in Accra that addresses high-profile crimes and a wide array of existing threats to U.S. national security posed by terrorist and criminal organizations.

- **Demand Reduction ($12.5 million):** Funding will address pressing regional and global drug-related threats posed by methamphetamine, opiates such as heroin and opium, crack cocaine, and high-risk drug-using behavior that promote HIV/AIDS. Funding supports an innovative training model to certify addiction counselors; sub-regional training centers that disseminate best-practice approaches; drug-free community coalitions that target illegal drugs; research and demonstration that improve women's treatment and minimize child addiction; and the development of scientific and technical methods to better detect, quantify, and understand drug use and its health-related consequences.

- **Anti-Crime Programs ($9.5 million):** Funding will support efforts to address corruption and kleptocracy, money laundering and financial crimes, border security and alien smuggling, intellectual property and cybercrime, and transnational and organized crime. Consistent with the President's Executive Order 13648 to combat wildlife trafficking, a portion of the transnational organized crime funding will support programs to reduce wildlife trafficking globally, including strengthening policies and legislative frameworks, enhancing investigative and law enforcement functions, supporting regional wildlife enforcement networks, and developing capacities to prosecute and adjudicate wildlife crimes and related corruption.

- **Critical Flight Safety Program ($7 million):** Funding will provide programmed depot-level maintenance and aircraft/aircrew safety of flight for the fixed- and rotary-wing aircraft fleet supporting countennarcotics and border security aviation programs worldwide.

- **Criminal Justice Assistance and Partnership ($3 million):** Funding will support a center of excellence to improve the Department's criminal justice sector programs and engagements, enhance pre-deployment training of law enforcement, justice, and corrections advisors, increase women's participation in criminal justice sector programs, improve the quality and consistency of curricula delivered in partner-country training, and expand domestic law enforcement, justice sector, and corrections partnerships for application in INCLE-funded programs globally.

- **International Police Peacekeeping Operations Support (IPPOS) Program ($2 million):** Funds will provide training and capacity building support for police-contributing-countries to deploy highly trained and well-equipped officers to peacekeeping and stabilization missions as well as help the United Nations with coordination, policy, and projects in support of police peacekeeping missions.

- **Office to Monitor and Combat Trafficking in Persons ($20.7 million):** INCLE funds will help stimulate governments to take action towards the eradication of trafficking in persons through criminal justice sector improvements including developing comprehensive legislation, strengthening anti-trafficking laws and enforcement strategies, training criminal justice officials on those laws and practices and how to implement them, supporting protection and assistance services to victims, developing victim-centered identification and assistance protocols and practices, and developing and implementing anti-trafficking public awareness campaigns. The resources requested will also enable the Office to Monitor and Combat Trafficking in Persons to lead the Department's efforts in carrying out the President's Executive Order on Strengthening Protections against Trafficking in Persons in Federal Contracts, including through support for partnerships with civil society, private sector, and multilateral organizations.

Details of the FY 2015 OCO Request for INCLE are addressed in the OCO chapter.

Nonproliferation, Anti-Terrorism, Demining and Related Programs

($ in thousands)	FY 2013 Actual[1/]	FY 2014 Estimate	FY 2015 Request	Increase / Decrease
Nonproliferation, Anti-Terrorism, Demining and Related Programs	674,862	700,000	605,400	-94,600
Enduring	560,270	630,000	605,400	-24,600
Overseas Contingency Operations	114,592	70,000	-	-70,000

The FY 2015 Nonproliferation, Anti-Terrorism, Demining and Related Programs (NADR) request of $605.4 million will support a broad range of U.S. national interests through critical, security-related programs that reduce threats posed by international terrorist activities; landmines and stockpiles of excess conventional weapons and munitions; and nuclear, chemical, biological, and other destabilizing weapons, missiles, and their associated technologies. A portion of the funding requested within this account is for Syria, including in anticipation of a transition requiring assistance. Areas for this assistance could include supporting multilateral efforts to standup a transition government's ability to manage its borders and deal with weapons management and destruction.

Highlights:

Nonproliferation Activities

- The voluntary contribution to the International Atomic Energy Agency ($83.6 million) supports programs that promote nuclear safeguards, nuclear safety and security, nuclear energy, and the peaceful use of nuclear science technologies.

- The Global Threat Reduction (GTR) program ($65.1 million) supports tailored activities aimed at reducing the threat of terrorist or state acquisition of WMD materials and expertise. Initiatives include strengthening security for dangerous biological materials and potentially dangerous chemicals, engaging with scientists with WMD-applicable expertise, and decreasing the likelihood that terrorists could gain the technical expertise needed to develop an improvised nuclear device. GTR priority countries include Yemen, Pakistan, and Iraq, where the combined risks of WMD proliferation and terrorism are greatest.

- The Export Control and Related Border Security program ($57 million) seeks to prevent states and terrorist organizations from acquiring WMD, their delivery systems, and destabilizing conventional weapons by helping partner countries to develop comprehensive strategic trade control and related border security systems. The program builds capacity to ensure that transfer authorizations support only legitimate trade and to detect and interdict illicit transfers at borders.

- The contribution to the Comprehensive Nuclear-Test-Ban Treaty Organization ($30.4 million) helps to fund the expansion, operation, and maintenance of the worldwide International Monitoring System as well as Preparatory Commission activities, including the development of the On-Site Inspection element of the Treaty's verification system. This contribution amount also includes funding for specific projects to increase the effectiveness and efficiency of the Treaty's verification regime.

- The Nonproliferation and Disarmament Fund (NDF) ($25 million) develops, negotiates, and implements carefully-vetted programs to destroy, secure, or prevent the proliferation of weapons of mass destruction (WMD), WMD-related materials and delivery systems, and destabilizing conventional weapons. NDF undertakes rapid-response activities to reduce threats that are unforeseen and unanticipated around the globe.

- The WMD Terrorism program ($4.8 million) undertakes specialized, targeted projects to improve international capacities to prepare for and respond to a terrorist attack involving weapons of mass destruction in support of the Global Initiative to Combat Nuclear Terrorism and to help develop capacity in key countries of concern to deter, detect, and respond to nuclear smuggling.

Anti -Terrorism Activities

- The Antiterrorism Assistance (ATA) program ($165.8 million) has long been the U.S. government's flagship program for counterterrorism law enforcement assistance to critical partner countries. ATA bilateral and regional programs provide training, mentoring, consultations, equipment, and infrastructure to help partner countries build or enhance a wide range of capabilities to detect, deter, and apprehend terrorists. This includes, but is not limited to law enforcement investigations, border security, protection of critical targets, leadership and management of counterterrorism incidents, regional coordination and cooperation, critical incident management, and cyber security. ATA capacity building fosters increased respect for human rights and the rule of law. The requested funds will build upon productive, strategic, and crucial existing partnerships with countries including Afghanistan, Indonesia, Iraq, Jordan, Kenya, Pakistan, the Philippines, and a number of other partners. The funds are also intended to address emerging counterterrorism needs in countries like Syria. Additionally, ATA funding supports the Regional Strategic Initiative, a global program that provides targeted, field-driven antiterrorism training and equipment to partner countries, improving their ability to respond to emerging, geographically diffuse threats and actors. The Countering Violent Extremism (CVE) program ($1.9 million) works in high-priority countries to build the capacities of partner country law enforcement institutions to work with at-risk communities, civil society groups, other counter-radicalization efforts, and in prisons on the rehabilitation and reintegration of violent extremist offenders. Focus countries in FY 2015 for CVE may include Indonesia, the Philippines, Bangladesh, Kenya, and Yemen.

- The Terrorist Interdiction Program/Personal Identification, Secure Comparison, & Evaluation System (TIP/PISCES) program ($25.1 million) provides state-of-the-art computerized screening systems, periodic hardware and software upgrades, and technical assistance and training to partner nations that enable immigration and border control officials to quickly identify suspect persons attempting to enter or leave their countries. The request provides funds for the deployment of PISCES installations, including biometric enhancements, to critical partner and candidate nations vulnerable to terrorist travel. There are 21 current partner nations, with PISCES systems installed at 140 Ports of Entry. Partners include critical nations with long established programs like Afghanistan, Iraq, Kenya, and Yemen as well as nations with newer programs initiated since 2012 in response to evolving terrorist threats, including Burkina Faso, Chad, the Maldives, and Niger. The funding also supports research, development and testing of enhanced capabilities to address evolving United States and host nation requests for customized interfaces with local and international databases, as well as deployment of portable and mobile PISCES systems for remote locations lacking infrastructure, while ensuring that the PISCES system maintains standards in accordance with international norms.

- The Counterterrorism Financing (CTF) program ($15 million) provides funding for anti-money laundering and counterterrorism finance (AML/CTF) training and technical assistance initiatives to enable frontline partners to detect, disrupt, and dismantle money laundering and terrorist financing networks. CTF capacity building efforts will include developing AML/CTF legal frameworks and regulatory structures, assisting in the development of national risk assessments, establishing effective financial investigative units, improving the effectiveness of other rule of law efforts to combat terrorist financing, and strengthening the capabilities of other relevant law enforcement, prosecutorial, and judicial institutions. The CTF program generally works through the interagency Terrorist Finance Working Group (TFWG) to leverage AML/CTF expertise across the U.S. government to develop and implement comprehensive AML/CTF training and technical assistance activities in those countries most threatened by terrorist financing.

- The Counterterrorism Engagement (CTE) program ($6 million) supports key bilateral, multilateral, and regional efforts to build political will among foreign government officials and civil societies to address shared counterterrorism challenges. By working with other government agencies and with nongovernmental organizations, CTE programs support initiatives and training, including through the United Nations and regional bodies, to promote the rule of law and human rights while countering terrorism and raising awareness of the UN Global Counterterrorism Strategy and implementation of UN counterterrorism resolutions. This funding will also support activities of the Global Counterterrorism Forum, a multilateral platform for senior counterterrorism policymakers and experts to engage on a sustained basis to build and mobilize the expertise and resources needed to identify and address critical civilian counterterrorism capacity-building challenges in key regions and countries around the globe. CTE funding will also go towards supporting the International Institute for Justice and the Rule of Law in Malta, with the primary mission of training police, prosecutors, parliamentarians, judges, and prison officials, particularly from transition countries, on how to prevent and respond to terrorist activity and other security challenges within a rule of law framework.

Regional Stability and Humanitarian Assistance

- The Conventional Weapons Destruction (CWD) program ($127.6 million) advances U.S. security and humanitarian interests by reducing the harmful worldwide effects of at-risk, illicitly-proliferated, and indiscriminately-used weapons of war. CWD activities mitigate security and public safety risks associated with excess, obsolete, unstable, or poorly-secured/maintained weapons and munitions stockpiles, including man-portable air defense systems (MANPADS), by assisting countries with destruction programs; improving physical security at storage facilities; and enhancing stockpile management practices. CWD also confronts the dangers posed by landmines and other explosive remnants of war (ERW) by surveying hazard areas, clearing landmines and ERW from affected areas, educating vulnerable populations, and assisting victims. CWD priorities for FY 2015 include preventing illicit small arms/light weapons (SA/LW) proliferation from Syria, clearing U.S.-origin ERW in Southeast Asia and the Pacific, denying SA/LW to destabilizing forces in North Africa and the Sahel, battle area clearance in South and Central Asia and Iraq, continued landmine and ERW clearance in Afghanistan, and reducing the threat of illicitly-held or at-risk MANPADS through safe and effective destruction efforts.

Peacekeeping Operations

($ in thousands)	FY 2013 Actual[1/]	FY 2014 Estimate	FY 2015 Request	Increase / Decrease
Peacekeeping Operations	490,197	435,600	336,150	-99,450
Enduring	287,508	235,600	221,150	-14,450
Overseas Contingency Operations	202,689	200,000	115,000	-85,000

1/ The FY 2013 OCO Actual reflects the following transfers: $87.14 million from the Foreign Military Financing account and $38.62 million from the International Narcotics Control and Law Enforcement account.

The FY 2015 enduring request for Peacekeeping Operations (PKO) of $221.2 million will help diminish and resolve conflict; enhance the ability of states to participate in peacekeeping and stability operations; address counterterrorism threats; and reform military establishments into professional military forces with respect for the rule of law in the aftermath of conflict.

The request supports two ongoing regional peacekeeping missions: the African Union Mission in Somalia (AMISOM), which is detailed in the Overseas Contingency Operations (OCO) section, and the Multinational Force and Observers (MFO) mission in the Sinai. The request also supports the ability of states to participate in peacekeeping operations through the Global Peace Operations Initiative (GPOI); enhances the ability of states to address counterterrorism threats through the Trans-Sahara Counterterrorism Partnership (TSCTP) and the Partnership for Regional East Africa Counter Terrorism (PREACT); supports long-term reforms to military forces in the aftermath of conflict to transform them into professional military forces with respect for the rule of law, including forces in South Sudan, Liberia, the Democratic Republic of the Congo, and Somalia (detailed in the OCO section); addresses regional conflict stabilization and border security issues in Africa; provides military professionalization institutional development; and provides regional maritime security training in Africa.

Highlights:

- **Global Peace Operations Initiative (GPOI) ($71 million):** FY 2015 funds will continue to support U.S. contributions to international peacekeeping capacity building by providing training, equipment, and other support for peacekeeping troops, with a focus on strengthening partner country capabilities to train their own peacekeeping units and achieve self-sufficiency. Funds will also support the deployment of troops to peace operations, enabling countries to respond to conflict-related crises worldwide. Finally, funds will continue an evaluation and metrics mechanism, including measures of effectiveness, to ensure GPOI is achieving its goals efficiently and effectively.

- **South Sudan ($36 million):** FY 2015 funds will be to support the rebuilding of a fractured military and support the Sudan People's Liberation Army (SPLA) continuing efforts to transform from an oversized disintegrated rebel force to an appropriately-sized professional military that respects human rights, represents its population, is accountable to elected leadership, protects the people of South Sudan, and encourages stability in the Horn of Africa. U.S. assistance is implemented through a "dual use" approach that builds the capacity of the SPLA in areas that will also directly benefit the citizens of South Sudan. In doing so, PKO-funded programs will provide technical training and non-lethal equipment to the military as well as expert advisors to assist both the military and the Ministry of Defense and Veteran's Affairs in the professionalization of the defense sector. If needed (depending on the security situation), funds may also support efforts to resolve or enforce stability in South Sudan.

- **Multinational Force and Observers ($28 million):** The FY 2015 request includes funds to continue the U.S. contribution to the Multinational Force and Observers mission in the Sinai, which supervises the implementation of the security provisions of the Egyptian-Israeli Peace Treaty, a fundamental element of regional stability.

- **Africa Regional ($23.6 million):** FY 2015 funds will be used to support the following programs:

  - *Partnership for Regional East Africa Counterterrorism (PREACT) ($10 million):* Funds will continue support for PREACT, an interagency initiative to build the capacity of governments in East Africa to counter terrorism. Funds will be used to enhance the tactical, strategic, and institutional capacity of PREACT partner militaries to respond to current and emergent terrorist threats, with an emphasis on border security, command-and-control, communications, civil-military operations, logistics, military intelligence, and special forces. Funds will support advisory assistance; modest infrastructure improvements; and training and equipping of counterterrorist military units in the East Africa region.

  - *Africa Conflict Stabilization and Border Security (ACSBS) ($8.6 million):* Funds will continue to support efforts to address and stabilize regional crises on the African continent. Specifically, funds will support activities in areas such as the Great Lakes region in Central Africa, the Mano River region in West Africa, and the Horn of Africa. Examples include countering the Lord's Resistance Army in Central and East Africa, and addressing conflict in the Central African Republic. Funds will support monitoring teams, advisory assistance, training, logistical support, infrastructure enhancements, and equipment. Funds will also support civil society engagement in the security sector and the military component of broader security sector reform efforts in Guinea and Cote d'Ivoire through training, advisory services, limited infrastructure projects, and non-lethal equipment.

  - *Africa Maritime Security Initiative (AMSI) ($2 million):* The request includes funds to increase African maritime security capabilities through the provision of regional training activities (including the training component of the Department of Defense's Africa Partnership Station program) and provide modest training equipment. By enhancing U.S. partners' maritime enforcement capabilities, the initiative helps to develop African maritime forces that can better respond to piracy, terrorist activity, illegal fishing, environmental threats, and trafficking in drugs, arms, and humans.

  - *Africa Military Education Program (AMEP) ($3 million):* The FY 2015 request will support professionalization at the institutional level of select African partner nations. This program will complement, but not duplicate, the International Military Education Training program, which focuses primarily on direct training of African military and select civilian personnel primarily in the United States. AMEP funds will provide training, advisory support, and potentially equipment and supplies to African military training institutions to enhance their ability to professionalize their militaries, including an appreciation of civilian control of the military, respect for the rule of law, and human rights.

- **Mali ($20.4 million):** Funds will continue to support defense sector reform efforts with the Government of Mali. Funds will concentrate on institutional reform, with a heavy focus on the proper role of the military, civil-military relations, and respect for human rights. Support may include training, advisory support, equipment, and potential refurbishment of facilities.

- **Trans-Sahara Counterterrorism Partnership (TSCTP) ($19.1 million):** The FY 2015 request continues support for the TSCTP, an interagency initiative designed to build the capacity and cooperation of governments across West and North Africa to counter terrorism. Funds will enhance the military capacity of TSCTP partners to respond to current and emerging threats, with an emphasis on border security, aerial mobility, military intelligence, logistics, institutional capacity, civil-military operations, military information support operations, and countering improvised explosive devices. Funds will support advisory assistance, modest infrastructure improvement, and training and equipping of counterterrorist military units in the West and North African regions. Funds will also have a new focus on institutional reform in the partner countries to ensure they can sustain and logistically support the new counterterrorism capabilities being developed.

- **Democratic Republic of the Congo ($11 million):** FY 2015 funds will be used to continue long-term efforts to reform the military in the Democratic Republic of the Congo (DRC) into a force capable of maintaining peace and security, to include the development of the military justice system and the Congolese military logistics system. Funds will support advisory assistance at the strategic and operational levels, training, equipment, and infrastructure improvements that contribute to the professionalization of the Congolese military.

- **Central African Republic ($10 million):** Requested funds will continue to support the African Union-led International Support Mission in the Central African Republic (MISCA), which began in December 2013 to stabilize the Central African Republic (CAR). Funds will support non-lethal equipment for Troop Contributing Countries (TCCs) and Police-Contributing Countries (PCCs), training of TCCs, possible advisory and logistics support, and strategic transport of personnel and equipment. Funds may also support security sector reform with the CAR military, including training, advisory support, and non-lethal equipment.

- **Liberia ($2 million):** The FY 2015 request continues to support the long-term effort to transform the Liberian military into a professional 2,100-member armed force that respects the rule of law and has the capacity to protect Liberia's borders and maintain adequate security in the country. Funds will primarily provide for operational support of existing infrastructure of the new military and some advisory and/or training support.

Details of the FY 2015 OCO Request for PKO are addressed in the OCO chapter

International Military Education and Training

($ in thousands)	FY 2013 Actual	FY 2014 Estimate	FY 2015 Request	Increase / Decrease
International Military Education and Training	100,432	105,573	107,474	1,901

The FY 2015 request for the International Military Education and Training (IMET) program is $107.5 million. As a key component of U.S. security assistance, IMET promotes regional stability and defense capabilities through professional military training and education. Through professional and technical courses and specialized instruction, most of which are conducted at military schoolhouses in the United States, the program provides students from allied and friendly nations with valuable training and education on U.S. military practices and standards. IMET students are exposed to the concepts of democratic values and respect for internationally-recognized standards of human rights, both through the courses they attend and through their experience of living in and being a part of local communities across the United States. IMET serves as an effective means to strengthen military alliances and international coalitions critical to U.S. national security goals. IMET also helps to develop a common understanding of shared international challenges, including terrorism, and fosters the relationships necessary to counter those challenges in a collaborative manner.

Highlights:

- **Africa ($13.3 million):** IMET programs for Africa focus on professionalizing defense forces in support of efforts to respond to regional crises and provide for long-term stability on the continent. Major IMET programs are focused on Kenya, Nigeria, Senegal, South Africa, and South Sudan – states critical to long-term regional peace and stability.

- **East Asia and the Pacific ($12.5 million):** IMET programs in East Asia and the Pacific focus on professionalizing the defense forces of regional partners, with a particular emphasis on building maritime security capability. Priority recipients include Indonesia, the Philippines, Thailand, and Vietnam.

- **Europe and Eurasia ($29.5 million):** IMET programs for this region enhance regional security and interoperability among U.S., NATO, and European armed forces. Importantly, these programs help to ensure that those nations that operate alongside the United States have officers that understand and appreciate the doctrine and operational tactics of the U.S. military. The largest programs include key strategic partners, such as Turkey, Poland, Bulgaria, Georgia, and the Czech Republic.

- **Near East ($19.6 million):** IMET programs for the Near East focus on critical countries, such as Egypt, Iraq, Jordan, Lebanon, Morocco, Oman, Tunisia, and Yemen, with the purpose of enhancing professionalism, providing the technical training necessary to maintain equipment of U.S. origin, and increasing awareness of international norms of human rights and civilian control of the military, topics that are critical for the development of security forces in the region in a time of change.

- **South and Central Asia ($13.3 million):** IMET programs in South and Central Asia focus on professionalizing the defense forces of regional partners, with a particular emphasis on English language training and respect for the rule of law, human rights, and civilian control of the military. Major IMET programs in this region include Pakistan, Afghanistan, India, and Bangladesh.

- **Western Hemisphere ($13.8 million):** IMET programs in the Western Hemisphere focus on professionalizing defense forces, institutionalizing respect for human rights and the rule of law, and enhancing the leadership and technical ability of partner nations to protect national territory and maritime borders against transnational threats. Priority programs include Colombia, El Salvador, Mexico, the Dominican Republic, and Honduras.

Foreign Military Financing

($ in thousands)	FY 2013 Actual[1]	FY 2014 Estimate	FY 2015 Request	Increase / Decrease
Foreign Military Financing	5,667,331	5,919,280	5,647,645	-271,635
Enduring	4,946,531	5,389,280	5,110,645	-278,635
Overseas Contingency Operations	720,800	530,000	537,000	7,000

1/ The FY 2013 OCO Actual level reflects the following transfers: $15 million to the Transition Initiatives account; $223.667 million to the Economic Support Fund account; and $87.14 million to the Peacekeeping Operations account.

The FY 2015 enduring request of $5,110.6 million for Foreign Military Financing (FMF) furthers U.S. interests around the world by helping ensure that coalition partners and friendly foreign governments are capable of working towards common security goals and sharing burdens in joint missions. FMF promotes U.S. national security by contributing to regional and global stability, strengthening military support for democratically-elected governments, and containing transnational threats, including terrorism and trafficking in narcotics, weapons, and persons. Increased military capabilities establish and strengthen multilateral coalitions with the United States and enable friends and allies to be interoperable with U.S., regional, and international military forces.

The FY 2015 FMF request is consistent with prior-year request levels for Israel, Egypt, and Jordan. The request continues funding for Pakistan and the planned reduction in funding for Iraq, both of which are detailed in the Overseas Contingency Operations (OCO) section. In addition, the request supports funding for coalition partners and allies, and is consistent with other requirements to promote U.S. national security, fight extremism, secure peace in the Middle East, and support the rebalance toward Asia. Increased funding for FMF administrative costs will support enhanced monitoring and evaluation efforts on military assistance programs.

Highlights:

- **Africa ($11.0 million):** In Africa, assistance will support defense reform, enhance counterterrorism and maritime security capabilities, promote interoperability, and expand recipient countries' capacity to participate in peacekeeping operations. FMF will support critical bilateral engagement in Djibouti, Ethiopia, Ghana, Kenya, Liberia, Nigeria, Senegal, South Africa, and Uganda as well as engagement through regional programs.

- **East Asia and the Pacific ($67.4 million):** Assistance will meet security challenges by enhancing ties with allies and partners. Programs will support the Administration's rebalance towards Asia by demonstrating U.S. commitment to priority regional security concerns of enhancing maritime security and freedom of navigation; disaster relief; enabling troop-contributing countries to participate in peacekeeping and coalition operations; increasing educational opportunities and English language capacity in support of deeper partnership with the United States; developing mutual understanding; and building the professionalization of partner nations' security forces, including strengthening democratic values and respect for human rights.

- **Europe and Eurasia ($66.9 million):** In Europe and Eurasia, FMF assistance furthers defense reform, military modernization, and interoperability of recipient country armed forces with the United States and NATO. A key focus of the program is helping ensure our European allies and partners, including Poland, Georgia, Romania, and Bulgaria, are ready and capable to undertake and sustain overseas deployments and peacekeeping missions, lessening the burden on U.S. forces.

- **Near East ($4,846.5 million):** The majority of FY 2015 FMF funding will provide continued assistance to the Middle East and North Africa region, including support for Israel in accordance with the Memorandum of Understanding; for Jordan' force modernization, border surveillance, and counterterrorism efforts; and for programs that consolidate gains in the development of counterterrorism capabilities and professional militaries. This request continues assistance to Egypt to further our shared security interests. Funds will also help the Government of Lebanon uphold its international obligations and improve its national defense capability. Since the political situation in the Middle East and North Africa remains fluid, program details will be reviewed in response to changing circumstances.

- **South and Central Asia ($7.9 million):** In South Asia, assistance will build land and maritime border security and disaster response capabilities. In Central Asia, assistance will strengthen capabilities to combat transnational threats such as terrorism and illicit trafficking in the wake of the U.S. drawdown in Afghanistan. Throughout the region, assistance will promote the professionalization of the security forces, with a particular focus on fostering respect for democratic governance, accountability, and international norms of human rights among our partners.

- **Western Hemisphere ($47.1 million):** FMF in the Western Hemisphere supports our partners' efforts to control national territory, modernize defense forces, and secure the southern approaches to the United States. FMF will continue to support Colombia's efforts to ensure that its security gains are irreversible and support the transition of the bilateral relationship toward that of a strategic partnership. FMF will also support Mexico's efforts to control national territory and enhance cooperation with the United States. Additionally, FMF funding for Central America will support partner efforts to control national territory and maritime borders, denying safe havens and operating areas to transnational criminal organizations and others who drive violence that threatens the security of our partners. FMF support through the Caribbean Basin Security Initiative will continue to build maritime security and support efforts in the region to identify, track and address transnational threats, such as illicit narcotics trafficking.

Details of the FY 2015 OCO Request for FMF are addressed in the OCO chapter.

Special Defense Acquisition Fund

($ in thousands)	FY 2013 Actual	FY 2014 Estimate	FY 2015 Request	Increase / Decrease
Special Defense Acquisition Fund	100,000	100,000	100,000	-
Foreign Military Sales Trust Fund offset	-	-	-	-
Offsetting Collections	-100,000	-100,000	-100,000	-
Net Cost for Special Defense Acquisition Fund	-	-	-	-

The Special Defense Acquisition Fund (SDAF) allows the United States to better support coalition and other partners, including those participating in U.S. overseas contingency and other operations, by expediting the procurement of defense articles for provision to foreign nations and international organizations.

The FY 2015 request reflects an additional $100 million in new SDAF obligation authority, to be funded by offsetting collections.   In FY 2015, offsetting collections will be derived from SDAF sales of stock as well as other receipts consistent with section 51(b) of the Arms Export Control Act.   The FY 2015 request will support advance purchases of high-demand equipment that have long procurement lead times. Long procurement lead times are often the main limiting factor in our ability to provide coalition partners with critical equipment to make them operationally effective in a timely manner.   Improving the mechanism for supporting U.S. partners is a high priority for the Departments of State and Defense.

Multilateral Assistance

($ in thousands)	FY 2013 Actual	FY 2014 Estimate	FY 2015 Request	Increase / Decrease
Multilateral Assistance	2,875,203	3,010,749	2,873,943	-136,806
International Organizations and Programs[1]	326,651	344,020	303,439	-40,581
International Development Association	1,351,018	1,355,000	1,290,600	-64,400
International Bank for Reconstruction and Development	180,993	186,957	192,921	5,964
Global Environment Facility	124,840	143,750	136,563	-7,187
African Development Fund	163,449	176,336	195,000	18,664
African Development Bank	30,717	32,418	34,119	1,701
Asian Development Fund	94,937	109,854	115,250	5,396
Asian Development Bank	101,190	106,586	112,194	5,608
Inter-American Development Bank	107,110	102,000	102,020	20
Enterprise of the Americas Multilateral Investment Fund	14,995	6,298	-	-6,298
Global Agriculture and Food Security Program[2]	128,165	133,000	-	-133,000
International Fund for Agricultural Development	28,481	30,000	30,000	-
Clean Technology Fund	175,283	184,630	201,253	16,623
Strategic Climate Fund	47,374	49,900	63,184	13,284
Transfer to Multilateral Trust Funds[3]	-	50,000	-	-50,000
IDA Multilateral Debt Relief Initiative	-	-	78,900	78,900
AfDF Multilateral Debt Relief Initiative	-	-	13,500	13,500
Middle East and North Africa Transition Fund	-	-	5,000	5,000

1/ The FY 2013 Enduring Actual level reflects the transfer of $4.4 million from the International Organizations and Programs account to the Global Health Programs - USAID account.

2/ For GAFSP, fundraising efforts are ongoing, with the goal of securing total contributions of at least $1.4 billion, including $475 million from the United States under our commitment to a 1:2 level against other donor pledges. For FY 2015, an $80 million request is included for GAFSP in the Administration's Opportunity, Growth, and Security Initiative.

3/ FY 2014 Estimate levels include an anticipated transfer of $50 million from the Economic Support Fund account in accordance with sec. 7060(c)(8) of the Consolidated Appropriations Act, 2014. Allocations to individual multilateral trust funds will be determined after consultation with the Committees on Appropriations.

International Organizations and Programs (IO&P)

The FY 2015 request of $303.4 million for the International Organizations and Programs (IO&P) account will advance U.S. strategic goals across a broad spectrum of critical areas by supporting and enhancing international coordination as well as leveraging resources from other countries. From this account, the United States provides voluntary contributions to international organizations to accomplish transnational goals where solutions to problems can best be addressed globally, such as protecting the ozone layer or safeguarding international air traffic. In other areas, such as development programs, the United States can multiply the influence and effectiveness of its own assistance through support for international programs that are attracting additional resources from other donors, leveraging other donors' contributions to advance U.S. strategic goals.

Highlights:

- **United Nations Children's Fund ($116.6 million):** U.S. voluntary contributions support the core budget of the United Nations Children's Fund (UNICEF), which provides goods and services directly to the world's neediest children, and contributes to the development of local institutional capacity. UNICEF's development work is closely coordinated with that of the U.S. government and international development agencies.

- **United Nations Development Program ($62.2 million):** U.S. voluntary contributions are provided for the United Nations Development Program (UNDP)'s regular budget, which supports its core administrative functions, basic development programming, and specific trust funds targeted in the areas of democratic governance and crisis prevention and recovery.

- **United Nations Population Fund ($35.3 million):** The United States continues to support the United Nations Population Fund (UNFPA). Contributions to UNFPA bolster its continued efforts to reduce poverty, improve the health of women and children, prevent HIV/AIDS, and provide family planning assistance to women in over 150 countries.

- **UN Women ($7.5 million):** Created in 2010, the UN Entity for Gender Equality and Women's Empowerment (UN Women) works to increase women's political participation, expand women's economic and educational opportunities, reduce violence against women, improve women's health, protect the rights of indigenous women and women with disabilities, facilitate women's political participation in all aspects of peace and security, and counter discrimination against women. This contribution to the core resources of UN Women will support programs and enable policies and programs related to women to be developed and implemented more efficiently.

- **International Conservation Programs ($7 million):** The United States is invested in several treaties on conservation. One of the key initiatives supported through the U.S. contribution to International Conservation Programs is the Convention on International Trade in Endangered Species of Wild Fauna and Flora (CITES). Other initiatives include the UN Convention to Combat Desertification, Ramsar Convention on Wetlands, the Intergovernmental Platform for Biodiversity and Ecosystem Services (IPBES), the UN Forum on Forests, International Tropical Timber Organization, and the FAO National Forest Program Facility.

Multilateral Development Banks

The FY 2015 request for the multilateral development banks (MDBs) is comprised of existing, previously authorized annual commitments as well as renewed pledges. The request for existing commitments includes the ongoing capital increases at the International Bank for Reconstruction and Development (IBRD), the Inter-American Development Bank (IDB), the African Development Bank (AfDB), and the Asian Development Bank (AsDB). Investments in these multilateral institutions remain a cost-effective way to promote U.S. national security, support broad-based and sustainable economic growth, and address key global challenges like environmental degradation, while fostering private sector development and entrepreneurship.

In addition to requesting funding for the annual commitment for each respective capital increase, Treasury is also requesting funding to address shortfalls caused by sequestration that would jeopardize U.S. shareholding and leadership at the MDBs. Addressing these shortfalls is necessary to ensure that the United States does not forfeit its leadership position at any of these institutions—a position that has greatly benefited both the MDBs and U.S. taxpayers for more than 60 years.

The FY 2015 request also includes funding for the concessional windows at the MDBs that provide grants and low-cost financing to the world's poorest countries. MDB concessional facilities are an important source of financing for the development needs of fragile and post-conflict states. The projects they support combat extreme hunger and poverty while promoting global stability, prosperity, and private sector growth. To continue the longstanding history of U.S. support for the MDBs, the FY 2015 request includes funding and authorization requests for the first of three installments to the seventeenth replenishment of the International Development Association (IDA) and the thirteenth replenishment of the African Development Fund (AfDF). In addition, Treasury is requesting funding for the U.S. commitment to the tenth replenishment of the Asian Development Fund (AsDF) and to meet a portion of U.S. unmet commitments to the institution, which currently total over $346 million.

Food Security

In addition to our core request, we are seeking $80 million for a contribution to the Global Agriculture and Food Security Program (GAFSP) as a part of the President's Opportunity, Growth, and Security Initiative. GAFSP continues to make major strides toward improving agricultural outcomes in countries seeking to reduce food insecurity. In 25 countries, more than ten million smallholder farmers and their families are expected to see significant increases in productivity on a per hectare basis with corresponding income gains. GAFSP is responsive to country needs and is aligned with each country's own homegrown strategies. It fosters cooperation among donors and allocates resources based on projected results.

The food security budget also includes $30 million for the third of three installments for the ninth replenishment of the International Fund for Agricultural Development (IFAD), the only global development finance institution solely dedicated to improving food security for the rural poor.

Environment and Clean Energy

Funding for multilateral environment programs helps to spur direct action and investment by developing countries to reduce their own pollution sources and advance ongoing global efforts. These global actions mitigate threats to our domestic environment that increasingly originate from beyond our own borders, enhancing our national security, and providing opportunities for U.S. businesses, especially in clean energy and other environmental technologies.

The FY 2015 request includes $264 million for the Clean Technology Fund (CTF), and three programs supported by the Strategic Climate Fund (SCF): the Pilot Program for Climate Resilience (PPCR), the Forest Investment Program (FIP), and the Program for Scaling up Renewable Energy in Low-Income Countries (SREP). These programs finance investments in other countries in clean energy, energy efficiency, and forest conservation, and in improving resilience to climate change impacts, such as drought.

The FY 2015 request also includes up to $136.6 million for the first installment of the sixth replenishment of the Global Environment Facility (GEF). The GEF replenishment negotiations are currently underway and expected to be completed in March 2014. Treasury will consult with Congress before finalizing the U.S. pledge to the new replenishment.

Debt Relief

The FY 2015 request includes $92.4 million to meet a portion of the U.S. commitment to the Multilateral Debt Relief Initiative (MDRI) at IDA and the AfDF. MDRI, together with associated debt relief efforts, reduced the debt burden for participating countries by about 90 percent as compared to their debt levels prior to entering the debt relief process. As a result, these countries have been able to increase poverty-reducing expenditures by an average of more than three percentage points of GDP over the past ten years.

In addition, the Budget includes transfer authority to allocate funding for bilateral debt relief under the Heavily Indebted Poor Countries (HIPC) Initiative for Sudan, should they meet the requirements to qualify.

Middle East and North Africa Transition Fund

The FY 2015 request includes $5 million for the Middle East and North Africa Transition Fund, a multi-donor trust fund administered by the World Bank and created under the U.S. chairmanship of the Group of 8 to assist countries that are members of the Deauville Partnership with Arab Countries in Transition (currently Egypt, Tunisia, Jordan, Morocco, Libya, and Yemen). The fund provides quick dispensation for small grants to help countries put in place economic policies and government reforms that will allow the countries to attract greater flows of capital as they address diverse economic challenges during their political transitions. A wide range of countries, including the United Kingdom, Saudi Arabia, Canada, France, Japan, Russia, Kuwait, and Qatar, have already provided or committed to provide funding.

International Monetary Fund

Treasury is seeking appropriations and authorization language within the FY 2015 request for the International Monetary Fund (IMF). In 2010, G-20 Leaders and the IMF membership decided on a set of quota and governance reforms designed to strengthen the IMF's critical role within the international system. The 2010 reforms are an important step in modernizing IMF governance to better reflect countries' economic weights in the global economy, while preserving U.S. leadership and veto power.

The proposed appropriations and authorization language would reduce U.S. participation in the IMF's New Arrangements to Borrow (NAB) by approximately $63 billion and increase the U.S. quota by an equal amount, for no net change in the overall U.S. financial commitment to the IMF. The proposal also authorizes the United States to accept an amendment to the IMF Articles of Agreement that will facilitate changes in the composition of the IMF Executive Board while preserving U.S. influence in the Board.

Completing the IMF reforms is a national security and economic policy priority for the United States. The Administration is putting forward a discretionary budget proposal, but we remain open to working with Congress on other approaches to get legislation passed as soon as possible, including mandatory spending approaches.

International Monetary Fund

($ in thousands)	FY 2013 Actual	FY 2014 Estimate	FY 2015 Request	Increase / Decrease
International Monetary Fund	-	-	16,000	16,000

International Monetary Fund

Treasury is seeking appropriations and authorization language within the FY 2015 request for the International Monetary Fund (IMF). In 2010, G-20 Leaders and the IMF membership decided on a set of quota and governance reforms designed to strengthen the IMF's critical role within the international system. The 2010 reforms are an important step in modernizing IMF governance to better reflect countries' economic weights in the global economy, while preserving U.S. leadership and veto power.

The proposed appropriations and authorization language would reduce U.S. participation in the IMF's New Arrangements to Borrow (NAB) by approximately $63 billion and increase the U.S. quota by an equal amount, for no net change in the overall U.S. financial commitment to the IMF. The proposal also authorizes the United States to accept an amendment to the IMF Articles of Agreement that will facilitate changes in the composition of the IMF Executive Board while preserving U.S. influence in the Board.

Completing the IMF reforms is a national security and economic policy priority for the United States. The Administration is proposing a discretionary funding approach, but we are willing to work with Congress on other approaches to get legislation passed as soon as possible, including mandatory funding approaches.

Export-Import Bank of the United States

($ in thousands)	FY 2013 Actual	FY 2014 Estimate	FY 2015 Request	Increase / Decrease
Export-Import Bank of the United States	-1,453,137	-864,500	-1,021,200	-156,700
Operations	-1,053,137	-841,500	-1,021,200	-179,700
Rescission	-400,000	-23,000	-	23,000

The FY 2015 Budget estimates that the Export-Import Bank of the United States (Ex-Im Bank) export credit support will total $37.6 billion in lending activity, and will be funded entirely by receipts collected from the Ex-Im Bank's customers. These receipts are expected to total $1,154.6 million in excess of estimated losses in FY 2015. These funds, treated as offsetting collections, will be used to pay $117.7 million for administrative expenses. The administrative expenses estimate includes funding for enhancing the Bank's comprehensive management framework and for upgrading the Bank's antiquated systems infrastructure. The Bank forecasts a net return of $1,021.2 million to the U.S. Treasury as receipts in excess of expenses or negative subsidy. The FY 2015 request for the Ex-Im Bank includes $5.8 million for the expenses of the Inspector General and $10.0 million in carryover authority.

The Ex-Im Bank is an independent, self-sustaining executive agency, and a wholly-owned U.S. Government corporation. As the official export credit agency of the United States, the mission of the Ex-Im Bank is to support U.S. exports by providing export financing through its loan, guarantee, and insurance programs. These programs are implemented in cases where the private sector is unable or unwilling to provide financing, and to ensure equitable competition in export sales between U.S. exporters and foreign exporters financed by their respective governments. By facilitating the financing of U.S. exports, Ex-Im Bank helps companies support and maintain U.S. jobs. The Ex-Im Bank actively assists small and medium sized businesses.

Overseas Private Investment Corporation

($ in thousands)	FY 2013 Actual	FY 2014 Estimate	FY 2015 Request	Increase / Decrease
Overseas Private Investment Corporation	-331,103	-211,055	-203,100	7,955

As the U.S. Government's development finance institution, the Overseas Private Investment Corporation (OPIC) is a critical development tool in fulfilling the President's national security, diplomacy and development commitments globally. OPIC mobilizes private capital to help address critical development challenges and in doing so, advances U.S. foreign policy. Because OPIC works with the U.S. private sector, it helps U.S. businesses gain footholds in emerging markets, catalyzing revenues, jobs and growth opportunities both at home and abroad. OPIC achieves its mission by providing investors with financing, guarantees, political risk insurance, and support for private equity investment funds.

OPIC's FY 2015 budget is fully self-funded and assumes continuation of OPIC's longstanding, thirty-six year consecutive track-record of positive contributions to the budget. From its FY 2015 estimated offsetting collections, OPIC is requesting to use $71.8 million for administrative expenses and $25 million for credit subsidy. OPIC expects these resources will support up to $4.2 billion in new direct loans, risk insurance and loan guarantees. The FY 2015 budget also includes $20 million in transfer authority and up to $10 million from OPIC's subsidy appropriation to implement OPIC's existing authority to execute a targeted equity financing program to fund limited partner interests in investment funds and to support limited investments in discrete and highly-developmental projects.

The requested resources are integral to OPIC's ability to continue to be a leading contributor to some of the Administration's most pressing foreign policy priorities. These resources build on OPIC's proven prudent business model which seeks to use limited public funds to mobilize private sector funds to address critical development challenges.

- **OPIC Delivers on U.S. Foreign Policy Priorities** – OPIC plays a critical role in fulfilling the President's commitments around the world, from Latin America to Africa, the Middle East and Asia. The Agency has supported economic reconstruction in Iraq, Afghanistan and Haiti, as well as economic development in the Middle East and North Africa following the Arab Spring. OPIC has also played a key role in supporting other initiatives such as the Power Africa Initiative, the U.S.-Asia Pacific Comprehensive Partnership for Sustainable Energy, the Global Climate Change Initiative, Feed the Future, and the Partnership for Growth.

- **OPIC is Playing a Key Role in Power Africa initiative** – OPIC, which has a long history of supporting projects in Sub-Saharan Africa, is playing a key role in a new U.S. initiative to double access to electricity in Sub-Saharan Africa. The region has in recent years seen strong economic growth and an expanding consumer class, but limited power remains a major problem, with more than two-thirds of the population lacking regular access to electricity.

- **OPIC Supports Small Businesses** – Nearly 75 percent of OPIC projects last fiscal year were in partnership with U.S. small businesses, accounting for $300 million in expected U.S. exports.

By balancing risks, returns and resources, OPIC generates returns to the budget, maintains itself as a fully self-sustaining Federal Corporation and consistently contributes to deficit reduction.

U.S. Trade and Development Agency

($ in thousands)	FY 2013 Actual	FY 2014 Estimate	FY 2015 Request	Increase / Decrease
U.S. Trade and Development Agency	47,469	55,073	67,700	12,627

The FY 2015 request for the U.S. Trade and Development Agency (USTDA) of $67.7 million will enable the Agency to continue its mission to help U.S. companies create jobs through the export of U.S. goods and services for priority development projects in emerging economies. USTDA links U.S. businesses to export opportunities by funding project planning activities, pilot projects, and reverse trade missions that create sustainable infrastructure and economic growth in its partner countries. In carrying out its mission, USTDA places particular emphasis on activities where there is a high likelihood for the export of U.S. goods and services during project implementation.

USTDA programs have a proven record of success. In FY 2013, USTDA identified nearly $3 billion in exports that were attributable to its activities. For the fifth year in a row, the Agency's measure of its return on investments increased, reaching $73 in U.S. exports for every dollar programmed. USTDA's success results, in part, from its rigorous, evidence-based decision-making processes. USTDA prioritizes funding for activities in markets and sectors that have strong opportunities for U.S. exports, where U.S. industry expertise can meet the development needs of its partner countries.

USTDA will continue to prioritize support for infrastructure development projects in the energy, transportation, and information and communications technology sectors, where the expertise of U.S. industry can best meet the development needs of USTDA's partner countries. USTDA's key markets will include Brazil, China, Colombia, Dominican Republic, Egypt, Ghana, India, Indonesia, Kazakhstan, Kenya, Mexico, Nigeria, Panama, the Philippines, Romania, South Africa, Turkey and Vietnam.

The FY 2015 budget request represents an increase of $12.6 million over the FY 2014 enacted level. This increase will allow USTDA to support critical Administration priorities and to level the playing field for U.S. companies in emerging markets. The additional funds will enable USTDA to: (1) provide critical project preparation assistance to support clean energy development as part of the Power Africa initiative; (2) catalyze investment from the U.S. private sector—leading to more exports and, ultimately, supporting more U.S. jobs — in support of the Administration's rebalance to the Asia-Pacific region; (3) increase its investment in clean energy development projects worldwide, including renewable and smart grid solutions; (4) address funding gaps in the life-cycle of sustainable infrastructure projects that impede implementation and hinder economic growth in emerging markets; and (5) educate public procurement officials in emerging economies about the benefits of structuring sustainable procurements that integrate life-cycle cost analyses and best-value determinations.

International Trade Commission

($ in thousands)	FY 2013 Actual	FY 2014 Estimate	FY 2015 Request	Increase / Decrease
International Trade Commission	79,517	83,257	86,459	3,202

The U.S. International Trade Commission (ITC) is an independent, nonpartisan, Federal agency with a wide range of trade-related mandates. The ITC makes determinations regarding unfair trade practices in import trade and conducts import-injury investigations. It also conducts economic research and fact-finding investigations of trade issues, maintains the Harmonized Tariff Schedule of the United States, participates in work on the international Harmonized System tariff nomenclature, and provides technical information and advice on trade matters to the Congress and the Administration.

The FY 2015 request of $86.5 million will fund activities related to these mandates.

Foreign Claims Settlement Commission

($ in thousands)	FY 2013 Actual	FY 2014 Estimate	FY 2015 Request	Increase / Decrease
Foreign Claims Settlement Commission	1,897	2,100	2,326	226

The Foreign Claims Settlement Commission (FCSC) is a quasi-judicial, independent agency within the Department of Justice. Its principle mission is to adjudicate claims of U.S. nationals against foreign governments, under specific jurisdiction conferred by Congress, pursuant to international claims settlement agreements, or at the request of the Secretary of State.

The FY 2015 request for FCSC provides $2.3 million to continue evaluating claims of U.S. nationals against foreign governments under current claims programs as well as maintaining the decisions and records of past claims programs, and continue building and modernizing both current and past claims programs records by creating and updating the relevant databases.

Food for Peace Title II

($ in thousands)	FY 2013 Actual	FY 2014 Estimate	FY 2015 Request	Increase / Decrease
Food for Peace Title II	1,359,358	1,466,000	1,400,000	-66,000

Title II of the Food for Peace Act (P.L. 83-480), as amended, formerly the Agricultural Trade Development and Assistance Act of 1954) authorizes the provision of U.S. food assistance to meet emergency food needs around the world, and funds development-oriented programs to help address the underlying causes of food insecurity. Funding for Title II, also known as P.L. 480 Title II, is appropriated to the U.S. Department of Agriculture and is administered by the U.S. Agency for International Development (USAID).

The FY 2015 Title II request of $1,400 million includes $270 million to be used for development programs. An additional $80 million is requested in the Development Assistance (DA) account under USAID's Community Development Fund, bringing the total funding for these types of programs to $350 million. Together, these resources support development food assistance programs' efforts to address chronic food insecurity in areas of recurrent crises using a multi-sectoral approach to reduce poverty and build resilience.

The balance of the FY 2015 Title II request, $1,130 million, will be used to provide emergency food assistance in response to natural disasters and complex emergencies. In an emergency, when people face the threat of imminent starvation, Title II emergency programs save lives, boost the resilience of disaster-affected communities, and support the transition from relief to recovery. This food, including specialized, processed commodities, provides life-saving assistance to millions of vulnerable people facing disasters overseas.

The request includes new authority to provide the flexibility to use up to 25 percent of these resources, valued at $350 million, for cash-based food assistance for emergencies. In these cases, interventions such as the local or regional procurement of agricultural commodities, use of food vouchers, or use of cash transfers, will allow USAID to make emergency food aid more timely and cost effective, improving program efficiencies and performance. It is estimated that this flexibility will allow USAID to assist approximately 2 million more emergency beneficiaries annually with the same level of resources.

This flexibility will help to mitigate the reduction in available resources for Title II programming due to the elimination of U.S. Maritime Administration (MARAD) reimbursements in the Bipartisan Budget Act of 2013. MARAD reimbursements, which helped USAID offset the increased cost of using U.S. flagged carriers versus foreign flagged carriers to deliver food aid around the world, contributed to USAID's annual operating budget and increased the reach of emergency food assistance.

McGovern-Dole International Food for Education and Child Nutrition Program

($ in thousands)	FY 2013 Actual	FY 2014 Estimate	FY 2015 Request	Increase / Decrease
McGovern-Dole International Food for Education and Child Nutrition Program	174,051	185,126	185,126	-

McGovern-Dole International Food for Education and Child Nutrition Program. The McGovern-Dole International Food for Education and Child Nutrition Program provides for the donation of U.S. agricultural commodities and associated financial and technical assistance to carry out preschool and school feeding programs in foreign countries. Maternal, infant, and child nutrition programs also are authorized under the program. Its purpose is to reduce the incidence of hunger and malnutrition and improve literacy and primary education. These measures contribute to a healthy, literate workforce that can support a more prosperous, sustainable economy and ensure long-term food security. The FY 2015 Budget proposes $185.1 million for the McGovern-Dole program. With this funding, the program is expected to assist more than 4 million women and children in 2015.

This page intentionally left blank.

FY 2015 INTERNATIONAL AFFAIRS OVERSEAS CONTINGENCY OPERATIONS (OCO)

STATE OPERATIONS and FOREIGN ASSISTANCE REQUEST
OVERSEAS CONTINGENCY OPERATIONS (OCO)
($000)

	FY 2013 OCO Actual[1]	FY 2014 Estimate OCO	FY 2015 Request OCO	Increase / Decrease
OVERSEAS CONTINGENCY OPERATIONS (OCO) TOTAL - STATE OPERATIONS and FOREIGN ASSISTANCE	10,822,173	6,520,000	5,912,525	(607,475)
STATE OPERATIONS & RELATED AGENCIES - OCO (With Rescissions)	3,495,040	1,390,407	2,021,125	630,718
Administration of Foreign Affairs	4,496,367	1,732,887	1,871,125	138,238
State Programs	3,178,992	1,391,109	1,553,425	162,316
Diplomatic and Consular Programs[2,3]	3,178,992	1,391,109	1,553,425	162,316
Ongoing Operations	2,269,613	490,835	563,719	72,884
Worldwide Security Protection	909,379	900,274	989,706	89,432
Embassy Security, Construction, and Maintenance	1,237,536	275,000	260,800	(14,200)
Ongoing Operations	1,237,536	275,000	10,800	(264,200)
Worldwide Security Upgrades	-	-	250,000	250,000
Other Administration of Foreign Affairs	79,839	66,778	56,900	(9,878)
Conflict Stabilization Operations (CSO)	8,075	8,500	-	(8,500)
Office of the Inspector General[4]	56,944	49,650	56,900	7,250
Educational and Cultural Exchange Programs[5]	14,820	8,628	-	(8,628)
International Organizations	96,205	74,400	150,000	75,600
Contributions to International Organizations (CIO)	96,205	74,400	-	(74,400)
Peacekeeping Response Mechanism	-	-	150,000	150,000
Broadcasting Board of Governors	4,180	4,400	-	(4,400)
International Broadcasting Operations	4,180	4,400	-	(4,400)
Other Programs	7,988	6,016	-	(6,016)
United States Institute of Peace	7,988	6,016	-	(6,016)
FOREIGN OPERATIONS - OCO	7,327,133	5,129,593	3,891,400	(1,238,193)
U.S Agency for International Development - OCO	246,457	91,038	65,000	(26,038)
USAID Operating Expenses (OE)	242,183	81,000	65,000	(16,000)
USAID Inspector General Operating Expenses	4,274	10,038	-	(10,038)
Bilateral Economic Assistance - OCO	5,188,054	3,894,165	2,778,400	(1,115,765)
International Disaster Assistance (IDA)	750,927	924,172	635,000	(289,172)
Transition Initiatives (TI)[6]	21,224	9,423	-	(9,423)
Complex Crises Fund (CCF)[7]	43,498	20,000	-	(20,000)
Economic Support Fund (ESF)[8,9,10]	3,293,886	1,656,215	1,678,400	22,185
Migration and Refugee Assistance (MRA)[9]	1,078,519	1,284,355	465,000	(819,355)
Department of Treasury	1,474	-	-	-
Treasury Technical Assistance	1,474	-	-	-

STATE OPERATIONS and FOREIGN ASSISTANCE REQUEST
OVERSEAS CONTINGENCY OPERATIONS (OCO)
($000)

	FY 2013 OCO Actual[1]	FY 2014 Estimate OCO	FY 2015 Request OCO	Increase / Decrease
International Security Assistance - OCO	**1,891,148**	**1,144,390**	**1,048,000**	**(96,390)**
International Narcotics Control and Law Enforcement (INCLE)[7, 10, 12]	853,067	344,390	396,000	51,610
Nonproliferation, Antiterrorism, Demining and Related Programs (NADR)	114,592	70,000	-	(70,000)
Peacekeeping Operations (PKO)[11, 12]	202,689	200,000	115,000	(85,000)
Foreign Military Financing (FMF)[6, 8, 11]	720,800	530,000	537,000	7,000
Rescissions				
Diplomatic & Consular Programs (D&CP)	**(1,109,700)**	**(427,296)**	**-**	**427,296**
Ongoing Operations Worldwide	(1,109,700)	(427,296)	-	427,296

Footnotes

1/ The FY 2013 Actual reflects the full-year continuing resolution, reduced by sequestration.

2/ The FY 2013 Actual reflects $22.6 million sequester reduction. The FY 2013 Actual includes $2.5 million transferred from Diplomatic and Consular Programs OCO to Educational and Cultural Exchange Programs.

3/ The FY 2014 Estimate excludes a rescission (ref P.L. 113-76) of $427.3 million in prior year balances.

4/ In FY 2013, funding was provided for the Special Inspector General for Iraq Reconstruction to sunset operations. In FY 2014 and FY 2015, funding is provided for the Special Inspector General for Afghanistan Reconstruction (SIGAR).

5/ The FY 2013 Actual includes $2.5 million transferred to Educational and Cultural Exchange Programs from Diplomatic and Consular Programs OCO.

6/ The FY 2013 OCO Actual level reflects the transfer of $15 million from the Foreign Military Financing account to the Transition Initiatives account.

7/ The FY 2013 OCO Actual level reflects the transfer of $15 million from the International Narcotics Control and Law Enforcement account to the Complex Crises Fund account.

8/ The FY 2013 OCO Actual level reflects the transfer of $223.667 million from the Foreign Military Financing account to the Economic Support Fund account.

9/ The FY 2013 OCO Actual level reflects the transfer of $35.5 million from the Migration and Refugee Assistance account to the Economic Support Fund account.

10/ The FY 2013 OCO Actual level reflects the transfer of $25.78 million from the International Narcotics Control and Law Enforcement account to the Economic Support Fund account.

11/ The FY 2013 OCO Actual level reflects the transfer of $87.14 million from the Foreign Military Financing account to the Peacekeeping Operations account.

12/ The FY 2013 OCO Actual level reflects the transfer of $38.62 million from the International Narcotics Control and Law Enforcement account to the Peacekeeping Operations account.

Overseas Contingency Operations Overview

The Administration's FY 2015 International Affairs request includes $5.9 billion for Overseas Contingency Operations (OCO). This funds the extraordinary costs of Department and U.S. Agency for International Development (USAID) operations and programs in in Afghanistan, Iraq, and Pakistan. It also supports our response to ongoing challenges presented by the Syria crisis and fund new peacekeeping missions in Africa and other areas of conflict. This approach is consistent with the practice of the past three years and allows the Department to deal with extraordinary activities that are critical to our immediate national security objectives without unnecessarily undermining funding for our longer-term efforts to sustain global order and tackle transnational challenges.

In FY 2015, OCO funds will continue to support a sovereign and self-reliant Iraq, promoting Iraq's security, stability, and growth. The request normalizes Mission Baghdad operations and will support staff and activities at Embassy Baghdad, as well as consulates in Erbil and Basrah. For Afghanistan, the OCO request sustains U.S. operations, diplomatic engagement, and assistance programs during a time when a newly elected Afghan President will be taking over the lead on managing the country through security, economic, and political transitions. The request for SIGAR provides for timely, effective oversight of these programs. For Pakistan, the OCO supports a robust diplomatic presence and critical assistance programs to support the government and its people following Pakistan's first democratic transition. These funds will help facilitate increased stability and prosperity in this strategically important nation and will enable us to sustain a presence necessary to achieve essential strategic priorities of eliminating terrorism and enhancing stability in Pakistan and the region following the transition in Afghanistan. The OCO resources will support critical U.S. activities such as sustaining close cooperation with Pakistan, ensuring the safety of Pakistani nuclear installations, working with Pakistan to facilitate the peace process in Afghanistan, and promoting improved relations with India.

For Syria, transition operations are underway along the country's northern border and the Department intends to counter sectarian strife and terrorism, and enable transition to peace and democracy. OCO funds will enable an ongoing U.S. response to the humanitarian crisis and provide support for the Syrian opposition.

Finally, the new Peacekeeping Response Mechanism request will address unanticipated peacekeeping requirements that emerge subsequent to transmittal of the President's Budget.

Diplomatic and Consular Programs - OCO

($ in thousands)	FY 2013 Actual[1]/	FY 2014 Estimate[2]/	FY 2015 Request	Increase / Decrease
Diplomatic and Consular Programs	3,178,992	1,391,109	1,553,425	162,316
Ongoing Operations	2,269,613	490,835	563,719	72,884
Worldwide Security Protection	909,379	900,274	989,706	89,432

1/ The FY 2013 Actual reflects $22.6 million sequester reduction. The FY 2013 Actual includes $2.5 million transferred from Diplomatic and Consular Programs OCO to Educational and Cultural Exchange Programs.

2/ The FY 2014 Estimate excludes a rescission (ref P.L. 113-76) of $427.3 million in prior year balances.

The FY 2015 Overseas Contingency Operations (OCO) request for Diplomatic and Consular Programs (D&CP) totals $1.6 billion, addressing the extraordinary and temporary costs of diplomatic operations in the Frontline States of Iraq, Afghanistan, and Pakistan, and transition operations related to Syria. This funding is critical to achieving U.S. national security goals: establishing a secure, stable, democratic, and self-reliant Iraq that will change the strategic landscape of the Middle East, defeating al-Qaida and its associates in Afghanistan while supporting the transition to full Afghan lead for security, and working to eliminate terrorist safe havens in Pakistan. The Department is also supporting a flexible diplomatic presence along Syria's borders to support humanitarian relief, counter sectarian strife and terrorism, and prepare for a peaceful transition.

D&CP - Ongoing Operations

For Iraq, the OCO request of $262.9 million supports the U.S. Mission's strategic partnership with Iraq, through which the U.S. can advance its economic and security interests in the region. Iraq is now a key U.S. ally in the region. Since the December 2011 departure of U.S. combat forces, the U.S. Mission in Iraq is now the foundation for all U.S. government programs and efforts. The D&CP Ongoing Operations request will support staff and activities at Embassy Baghdad, as well as consulates in Erbil and Basrah. The Department is normalizing its presence in Iraq to achieve a more flexible, less visible footprint. The request is $82.1 million above the FY 2014 due to reduced OCO carryover levels. Also, the request is $210.1 million below the FY 2013 actual level due to the realignment of Iraq security costs to Worldwide Security Protection in FY 2014.

For Afghanistan, the OCO request of $214.3 million supports the accelerating shift from a military to civilian-lead U.S. presence. Department personnel are engaged in capacity building, stabilization, and development programs that are essential to strengthening the ability of Afghanistan to take full responsibility for its security and growth. The request is $22.4 million below the FY 2014 level as the number of Department and interagency personnel is decreasing, primarily in the provinces.

For Pakistan, the OCO request of $39.7 million supports a robust diplomatic presence that will help create a durable stability in this strategically important nation. Pakistan lies at the heart of the U.S. counterterrorism strategy, the peace process in Afghanistan, nuclear non-proliferation efforts, and economic integration in South and Central Asia. OCO resources will support critical U.S. activities such as sustaining close cooperation with Pakistan, ensuring the safety of Pakistani nuclear installations, working with Pakistan to facilitate the peace process in Afghanistan, and promoting improved relations with India. The request is $33.7 million below the FY 2014 enacted level due to inclusion of salary costs in Enduring and the non-recurral of one-time costs.

For Syria, transition operations are underway along the country's northern border. Mission-specific office space has been identified in Gaziantep, Turkey, with additional renovations to Consulate Adana for personnel supporting U.S. government humanitarian and diplomatic efforts. The FY 2015 request of $46.9 million in OCO funding will support additional office space capacity, ongoing maintenance and operations, communications, information technology, life support, and transportation; as well as public diplomacy outreach to refugee and exile communities.

D&CP – Worldwide Security Protection

In Iraq, OCO funding of $501.4 million supports operational requirements, movement security, equipment and associated Operation and Maintenance, physical and technical security, static guards, and security operations in Basrah and Erbil. The request is $4.4 million above the FY 2014 level and funded through Worldwide Security Protection, consistent with FY 2014 Congressional action.

In Afghanistan, OCO funding of $473.0 million for WSP is an increase of $88.8 million above the FY 2014 level. This increase includes costs for general support operation expenses, equipment for the Tactical Operations Center, physical and technical security equipment such as Unmanned Aerial Vehicles, and regional security-related costs.

In Pakistan, OCO funding of $15.3 million for WSP similarly provides for overseas protective operations of U.S. civilians at the Embassy and consulates. The request is -$3.8 million below the FY 2014 level and includes lower costs for armored vehicles, a reduction in regional director costs, and lower costs to support Temporary Duty (TDY) personnel in Pakistan.

Embassy Security, Construction and Maintenance - OCO

($ in thousands)	FY 2013 Actual	FY 2014 Estimate	FY 2015 Request	Increase / Decrease
Embassy Security, Construction and Maintenance	1,237,536	275,000	260,800	-14,200

The Bureau of Overseas Buildings Operations (OBO), funded through the Embassy Security, Construction, and Maintenance (ESCM) appropriation, is responsible for providing U.S. Diplomatic and Consular missions overseas with secure, safe, and functional facilities to assist them in achieving the foreign policy objectives of the United States.

The FY 2015 Request represents an overall decrease of $14 million below the FY 2014 Estimate level. The funding covers lease costs for properties in Iraq ($10.8 million) and the construction of a new consulate compound in Basrah ($250 million). The compound will include a new consulate office building, general services support buildings, consul general residence, recreation facilities, parking and vehicular/pedestrian screening facilities. Consulate General Basrah serves Iraq's Shi'a heartland, which is the home of 80 percent of Iraq's known oil and gas reserves. Iraq's hydrocarbons represent approximately 70 percent of the country's GDP and more than 90 percent of Iraqi government revenues. Development of the resources in this region provides Iraq the best long-term opportunity to diversify its economy, improve basic services, and invest in its own reconstruction.

Office of Inspector General - OCO

($ in thousands)	FY 2013 Actual[1]/	FY 2014 Estimate	FY 2015 Request	Increase / Decrease
Office of Inspector General	56,944	49,650	56,900	7,250
Special Inspector General for Afghanistan Reconstruction	48,039	49,650	56,900	7,250
Special Inspector General for Iraq Reconstruction	5,776	-	-	-
Office of the Inspector General - MERO	3,129	-	-	-

1/ In FY 2013, funding was provided for the Special Inspector General for Iraq Reconstruction to sunset operations. In FY 2014, and FY 2015, funding is provided for the Special Inspector General for Afghanistan Reconstruction (SIGAR).

The FY 2015 request of $56.9 million for the Special Inspector General for Afghanistan Reconstruction (SIGAR) will enable the organization to perform independent and objective oversight of reconstruction and security programs. SIGAR will continue to address emergent reconstruction issues, coordinate with experts from multiple SIGAR Directorates, and quickly address matters before they mature into significant issues that negatively impact the reconstruction.

Peacekeeping Response Mechanism - OCO

($ in thousands)	FY 2013 Actual	FY 2014 Estimate	FY 2015 Request	Increase / Decrease
Peacekeeping Response Mechanism	-	-	150,000	150,000

The proposed Peacekeeping Response Mechanism (PKRM) Overseas Contingency Operations account will support critical requirements for peacekeeping operations and activities that emerge outside of the regular budget cycle. Such missions may involve the United Nations (UN), regional security partnerships, coalition peacekeeping efforts, or forces which promote the peaceful resolution of conflict.

Allocation of PKRM funding is subject to a determination by the Secretary that additional resources are necessary to support new or expanded peacekeeping operations or peacekeeping activities above the program level recommended in the FY 2015 budget submission to the Congress in the Peacekeeping Operations (PKO) or Contributions for International Peacekeeping Activities (CIPA) accounts. The PKRM request includes transfer authority to the PKO and CIPA accounts to provide flexibility for new UN or non-UN peacekeeping missions including significant troop level or mission expansions approved by the relevant governing bodies.

The PKRM will allow the United States to respond more rapidly and effectively to unanticipated peacekeeping requirements without disrupting important, ongoing missions and programs. Unanticipated peacekeeping requirements in Africa over the past several years demonstrate the need for such a mechanism, which would enable the United States to respond to future missions in Africa, Syria, or other needs around the world.

USAID Operating Expenses - OCO

($ in thousands)	FY 2013 Actual	FY 2014 Estimate	FY 2015 Request	Increase / Decrease
USAID Operating Expenses	242,183	81,000	65,000	-16,000

The Quadrennial Diplomacy and Development Review calls for "elevating American 'civilian power' to better advance our national interests and be a better partner with the U.S. military." The U.S. Agency for International Development (USAID) Overseas Contingency Operations (OCO) Operating Expense (OE) request provides the resources to respond to this challenge. It funds the extraordinary costs of operations in the frontline state of Afghanistan.

For FY 2015, the request of $65 million in USAID OCO OE will support 110 U.S. Direct Hires (USDHs) and 20 U.S./Third Country National (TCN) personal services contractors projected for Afghanistan. For the 110 USDHs, OCO OE will cover that portion of support costs that exceed the average for USDHs in non-frontline states.

Economic Support Fund - OCO

($ in thousands)	FY 2013 Actual[1/]	FY 2014 Estimate	FY 2015 Request	Increase / Decrease
Economic Support Fund	3,293,886	1,656,215	1,678,400	22,185

1/ The FY 2013 OCO Actual level reflects the following transfers: $223.667 million from the Foreign Military Financing account; $35.5 million from the Migration and Refugee Assistance account; and $25.78 million from the International Narcotics Control and Law Enforcement account to the Economic Support Fund account.

The Economic Support Fund Overseas Contingency Operations account includes the extraordinary costs of our involvement in Afghanistan, Pakistan, and Syria.

South and Central Asia – Overseas Contingency Operations ($1,553.4 million): The FY 2015 request includes funding to support extraordinary and temporary needs that will help stabilize conflict areas and aid in the transition to long-term sustainable and durable development of Afghanistan and Pakistan.

- **Afghanistan ($1,107.4 million):** FY 2015 resources are necessary for the continued security and economic transitions, perhaps the most critical phase of solidifying the progress made over the last decade and helping establish Afghanistan as a stable, prosperous, secure nation in a stable, prosperous, secure region. OCO funding will prioritize those areas critical to sustaining transition gains and objectives while continuing to lay the foundation for sustained economic, political, and social sector development. FY 2015 assistance will focus on promoting economic growth by investing in viable sectors including agriculture and extractives, improved governance, a better system of justice, and alternatives to the illicit production of narcotics. The United States will work with international partners to sustain gains in health and education and will support women and girls through the critical transition period and beyond. The United States and the Government of Afghanistan are working together to make progress on the fundamental reforms objectives laid out in the Tokyo Mutual Accountability Framework. Assistance funds will help support progress in these areas and the United States is working in coordination with other major donors to create incentives for government enactment and implementation of reforms including respect for the rights of women and minorities, improved governance, anti-corruption efforts and improved legislation to support private investment.

  OCO resources in FY 2015 are essential to a successful ongoing security transition and to the continued stability of Afghanistan. They will be used to solidify gains in areas still vulnerable to unrest. Infrastructure funding will help finalize and maintain investments in core projects that will bring sustainable power to the North and South – a critical component of the U.S. government stabilization and economic growth strategies for Afghanistan. OCO funds will also support government reform efforts through the Afghan Reconstruction Trust Fund and through other programs.

- **Pakistan ($446 million):** FY 2015 funding for Pakistan is crucial to meeting key U.S. strategic priorities of combatting terrorism, strengthening security in both Pakistan and the region, and maintaining stability in Afghanistan post-transition. OCO funding will support stabilization, infrastructure, and regional trade, particularly in the tribal areas and border regions with Afghanistan. These resources will expand the reach of the government, increase economic opportunities in areas prone to instability, improve governance and strengthen the delivery of essential services, including those of health and education. In addition to community development and the construction and rehabilitation of roads, bridges, and other infrastructure that will increase security and stability in key areas afflicted by extremism, FY 2015 assistance will support energy investments, a top priority for both the U.S. government and the Government of Pakistan. These projects will increase power generation and improve the efficiency and regulation of the energy sector, promoting stability and economic growth in Pakistan and the broader region.

Near East – Overseas Contingency Operations ($125 million): The FY 2015 ESF-OCO request includes extraordinary funding to continue opposition support efforts inside Syria.

- **Syria Response ($125 million):** The United States has already provided significant funding to Syrian opposition groups and Syria's neighbors to address critical needs resulting from the ongoing Syria crisis, and will continue this support in FY 2015. U.S. leadership will remain critical through FY 2015 and this request will help the United States support a political transition, counter violent extremism, support local communities in liberated areas to maintain basic services and help preserve U.S. national security interests in the region. Specifically, this request will continue ongoing efforts to support the opposition, including support to national and local-level opposition groups as they strive to achieve a negotiated political solution to this conflict; provide goods and services to their communities; and jumpstart local economies. As the Administration has stated, the only way to end this conflict is through a negotiated political solution that results in a transitional governing body. As negotiations progress, and should a transition occur, U.S. assistance will focus on helping consolidate the political transition, support the democratic process, and enable reconstruction and recovery efforts, in coordination with the other international donors.

International Disaster Assistance - OCO

($ in thousands)	FY 2013 Actual	FY 2014 Estimate	FY 2015 Request	Increase / Decrease
International Disaster Assistance	750,927	924,172	635,000	-289,172

With over 9.3 million conflict-affected people inside Syria and nearly 2.4 million Syrian refugees throughout the region, humanitarian needs related to the Syria crisis are expected to remain high in FY 2015. The FY 2015 International Disaster Assistance (IDA) Overseas Contingency Operations (OCO) request of $635 million will provide funds to save lives and reduce suffering through the provision of mainly food assistance, emergency medical care, and protection assistance to those most vulnerable inside Syria and to those who have fled to neighboring countries. This request includes $335 million to be administered by the U.S. Agency for International Development's (USAID) Office of U.S. Foreign Disaster Assistance for disaster response and $300 million to be administered by USAID's Office of Food for Peace for emergency food assistance. The U.S. government has been the largest donor for Syrian humanitarian needs, providing more than $1.7 billion since the crisis began.

Migration and Refugee Assistance - OCO

($ in thousands)	FY 2013 Actual[1]	FY 2014 Estimate	FY 2015 Request	Increase / Decrease
Migration and Refugee Assistance	1,078,519	1,284,355	465,000	-819,355

1/ The FY 2013 OCO Actual level reflects the transfer of $35.5 million from the Migration and Refugee Assistance account to the Economic Support Fund account.

With over 9.3 million conflict-affected people inside Syria and nearly 2.4 million Syrian refugees throughout the region, humanitarian needs related to the Syria crisis are expected to remain high in FY 2015. The FY 2015 Migration and Refugee Assistance (MRA) Overseas Contingency Operations (OCO) request of $465 million will fund humanitarian assistance programs that meet basic needs to sustain life; support emergency medical care and provide protection and assistance to the most vulnerable, including assisting those affected by gender-based violence; and help ease the burden of host communities supporting refugees from Syria. These funds will support the humanitarian response efforts of several international organizations, including the UN High Commissioner for Refugees and the International Committee of the Red Cross, as well as non-governmental organization partners to address the immense humanitarian needs of individuals inside Syria and refugees throughout the region. The U.S. government is already providing more than $1.7 billion as part of the humanitarian response to the crisis.

International Narcotics Control and Law Enforcement - OCO

($ in thousands)	FY 2013 Actual[1]	FY 2014 Estimate	FY 2015 Request	Increase / Decrease
International Narcotics Control and Law Enforcement	853,067	344,390	396,000	51,610

1/ The FY 2013 OCO Actual level reflects the following transfers: $15 million to the Complex Crises Fund account; $25.78 million to the Economic Support Fund account; and $38.62 million to the Peacekeeping Operations account.

The FY 2015 International Narcotics Control and Law Enforcement (INCLE) request of $396 million includes funding for Overseas Contingency Operations (OCO) for Afghanistan, Pakistan, Syria, and the Middle East North Africa Initiative. The request of $325 million for Afghanistan includes a full year of operations for the interdiction, justice, corrections, and various support programs in Afghanistan. The $41 million request for Pakistan will support efforts to increase the reach of Pakistani law enforcement into the unstable areas bordering Afghanistan. The $30 million request for Syria and the Middle East and North Africa (MENA) will support security sector reform, judicial reform, and corrections reform across the region.

Near East

- **Syria ($10 million):** The OCO request will strengthen criminal justice institutions within Syria, either as part of a transitional government or as support to moderate local governments in liberated areas. This temporary and extraordinary assistance will focus on short-term, high-impact security sector, judicial, and corrections reform. The goal will be to prevent a security vacuum and support functioning rule of law systems in Syria where citizens would no longer fear state-run security services and have confidence in a transparent and independent judiciary and corrections system.

- **MENA Initiative Contingencies ($20 million):** Temporary and extraordinary funding is requested under the OCO heading to enable the United States to address needs resulting from the crisis in Syria and spillover effects in the region, including: transitional justice, short-term, high-impact judicial sector capacity building, security sector reform, combatting trafficking in persons, and anti-corruption. Programs would also help institute reforms that promote minority and women's rights, and increase access to justice for vulnerable populations.

South and Central Asia

- **Afghanistan ($325 million):** OCO funds in this request will continue projects supporting the capacity of the Afghan government to provide justice services and the capacity of civil society and other actors to advocate for and raise awareness of legal rights. These projects will be carried out with fewer international staff, more Afghan leadership, and in some cases will consist of Afghan government implementation with financial support from the U.S. government. Funding will be used to continue providing professional justice sector training, mentoring, capacity building, and access to justice programs on a nationwide basis with a heavy focus on creating sustainable Afghan solutions. In many cases, programs will be facilitated by organizations staffed with Afghan legal experts who have benefitted from both educational opportunities and previous work experience provided by U.S. implementers. Programming to combat narcotics, corruption, and national security crimes will continue, including through support for the Counternarcotics Justice Center as well as Department of Justice mentors. By 2015, efforts will focus on corrections support through a core cadre of highly specialized international corrections advisors in Kabul and enduring sites. These advisors, working with Afghan professional staff, will mentor the Afghan corrections system leadership, provincial prison commanders and corrections personnel with targeted training and mentoring sessions. Funding will continue to support an embedded capacity building team at the General Directorate of Prisons and Detention Centers (GDPDC) headquarters, which will work with GDPDC staff in developing prison industries and vocational programs, supporting vulnerable populations including juveniles and women, and managing security threats.

Additionally, FY 2015 OCO funds will support Afghan-led initiatives to reduce the supply of opiates originating in Afghanistan, including by enhancing Afghan-led eradication programs. Funds will continue to support the specialized units of the Counternarcotics Police of Afghanistan to disrupt insurgency revenue sources derived from the illicit narcotics trade. Funding will promote stabilization by incentivizing provincial governors' counternarcotics and supply reduction activities, including through support for sustainable, community-led development projects in provinces that have successfully reduced or eliminated poppy cultivation.

- **Pakistan ($41 million):** OCO funding for Pakistan will continue support for Government of Pakistan initiatives to enhance stability, security, and justice in Pakistan. Assistance will support law enforcement and border security efforts that strengthen the presence, reach, and operational capabilities of Pakistani law enforcement throughout Pakistan, especially in the challenging terrain bordering Afghanistan. Specifically, funding will support equipment and infrastructure for law enforcement entities in the Federally Administered Tribal Areas (FATA) and Khyber Pakhtunkhwa province to help extend the reach of law enforcement into typically inaccessible areas. Funds will also support the Ministry of Interior Air Wing which enhances law enforcement operations nationwide against traffickers, militants, and criminals, as well as counternarcotics activities and programs to strengthen Pakistan's justice and corrections sectors.

Peacekeeping Operations - OCO

($ in thousands)	FY 2013 Actual[1/]	FY 2014 Estimate	FY 2015 Request	Increase / Decrease
Peacekeeping Operations	202,689	200,000	115,000	-85,000

1/ The FY 2013 OCO Actual reflects the following transfers: $87.14 million from the Foreign Military Financing account and $38.62 million from the International Narcotics Control and Law Enforcement account.

The FY 2015 Peacekeeping Operations (PKO) Overseas Contingency Operations (OCO) request of $115 million will support programming related to Somalia. FY 2015 funds will be used to continue voluntary support to the African Union Mission in Somalia (AMISOM), including training and advisory services, equipment, and transportation of personnel/goods from current and new force-contributing countries not covered by the UN Support Office for the AMISOM (UNSOA). Given the newly recognized government of Somalia and the security gains and expansion made by AMISOM, increased support to the national Somali military forces is critically important. Accordingly, PKO funds will also be used to professionalize, and provide logistical, operational, and facilities maintenance support to Somali military forces to ensure they have the capability to contribute to national peace and security in support of the international peace process efforts, and as part of a multi-sector approach to post-conflict security sector reform. Programming will emphasize human rights and civil-military relations. Funds to pay the United States' portion of the UN assessment for UNSOA are requested separately in the Contributions for International Peacekeeping Activities account.

Foreign Military Financing - OCO

($ in thousands)	FY 2013 Actual[1/]	FY 2014 Estimate	FY 2015 Request	Increase / Decrease
Foreign Military Financing	720,800	530,000	537,000	7,000

1/ The FY 2013 OCO Actual level reflects the following transfers: $15 million to the Transition Initiatives account; $223.667 million to the Economic Support Fund account; and $87.14 million to the Peacekeeping Operations account.

The FY 2015 Foreign Military Financing (FMF) Overseas Contingency Operations (OCO) request of $537 million is for Iraq and Pakistan.

- **Pakistan ($280 million):** Given the ongoing transition in Afghanistan and continued terrorist attacks against civilian and military targets throughout Pakistan, FMF is essential to Pakistan's efforts to increase stability in its western border region and ensure overall stability within its own borders. The $280 million Pakistan request will enhance the Pakistan Army, Frontier Corps, Air Force, and Navy's ability to conduct counterinsurgency (COIN) and counterterrorism (CT) operations against militants throughout its borders, especially in the Federally Administered Tribal Areas and Khyber-Pakhtunkhwa, improve Pakistan's ability to deter threats emanating from those areas, and encourage continued U.S.-Pakistan military-to-military engagement. FMF will continue to focus on seven priority areas identified and agreed to with the Government of Pakistan, including precision strike; air mobility and combat search and rescue; counter-improvised explosive devise and battlefield survivability; battlefield communications; night operations; border security; and maritime security/counternarcotics in support of CT aims.

- **Iraq ($267 million):** The $257 million requested for Iraq in FY 2015 broadly focuses on helping the Iraqis improve the capability and professionalism of their military and builds upon the efforts made since 2003 by the U.S. military, coalition forces, and Iraqi military operations and initiatives. Of the Iraq request, $7 million will fund administrative costs associated with the Office of Security Cooperation in Iraq, which also supports implementation of Iraq's own significant and ongoing purchases through the Foreign Military Sales program. FMF will help ensure that a strong U.S.-Iraq relationship is in place as Iraq continues to rely on its own fiscal resources to contribute to peace and security in the region. The program will focus on the development of enduring logistics capabilities and institutions to sustain U.S. and Iraqi post-war investments; professionalizing the security forces; and strengthening the United States' long-term strategic partnership with Iraq.

ACCOUNT TABLES

Global Health Programs - USAID
($ in thousands)

	FY 2013 Actual[1,2]	FY 2014 Estimate	FY 2015 Request
TOTAL	2,626,059	2,769,450	2,680,000
Africa	1,419,284	1,463,710	1,451,270
Angola	38,266	38,400	38,700
Benin	23,466	23,100	23,500
Burkina Faso	9,421	9,500	9,000
Burundi	17,740	18,000	17,500
Cameroon	1,500	1,500	1,500
Democratic Republic of the Congo	114,616	126,650	127,200
Ethiopia	131,546	138,365	137,200
Ghana	61,567	61,500	61,500
Guinea	17,880	17,850	17,500
Kenya	78,324	83,000	81,400
Lesotho	6,400	6,400	6,400
Liberia	33,112	32,700	32,700
Madagascar	48,640	49,000	49,000
Malawi	69,493	71,200	72,400
Mali	56,679	57,650	56,850
Mozambique	63,965	68,700	68,100
Nigeria	165,451	173,500	173,500
Rwanda	42,397	43,500	44,000
Senegal	54,757	57,000	56,000
South Africa	12,009	12,000	10,000
South Sudan	38,541	35,510	35,510
Swaziland	6,900	6,900	6,900
Tanzania	96,084	98,335	98,335
Uganda	84,955	90,500	88,200
Zambia	56,969	58,800	56,875
Zimbabwe	42,550	42,500	41,500
Africa Regional	15,800	14,100	13,500
East Africa Regional	9,365	8,650	7,800
Sahel Regional Program	2,512	2,800	2,300
Southern Africa Regional	2,000	2,000	2,000
West Africa Regional	16,379	14,100	14,400
East Asia and Pacific	134,024	141,750	130,450
Burma	11,848	22,000	15,500
Cambodia	32,214	32,500	30,500
Indonesia	41,264	41,250	39,750
Papua New Guinea	2,500	2,500	2,500
Philippines	32,810	32,500	31,200
Timor-Leste	2,013	2,000	2,000
Regional Development Mission-Asia (RDM/A)	11,375	9,000	9,000
Europe and Eurasia	14,392	9,000	7,500
Armenia	2,386	-	-
Georgia	3,664	-	-
Ukraine	7,724	7,500	6,500

Global Health Programs - USAID
($ in thousands)

	FY 2013 Actual[1, 2]	FY 2014 Estimate	FY 2015 Request
Europe and Eurasia Regional	618	1,500	1,000
Near East	8,345	9,000	9,500
Yemen	8,345	9,000	9,500
South and Central Asia	182,032	184,700	167,900
Bangladesh	74,005	79,500	78,200
India	50,910	48,000	36,000
Kazakhstan	2,234	-	-
Kyrgyz Republic	4,282	4,300	3,750
Nepal	39,056	40,900	40,200
Tajikistan	7,500	7,000	5,750
Uzbekistan	3,045	4,000	3,000
Central Asia Regional	1,000	1,000	1,000
Western Hemisphere	78,948	68,791	65,541
Dominican Republic	6,702	5,750	5,750
Guatemala	16,796	15,000	13,000
Haiti	25,017	25,200	25,200
Honduras	3,578	-	-
Barbados and Eastern Caribbean	6,950	6,950	6,950
Central America Regional	8,391	8,391	8,391
Latin America and Caribbean Regional	7,993	4,000	2,750
South America Regional	3,521	3,500	3,500
Asia Regional	-	4,750	3,250
Asia Middle East Regional	4,805	-	-
DCHA - Democracy, Conflict, and Humanitarian Assistance	14,269	13,000	13,000
Special Protection and Assistance Needs of Survivors (SPANS)	14,269	13,000	13,000
GH - Global Health	370,331	399,054	373,244
GH - International Partnerships	392,017	468,695	453,345
Blind Children	2,378	2,500	-
Children in Adversity	-	-	1,500
Commodity Fund	19,350	20,335	20,335
Global Alliance for Vaccine Immunization (GAVI)	137,979	175,000	200,000
International AIDS Vaccine Initiative (IAVI)	27,320	28,710	28,710
Iodine Deficiency Disorder (IDD)	1,902	2,500	2,000
Microbicides	42,807	45,000	45,000
Neglected Tropical Diseases (NTD)	85,371	99,750	86,500
Pandemic Influenza and Other Emerging Threats	54,931	72,100	50,000
TB Drug Facility	14,269	15,000	13,500
MDR Financing	2,855	5,000	3,000
New Partners Fund	2,855	2,800	2,800
IDEA - Office of Innovation and Development Alliances	3,806	-	-
LAB - Global Development Lab	-	7,000	5,000
OST - Office of Science and Technology	3,806	-	-

1/ The FY 2013 Actual reflects the full-year continuing resolution, reduced by the 0.032% rescission and sequestration.

2/ The FY 2013 Enduring Actual level reflects the transfer of $4.4 million from the International Organizations and Programs account to the Global Health Programs - USAID account.

Global Health Programs - State

($ in thousands)

	FY 2013 Actual[1]	FY 2014 Estimate	FY 2015 Request
TOTAL	5,439,829	5,670,000	5,370,000
Africa	3,173,623	3,357,686	3,332,686
Angola	7,291	9,899	12,899
Botswana	54,269	57,804	57,804
Burundi	15,360	15,360	15,360
Cameroon	23,825	34,175	34,175
Cote d'Ivoire	134,769	118,405	138,405
Democratic Republic of the Congo	34,754	51,975	59,975
Djibouti	1,800	1,800	1,800
Ethiopia	156,792	132,213	147,213
Ghana	6,670	6,797	6,797
Kenya	269,585	371,680	371,680
Lesotho	26,765	27,288	27,288
Liberia	800	800	800
Malawi	58,013	67,988	67,988
Mali	1,352	1,500	1,500
Mozambique	257,100	274,001	274,001
Nam bia	32,126	58,513	43,513
Nigeria	455,746	456,652	456,652
Rwanda	92,100	88,559	78,559
Senegal	1,538	1,535	1,535
Sierra Leone	500	500	500
South Africa	477,335	455,550	409,550
South Sudan	13,689	11,790	11,790
Swaziland	19,154	36,413	36,413
Tanzania	340,670	372,381	372,381
Uganda	316,140	320,176	320,176
Zambia	301,225	304,282	304,282
Zimbabwe	71,855	77,250	77,250
East Africa Regional	800	800	800
Southern Africa Regional	1,600	1,600	1,600
East Asia and Pacific	87,556	88,627	83,627
Burma	9,000	9,000	9,000
Cambodia	4,745	5,122	5,122
China	2,977	1,500	1,500
Indonesia	250	250	250
Papua New Guinea	2,353	3,700	3,700
Vietnam	65,676	63,142	58,142
Regional Development Mission-Asia (RDM/A)	2,555	5,913	5,913
Europe and Eurasia	11,863	12,015	22,015
Ukraine	11,863	12,015	22,015
South and Central Asia	17,622	38,494	38,494
India	7,407	26,000	26,000
Central Asia Regional	10,215	12,494	12,494
Western Hemisphere	173,496	162,443	167,444
Brazil	881	500	500

Global Health Programs - State

($ in thousands)

	FY 2013 Actual[1]	FY 2014 Estimate	FY 2015 Request
Dominican Republic	7,122	8,363	8,363
Guyana	8,866	6,636	6,636
Haiti	129,865	124,013	124,013
Barbados and Eastern Caribbean	14,509	10,331	15,331
Central America Regional	12,253	12,600	12,601
S/GAC - Office of the Global AIDS Coordinator	1,975,669	2,010,735	1,725,734
Additional Funding for Country Programs	93,137	100,566	115,565
International Partnerships	1,611,837	1,695,000	1,395,000
Oversight/Management	159,138	135,169	135,169
Technical Support//Strategic Information/Evaluation	111,557	80,000	80,000

1/ The FY 2013 Actual reflects the full-year continuing resolution, reduced by the 0.032% rescission and sequestration.

Development Assistance
($ in thousands)

	FY 2013 Actual[1]	FY 2014 Estimate	FY 2015 Request
TOTAL	2,717,671	2,507,001	2,619,984
Africa	1,170,113	1,139,240	1,073,448
Democratic Republic of the Congo	7,930	-	-
Djibouti	1,911	-	10,000
Ethiopia	94,490	100,000	89,838
Ghana	85,309	85,100	89,824
Guinea	2,003	-	-
Kenya	97,211	95,000	90,861
Liberia	50,078	-	-
Malawi	49,747	50,500	38,000
Mali	39,173	53,210	42,644
Mauritania	1,907	-	1,615
Mozambique	56,667	60,500	46,276
Niger	955	-	-
Nigeria	76,920	71,000	89,440
Rwanda	61,912	65,000	48,109
Senegal	47,756	55,621	39,880
Somalia	4,777	-	-
South Africa	16,475	19,000	16,200
Tanzania	122,550	115,734	118,145
Uganda	67,512	68,270	55,658
Zambia	36,784	42,500	19,458
Africa Regional	86,026	88,750	113,349
Central Africa Regional	30,679	39,400	16,087
East Africa Regional	40,971	41,161	52,194
Sahel Regional Program	5,064	15,600	24,000
Southern Africa Regional	22,518	21,911	19,972
West Africa Regional	62,788	50,983	51,898
East Asia and Pacific	275,442	254,825	345,638
Cambodia	27,087	26,456	31,250
Indonesia	89,046	69,920	104,500
Laos	1,290	1,300	4,000
Marshall Islands	470	500	500
Micronesia	470	500	500
Mongolia	5,159	5,000	6,000
Philippines	85,755	87,682	115,182
Thailand	4,826	4,000	5,000
Timor-Leste	10,032	6,500	10,200
Vietnam	17,198	20,445	37,800
Regional Development Mission-Asia (RDM/A)	34,109	32,522	30,706
Near East	25,032	-	-
Morocco	16,720	-	-
Yemen	8,312	-	-
South and Central Asia	125,162	111,857	126,165
Bangladesh	79,301	81,578	82,400
India	15,287	19,000	18,229
Maldives	2,866	2,000	2,000

Development Assistance
($ in thousands)

	FY 2013 Actual[1]	FY 2014 Estimate	FY 2015 Request
Nepal	21,020	7,279	19,500
Sri Lanka	5,733	2,000	3,229
South Asia Regional	955	-	807
Western Hemisphere	305,945	219,520	282,390
Brazil	11,462	12,500	2,000
Dominican Republic	11,864	10,300	10,830
Ecuador	13,376	-	-
El Salvador	21,426	19,281	25,000
Guatemala	45,861	42,789	57,387
Honduras	44,428	36,700	44,326
Jamaica	6,688	6,000	5,500
Mexico	26,224	-	12,500
Nicaragua	8,599	7,400	8,000
Paraguay	4,777	6,000	8,073
Peru	49,140	18,500	54,000
Barbados and Eastern Caribbean	10,032	7,500	10,000
Central America Regional	12,421	11,500	11,000
Latin America and Car bbean Regional	30,096	28,050	31,774
South America Regional	9,551	13,000	2,000
USAID Asia Regional	-	7,180	9,296
Asia Middle East Regional	14,331	-	-
BFS - Bureau for Food Security	316,559	328,535	348,900
DCHA - Democracy, Conflict, and Humanitarian Assistance	122,562	120,530	95,661
Special Protection and Assistance Needs of Survivors (SPANS)	21,968	23,700	4,880
E3 - Economic Growth, Education, and Environment	187,959	191,520	170,547
IDEA - Office of Innovation and Development Alliances	99,931	-	-
LAB - Global Development Lab	-	105,000	146,300
OST - Office of Science and Technology	40,767	-	-
Other Funding	11,320	5,794	-
To Be Programmed	11,320	5,794	-
PPL - Policy, Planning and Learning	21,975	21,000	20,500
USAID Program Management Initiatives	573	2,000	1,139

1/ The FY 2013 Actual reflects the full-year continuing resolution, reduced by the 0.032% rescission and sequestration.

Economic Support Fund
($ in thousands)

	FY 2013 Actual[1, 2, 3, 4]	FY 2014 Estimate[5, 6]	FY 2015 Request
TOTAL - ESF	5,867,473	4,589,182	5,077,094
Total Enduring - ESF	2,573,587	2,932,967	3,398,694
Africa	352,830	424,509	521,100
Central African Republic	-	2,000	-
Cote d'Ivoire	9,748	-	7,000
Additional FY 2013 OCO[7]	-	[7,500]	-
Democratic Republic of the Congo	29,197	51,385	71,440
Dj bouti	-	5,000	-
Additional FY 2013 OCO[7]	-	[5,000]	-
L beria	65,191	89,138	82,600
Sierra Leone	2,981	1,600	-
Somalia	-	21,067	79,217
Additional FY 2013 OCO[7]	-	[13,000]	-
South Sudan	201,094	183,241	225,400
Sudan	10,708	9,197	9,500
Zimbabwe	16,943	19,575	19,043
African Union	733	774	800
Africa Regional	16,235	21,532	26,100
Trans Sahara Counter-Terrorism Partnership (TSCTP)	-	*	[7,000]
East Africa Regional	-	20,000	-
East Asia and Pacific	98,966	139,465	99,200
Burma	41,037	61,200	58,700
Cambodia	6,751	5,000	5,000
China	10,124	22,900	4,500
Indonesia	5,883	-	-
Vietnam	14,462	22,000	-
East Asia and Pacific Regional	13,960	22,348	26,000
Regional Development Mission-Asia (RDM/A)	6,749	6,017	5,000
Europe and Eurasia	368,552	324,567	316,074
Albania	10,378	6,000	6,872
Armenia	27,026	20,000	20,700
Azerbaijan	11,029	9,000	9,600
Belarus	11,001	12,700	9,000
Bosnia and Herzegovina	28,416	22,000	23,300
Cyprus	2,925	-	-
Georgia	42,468	39,000	38,266
Kosovo	46,151	41,014	35,450
Macedonia	10,187	5,000	5,628
Moldova	16,481	15,050	15,050
Montenegro	823	200	200
Poland	5,893	-	-
Serbia	22,271	16,103	9,250
Ukraine	56,939	54,000	56,958
Europe and Eurasia Regional	58,029	59,000	61,800
International Fund for Ireland	2,090	2,500	-
Organization for Security and Cooperation in Europe (OSCE)	16,445	23,000	24,000

Economic Support Fund
($ in thousands)

	FY 2013 Actual[1, 2, 3, 4]	FY 2014 Estimate[5, 6]	FY 2015 Request
Near East	973,414	1,100,901	1,492,844
Egypt	241,032	200,000	200,000
Iraq	-	-	22,500
Jordan	347,961	360,000	360,000
Lebanon	7,952	48,163	58,000
Additional FY 2013 OCO[7]	-	[10,000]	-
Morocco	1,929	20,896	20,000
Tunisia	-	30,000	30,000
West Bank and Gaza	356,727	264,042	370,000
Additional FY 2013 OCO[7]	-	[105,958]	-
Yemen	12,000	45,000	64,500
MENA Initiative	-	-	225,000
Middle East Multilaterals (MEM)	993	800	1,200
Middle East Partnership Initiative (MEPI)	-	75,000	70,000
Middle East Regional Cooperation (MERC)	4,820	5,000	5,000
Near East Regional Democracy	-	32,000	30,000
Trans-Sahara Counter-Terrorism Partnership (TSCTP)	-	-	6,644
Middle East Regional (MER)	-	20,000	30,000
South and Central Asia	64,001	273,739	317,200
Afghanistan	21,700	100,000	117,600
India	-	-	3,000
Kazakhstan	-	6,354	6,200
Kyrgyz Republic	-	32,937	33,100
Nepal	19,830	26,654	12,500
Pakistan	19,578	60,122	100,000
Tajikistan	-	18,439	15,900
Turkmenistan	-	3,988	4,100
Uzbekistan	-	4,738	4,900
Central Asia Regional	-	17,928	16,900
South and Central Asia Regional	2,893	2,579	3,000
Western Hemisphere	447,503	456,159	392,876
Colombia	165,883	141,500	132,876
Cuba	19,283	20,000	20,000
El Salvador	3,354	-	-
Haiti	135,985	119,477	110,000
Mexico	32,067	46,100	35,000
Peru	2,834	20,000	-
Venezuela	5,786	4,298	5,000
Western Hemisphere Regional	82,311	104,784	90,000
Caribbean Basin Security Initiative (CBSI)	[18,802]	*	[28,000]
Central American Regional Security Initiative (CARSI)	[50,619]	*	[60,000]
CT - Counterterrorism	-	-	10,000
DCHA - Democracy, Conflict, and Humanitarian Assistance	22,174	19,900	-
Special Protection and Assistance Needs of Survivors (SPANS)	9,641	5,000	-
DRL - Democracy, Human Rights and Labor	1,446	-	60,000
E3 - Economic Growth, Education, and Environment	5,771	10,000	12,000
ECA - Educational and Cultural Affairs	8,822	-	

Economic Support Fund
($ in thousands)

	FY 2013 Actual[1, 2, 3, 4]	FY 2014 Estimate[5, 6]	FY 2015 Request
ENR - Energy Resources	9,620	11,800	11,800
OES - Oceans and International Environmental and Scientific Affairs	115,771	115,807	149,000
Office of U.S. Foreign Assistance Resources	497	4,300	2,500
Other Funding	94,152	29,475	-
OPIC/State Regional Economic Partnership	-	4,000	-
To Be Programmed	10,485	25,475	-
Treasury GCC Transfer	83,667	-	
Special Representatives	10,068	22,345	14,100
S/CCI - Office of the Coordinator for Cyber Issues	-	480	400
S/GPI - Special Representative for Global Partnerships	909	1,000	1,000
S/GWI - Ambassador-at-Large for Global Women's Issues	8,195	20,000	12,000
S/SACSED - Senior Advisor for Civil Society and Emerging Democracies	482	480	400
S/SRMC - Special Representative to Muslim Communities	482	385	300

	FY 2013 Actual	FY 2014 Estimate	FY 2015 Request
Total Overseas Contingency Operations - ESF	3,293,886	1,656,215	1,678,400
Africa	148,612	-	
Democratic Republic of the Congo	35,144	-	-
Kenya	5,844	-	-
Somalia	14,277	-	-
South Sudan	83,667	-	-
State Africa Regional (AF)	3,858	-	-
USAID East Africa Regional	5,822	-	-
East Asia and Pacific	15,500	-	
Philippines	15,500	-	-
Near East	737,220	384,337	125,000
Iraq	72,333	22,500	
Jordan	216,443	340,000	
Lebanon	73,251	11,837	
L bya	5,000	-	
Syria	20,780	-	125,000
Tunisia	14,467	-	
West Bank and Gaza	10,000	-	
Yemen	4,881	-	
MENA Initiative	202,531	-	
Middle East Partnership Initiative (MEPI)	67,510	-	
Near East Regional Democracy	30,862	-	
Trans-Sahara Counter-Terrorism Partnership (TSCTP)	1,447	-	
USAID Middle East Regional (MER)	17,715	10,000	-
South and Central Asia	2,387,249	1,271,878	1,553,400
Afghanistan	1,601,445	752,000	1,107,400
Kazakhstan	6,892	-	
Kyrgyz Republic	35,731	-	
Pakistan	703,749	519,878	446,000
Tajikistan	21,365	-	
Turkmenistan	4,640	-	
Uzbekistan	5,366	-	
Central Asia Regional	8,061	-	

Economic Support Fund

($ in thousands)

	FY 2013 Actual[1,2,3,4]	FY 2014 Estimate[5,6]	FY 2015 Request
CT - Counterterrorism	3,858	-	-
Special Representatives	1,447	-	-
S/CCI - Office of the Coordinator for Cyber Issues	1,447	-	-

1/ The FY 2013 Actual Enduring reflects the full-year continuing resolution, reduced by the 0.032% rescission and sequestration. The FY 2013 Actual OCO reflects the full year Continuing Resolution reduced by sequestration.

2/ The FY 2013 OCO Actual level reflects the transfer of $223.667 million from the Foreign Military Financing account to the Economic Support Fund account.

3/ The FY 2013 OCO Actual level reflects the transfer of $35.5 million from the Migration and Refugee Assistance account to the Economic Support Fund account.

4/ The FY 2013 OCO Actual level reflects the transfer of $25.78 million from the International Narcotics Control and Law Enforcement account to the Economic Support Fund account.

5/ FY 2014 Estimate levels include an anticipated transfer of $50 million from the Economic Support Fund account to the Multilateral Development Banks in accordance with sec. 7060(c)(8) of the Consolidated Appropriations Act, 2014.

6/ The FY 2014 Estimate reflects the estimated funding level for FY 2014 at the Account and Operating Unit level and are subject to change. Detailed allocations below the Account and Operating Unit level are not available.

7/ In order to offset reductions to programs in FY 2014, additional FY 2013 ESF OCO will be provided to the countries identifed.

Migration and Refugee Assistance & U.S. Emergency Refugee and Migration Assistance Fund

($ in thousands)

	FY 2013 Actual[1,2]	FY 2014 Estimate	FY 2015 Request
TOTAL - MRA	2,668,665	2,743,100	2,047,374
Total Enduring - MRA	1,590,146	1,458,745	1,582,374
PRM - Population, Refugee, and Migration	1,590,146	1,458,745	1,582,374
Africa	414,675	408,648	418,000
East Asia	65,650	69,332	54,600
Europe	44,700	48,651	31,000
Migration	21,550	27,500	20,000
Near East	351,407	480,909	362,400
Protection Priorities	220,252	215,450	140,200
South Asia	55,355	66,875	105,800
Western Hemisphere	53,237	61,100	45,374
Administrative Expenses	34,000	34,500	35,000
Humanitarian Migrants to Israel	19,320	10,680	10,000
Refugee Admissions	310,000	35,100	360,000
Total Overseas Contingency Operations - MRA[1]	1,078,519	1,284,355	465,000
Other Funding	326,825	-	-
To Be Programmed	326,825	-	-
PRM - Population, Refugees, and Migration	751,694	1,284,355	465,000
U.S. Emergency Refugee and Migration Assistance	25,823	50,000	50,000

1/ The FY 2013 Actual Enduring reflects the full-year continuing resolution, reduced by the 0.032% rescission and sequestration. The FY 2013 Actual OCO reflects the full year Continuing Resolution reduced by sequestration.

2/ The FY 2013 OCO Actual level reflects the transfer of $35.5 million from the Migration and Refugee Assistance account to the Economic Support Fund account.

International Narcotics Control and Law Enforcement
($ in thousands)

	FY 2013 Actual [1, 2, 3, 4]	FY 2014 Estimate [5]	FY 2015 Request
TOTAL - INCLE	1,858,678	1,350,000	1,117,911

	FY 2013 Actual [1, 2, 3, 4]	FY 2014 Estimate [5]	FY 2015 Request
Total Enduring - INCLE	1,005,611	1,005,610	721,911
Africa	53,262	66,169	54,650
Democratic Republic of the Congo	5,996	3,250	2,000
Kenya	4,996	2,000	1,000
L beria	16,250	11,700	11,500
Mozambique	598	500	-
Somalia	-	1,700	1,700
South Africa	6,155	2,000	1,000
South Sudan	-	20,599	20,000
Tanzania	448	450	450
Uganda	598	-	-
Africa Regional	18,221	23,970	17,000
Trans Sahara Counter-Terrorism Partnership (TSCTP)	-	*	*[4,000]*
East Asia and Pacific	25,050	32,232	31,000
Burma	-	-	3,000
China	823	800	825
Indonesia	10,049	10,066	10,025
Laos	1,000	1,000	1,000
Malaysia	800	800	-
Philippines	2,996	8,000	9,000
Thailand	1,740	1,466	1,900
Timor-Leste	800	660	800
Vietnam	450	450	450
East Asia and Pacific Regional	6,392	8,990	4,000
Europe and Eurasia	53,703	43,798	30,700
Albania	4,445	4,450	2,650
Armenia	3,009	2,824	1,700
Azerbaijan	1,262	1,226	800
Bosnia and Herzegovina	7,535	6,735	3,800
Georgia	5,565	3,947	3,500
Kosovo	11,751	10,674	6,800
Macedonia	1,893	1,786	1,600
Moldova	3,062	3,230	2,800
Montenegro	1,831	1,826	1,500
Serbia	3,517	3,000	2,250
Ukraine	4,408	4,100	2,500
Europe and Eurasia Regional	5,425	-	800
Near East	93,959	104,394	106,000
Egypt	5,001	3,000	1,000
Iraq	-	-	11,000
Lebanon	15,460	13,894	10,000
L bya	-	1,500	1,000
Morocco	1,500	3,000	3,000
Tunisia	1,998	9,000	7,000

International Narcotics Control and Law Enforcement
($ in thousands)

	FY 2013 Actual[1, 2, 3, 4]	FY 2014 Estimate[5]	FY 2015 Request
West Bank and Gaza	70,000	70,000	70,000
Yemen	-	3,000	1,000
Trans-Sahara Counter-Terrorism Partnership (TSCTP)	-	1,000	2,000
South and Central Asia	30,947	98,260	16,360
Afghanistan	-	45,000	-
Additional FY 2013 OCO[6]	-	[25,000]	-
Bangladesh	2,000	2,600	1,250
Kazakhstan	1,801	1,200	600
Kyrgyz Republic	5,536	6,000	2,400
Maldives	-	1,200	640
Nepal	4,000	3,300	2,230
Pakistan	-	23,000	-
Sri Lanka	720	720	-
Tajikistan	7,252	7,000	4,000
Turkmenistan	550	500	500
Uzbekistan	1,044	740	740
Central Asia Regional	8,044	7,000	4,000
Western Hemisphere	550,942	467,131	332,000
Bolivia	4,996	-	-
Brazil	2,000	-	-
Colombia	152,322	149,000	117,000
Ecuador	4,503	-	-
Guatemala	4,846	-	-
Haiti	17,448	12,000	6,000
Mexico	195,077	148,131	80,000
Paraguay	500	-	-
Peru	44,250	33,000	37,000
Western Hemisphere Regional	125,000	125,000	92,000
Caribbean Basin Security Initiative (CBSI)	[30,000]	*	[22,000]
INL - International Narcotics and Law Enforcement Affairs	177,025	169,585	130,478
Alien Smuggling/Border Security	1,000	750	500
Anti-Money Laundering Programs	4,148	3,600	2,500
Critical Flight Safety Program (CFSP)	12,385	11,085	7,000
Criminal Justice Assistance and Partnership	4,200	9,517	3,000
Criminal Youth Gangs	3,000	-	-
Cyber Crime and IPR	4,739	5,000	2,000
Demand Reduction	12,499	12,500	12,500
Fighting Corruption	5,001	3,900	3,500
International Law Enforcement Academy (ILEA)	27,000	31,300	24,000
Inter-regional Aviation Support	46,329	40,000	38,478
International Organizations	5,000	3,869	4,000
International Organized Crime	5,000	8,750	1,000
International Police Peacekeeping Operations Support (IPPOS)	7,500	2,500	2,000
Program Development and Support	39,224	36,814	30,000
J/TIP - Office to Monitor and Combat Trafficking In Persons	20,723	24,041	20,723

International Narcotics Control and Law Enforcement

($ in thousands)

	FY 2013 Actual[1, 2, 3, 4]	FY 2014 Estimate[5]	FY 2015 Request
Total Overseas Contingency Operations - INCLE	853,067	344,390	396,000
Africa	34,978	-	-
Somalia	2,095	-	-
South Sudan	28,882	-	-
Africa Regional	4,001	-	-
Near East	28,345	23,052	30,000
Iraq	13,499	23,052	-
Syria		-	10,000
Tunisia	6,001	-	-
Yemen	5,001	-	-
MENA Initiative		-	20,000
Trans-Sahara Counter-Terrorism Partnership (TSCTP)	3,844	-	
South and Central Asia	626,206	214,400	366,000
Afghanistan	568,806	180,000	325,000
Pakistan	57,400	34,400	41,000
Office of U.S. Foreign Assistance Resources	-	10,000	-
Complex Crises Fund (CCF)	-	10,000	-
Other Funding	163,538	96,938	-
To Be Programmed	163,538	96,938	-

1/ The FY 2013 Actual Enduring reflects the full-year continuing resolution, reduced by the 0.032% rescission and sequestration. The FY 2013 Actual OCO reflects the full year Continuing Resolution reduced by sequestration.

2/ The FY 2013 OCO Actual level reflects the transfer of $15 million from the International Narcotics Control and Law Enforcement account to the Complex Crises Fund account.

3/ The FY 2013 OCO Actual level reflects the transfer of $25.78 million from the International Narcotics Control and Law Enforcement account to the Economic Support Fund account.

4/ The FY 2013 OCO Actual level reflects the transfer of $38.62 million from the International Narcotics Control and Law Enforcement account to the Peacekeeping Operations account.

5/ The FY 2014 Estimate reflects the estimated funding level for FY 2014 at the Account and Operating Unit level and are subject to change. Detailed allocations below the Account and Operating Unit level are not available.

6/ In order to offset reductions to the Afghanistan program in FY 2014, additional FY 2013 INCLE OCO will be provided.

Nonproliferation, Antiterrorism, Demining and Related Programs

($ in thousands)

Summary by Sub-Account

	FY 2013 Actual[1]	FY 2014 Estimate	FY 2015 Request
NADR Total	674,862	700,000	605,400
Total - Enduring	560,270	630,000	605,400
Nonproliferation Programs	281,059	298,369	265,880
Nonproliferation and Disarmament Fund	27,020	30,000	25,000
Export Control and Related Border Security Assistance	55,597	64,000	56,990
Global Threat Reduction	64,487	77,369	65,140
IAEA Voluntary Contribution	90,035	90,000	83,600
CTBT International Monitoring System	31,331	31,000	30,300
Weapons of Mass Destruction Terrorism	5,468	5,000	4,750
UN Security Council Resolution 1540 Trust Fund	-	-	-
CTBTO Preparatory Commission-Special Contributions	7,121	1,000	100
Anti-terrorism Programs	138,887	152,631	211,925
Antiterrorism Assistance	75,275	102,540	165,834
Terrorist Interdiction Program	39,876	25,091	25,091
CT Engagement with Allies	7,595	10,000	6,000
Counterterrorism Financing	16,141	15,000	15,000
Regional Stability and Humanitarian Assistance	140,324	179,000	127,595
Conventional Weapons Destruction	140,324	179,000	127,595
Total - Overseas Contingency Operations	114,592	70,000	-
Antiterrorism Assistance - OCO	112,502	70,000	-
Conventional Weapons Destruction - OCO	2,090	-	-

1/ The FY 2013 Actual Enduring reflects the full-year continuing resolution, reduced by the 0.032% rescission and sequestration. The FY 2013 Actual OCO reflects the full year Continuing Resolution reduced by sequestration.

Peacekeeping Operations

($ in thousands)

	FY 2013 Actual[1,2,3]	FY 2014 Estimate	FY 2015 Request
TOTAL - PKO	490,197	435,600	336,150
Total Enduring - PKO	287,508	235,600	221,150
Africa	169,815	112,500	103,050
Central African Republic	-	-	10,000
Cote d'Ivoire	500	1,000	-
Democratic Republic of the Congo	12,000	10,000	11,000
Liberia	2,000	2,000	2,000
Mali	7,168	3,000	20,445
Somalia	106,947	42,350	-
South Sudan	19,200	33,000	36,000
Africa Regional	22,000	21,150	23,605
Near East	26,593	36,000	28,000
Multinational Force and Observers (MFO)	26,593	36,000	28,000
PM - Political-Military Affairs	91,100	87,100	90,100
Trans-Sahara Counter-Terrorism Partnership (TSCTP)	16,100	16,100	19,100
Global Police Operations Initiative (GPOI)	75,000	71,000	71,000
Total Overseas Contingency Operations - PKO	202,689	200,000	115,000
Africa	164,069	180,000	115,000
Central African Republic	23,400	10,000	-
Mali	12,740	-	-
Somalia	121,929	170,000	115,000
South Sudan	6,000	-	-
Near East	38,620	-	-
Syria	38,620	-	-
PM - Political-Military Affairs	-	20,000	-
Peacekeeping Response	-	20,000	-

1/ The FY 2013 Actual Enduring reflects the full-year continuing resolution, reduced by the 0.032% rescission and sequestration. The FY 2013 Actual OCO reflects the full year Continuing Resolution reduced by sequestration.

2/ The FY 2013 OCO Actual level reflects the transfer of $87.14 million from the Foreign Military Financing account to the Peacekeeping Operations account.

3/ The FY 2013 OCO Actual level reflects the transfer of $38.62 million from the International Narcotics Control and Law Enforcement account to the Peacekeeping Operations account.

International Military Education and Training
($ in thousands)

	FY 2013 Actual[1]	FY 2014 Estimate	FY 2015 Request
TOTAL	100,432	105,573	107,474
Africa	13,602	13,530	13,290
Angola	488	360	360
Benin	241	210	200
Botswana	543	560	525
Burkina Faso	223	250	250
Burundi	357	325	325
Cabo Verde	92	100	100
Cameroon	237	300	240
Central African Republic	-	-	100
Chad	300	280	280
Comoros	122	100	100
Cote d'Ivoire	244	280	240
Democratic Republic of the Congo	324	375	350
Djibouti	470	335	335
Ethiopia	541	570	500
Gabon	341	230	180
Ghana	651	670	650
Guinea	279	280	240
Kenya	721	760	700
Lesotho	-	100	100
Liberia	487	420	360
Malawi	266	240	240
Mali	-	150	280
Mauritania	309	300	300
Mauritius	94	110	100
Mozambique	423	375	340
Namibia	113	120	110
Niger	273	300	300
Nigeria	712	730	700
Republic of the Congo	38	100	100
Rwanda	282	-	350
Sao Tome and Principe	253	100	100
Senegal	717	770	700
Seychelles	132	140	130
Sierra Leone	343	310	280
Somalia	-	200	200
South Africa	613	650	650
South Sudan	759	800	650
Swaziland	90	100	90
Tanzania	356	400	375
The Gambia	82	90	90
Togo	155	200	200
Uganda	536	520	550
Zambia	395	320	320
East Asia and Pacific	8,522	9,290	12,500
Burma	-	-	250

International Military Education and Training

($ in thousands)

	FY 2013 Actual[1]	FY 2014 Estimate	FY 2015 Request
Cambodia	383	450	450
Indonesia	1,660	1,700	2,400
Laos	-	400	500
Malaysia	967	900	1,050
Marshall Islands	13	50	100
Mongolia	755	850	1,150
Papua New Guinea	-	250	250
Philippines	1,614	1,700	2,000
Samoa	37	40	100
Thailand	1,319	1,300	2,100
Timor-Leste	379	400	400
Tonga	-	250	250
Vietnam	901	1,000	1,500
East Asia and Pacific Regional	494	-	-
Europe and Eurasia	28,772	29,550	29,500
Albania	983	1,000	1,000
Armenia	680	600	600
Azerbaijan	576	600	600
Bosnia and Herzegovina	872	1,000	1,000
Bulgaria	1,996	2,000	2,000
Croatia	1,024	1,100	1,100
Czech Republic	1,752	1,800	1,800
Estonia	1,134	1,200	1,200
Georgia	1,799	1,800	1,800
Greece	93	100	100
Hungary	1,044	1,000	1,000
Kosovo	819	750	750
Latvia	1,151	1,200	1,200
Lithuania	1,140	1,200	1,200
Macedonia	1,002	1,100	1,100
Malta	152	150	100
Moldova	725	750	750
Montenegro	569	600	600
Poland	1,895	2,000	2,000
Portugal	93	100	100
Romania	1,614	1,700	1,700
Serbia	875	1,050	1,050
Slovakia	946	900	900
Slovenia	612	650	650
Turkey	3,415	3,300	3,300
Ukraine	1,811	1,900	1,900

International Military Education and Training
($ in thousands)

	FY 2013 Actual[1]	FY 2014 Estimate	FY 2015 Request
Near East	16,641	20,495	19,561
Algeria	1,259	1,300	1,100
Bahrain	487	725	801
Egypt	474	1,800	1,700
Iraq	1,116	2,000	1,400
Jordan	3,608	3,800	3,800
Lebanon	2,849	2,250	2,250
Libya	142	1,500	1,750
Morocco	1,677	1,710	1,650
Oman	1,935	2,000	1,900
Saudi Arabia	9	10	10
Tunisia	2,155	2,300	2,000
Yemen	930	1,100	1,200
South and Central Asia	13,268	13,309	13,333
Afghanistan	1,424	1,500	1,400
Bangladesh	1,067	1,000	1,500
India	1,267	1,260	1,260
Kazakhstan	744	707	707
Kyrgyz Republic	906	1,000	800
Maldives	216	176	326
Nepal	977	900	900
Pakistan	5,000	5,000	4,800
Sri Lanka	591	626	500
Taj kistan	499	540	540
Turkmenistan	278	300	150
Uzbekistan	299	300	450
Western Hemisphere	12,892	13,896	13,770
Argentina	495	350	350
Belize	205	180	205
Bolivia	175	-	-
Brazil	572	625	625
Chile	768	810	760
Colombia	1,485	1,517	1,450
Costa Rica	293	350	400
Dominican Republic	719	765	765
Ecuador	340	360	360
El Salvador	1,077	1,100	1,000
Guatemala	688	720	720
Guyana	284	300	300
Haiti	208	220	300
Honduras	626	650	750
Jamaica	373	700	600
Mexico	1,239	1,449	1,500
Nicaragua	-	200	200
Panama	655	720	720
Paraguay	432	460	360
Peru	530	585	605

International Military Education and Training

(\$ in thousands)

	FY 2013 Actual[1]	FY 2014 Estimate	FY 2015 Request
Suriname	213	225	200
The Bahamas	164	180	200
Trinidad and Tobago	167	180	200
Uruguay	427	450	500
Barbados and Eastern Caribbean	757	800	700
Other Funding	1,235	-	-
To Be Programmed	1,235	-	-
PM - Political-Military Affairs	5,500	5,503	5,520
IMET Administrative Expenses	5,500	5,503	5,520

1/ The FY 2013 Actual reflects the full-year continuing resolution, reduced by the 0.032% rescission and sequestration.

Foreign Military Financing
($ in thousands)

	FY 2013 Actual[1, 2, 3, 4]	FY 2014 Estimate[5]	FY 2015 Request
TOTAL - FMF	5,667,331	5,919,280	5,647,645
Total Enduring - FMF	4,946,531	5,389,280	5,110,645
Africa	15,775	15,321	10,950
Botswana	190	200	-
Burundi	500	-	-
Cote d'Ivoire	109	200	-
Djibouti	949	1,000	700
Ethiopia	799	843	700
Ghana	332	350	300
Guinea	190	200	-
Kenya	1,041	1,178	1,200
Liberia	4,421	4,000	2,500
Nigeria	949	1,000	600
Senegal	293	325	300
South Africa	665	700	450
Tanzania	-	200	-
Uganda	190	200	200
Africa Regional	5,147	4,925	4,000
East Asia and Pacific	53,316	78,488	67,400
Cambodia	475	500	-
Indonesia	13,292	14,000	14,000
Laos	-	288	200
Mongolia	3,048	2,400	2,000
Philippines	25,483	50,000	40,000
Thailand	1,424	1,000	900
Timor-Leste	100	300	300
Vietnam	9,494	10,000	10,000
Europe and Eurasia	96,837	86,600	66,850
Albania	2,848	2,600	2,400
Armenia	2,564	2,700	1,700
Azerbaijan	2,564	2,700	1,700
Bosnia and Herzegovina	4,272	4,500	4,000
Bulgaria	7,406	7,000	5,000
Croatia	2,374	2,500	2,500
Czech Republic	4,747	3,000	1,000
Estonia	2,279	2,400	1,500
Georgia	13,672	12,000	10,000
Hungary	854	450	-
Kosovo	2,848	4,000	4,400
Latvia	2,134	2,250	1,500
Lithuania	2,420	2,550	1,500
Macedonia	3,418	3,600	4,000
Moldova	1,187	1,250	1,250
Montenegro	1,139	1,200	1,200
Poland	18,989	14,000	9,000

Foreign Military Financing
($ in thousands)

	FY 2013 Actual[1, 2, 3, 4]	FY 2014 Estimate[5]	FY 2015 Request
Romania	11,391	8,000	5,400
Serbia	1,709	1,800	1,800
Slovakia	949	450	-
Slovenia	427	450	-
Ukraine	6,646	4,200	2,000
Europe and Eurasia Regional	-	3,000	5,000
Near East	4,639,077	4,840,000	4,846,500
Bahrain	12,575	10,000	7,500
Egypt	1,234,259	1,300,000	1,300,000
Iraq	37,291	-	-
Israel	2,943,234	3,100,000	3,100,000
Jordan	284,829	300,000	300,000
Lebanon	71,207	75,000	80,000
Libya	949	-	-
Morocco	7,595	7,000	5,000
Oman	7,595	8,000	4,000
Tunisia	20,554	20,000	25,000
Yemen	18,989	20,000	25,000
South and Central Asia	9,914	248,656	7,900
Bangladesh	2,848	2,500	2,000
Kazakhstan	855	1,500	800
Kyrgyz Republic	655	1,050	-
Maldives	380	400	400
Nepal	2,274	1,300	1,300
Pakistan	-	237,771	-
Sri Lanka	424	450	-
Taj kistan	854	1,500	700
Turkmenistan	-	685	100
Uzbekistan	1,624	1,500	700
Central Asia Regional	-	-	1,900
Western Hemisphere	59,226	60,215	47,100
Belize	807	1,000	800
Colombia	28,862	28,500	25,000
Costa Rica	1,331	1,400	1,200
Ecuador	427	450	-
El Salvador	1,709	1,900	1,600
Guatemala	712	1,740	1,000
Haiti	1,519	1,600	800
Honduras	2,848	4,500	3,100
Mexico	6,646	7,000	5,000
Panama	2,659	2,125	1,800
Paraguay	332	-	-
Peru	1,880	2,500	1,800
Western Hemisphere Regional	9,494	7,500	5,000
Caribbean Basin Security Initiative (CBSI)	*[9,494]*	*	*[5,000]*

Foreign Military Financing

($ in thousands)

	FY 2013 Actual[1,2,3,4]	FY 2014 Estimate[5]	FY 2015 Request
PM - Political-Military Affairs	72,386	60,000	63,945
FMF Administrative Expenses	72,386	60,000	63,945
Total Overseas Contingency Operations - FMF	720,800	530,000	537,000
Near East	434,029	300,000	250,000
Iraq	434,029	300,000	250,000
South and Central Asia	280,171	42,229	280,000
Pakistan	280,171	42,229	280,000
Office of U.S. Foreign Assistance Resources	-	50,000	-
Complex Crises Fund (CCF)	-	50,000	-
Other Funding	6,600	126,771	-
Global Security Contingency Fund	-	25,000	-
To Be Programmed	6,600	101,771	-
PM - Political-Military Affairs	-	11,000	7,000
FMF Administrative Expenses	-	11,000	7,000

1/ The FY 2013 Actual Enduring reflects the full-year continuing resolution, reduced by the 0.032% rescission and sequestration. The FY 2013 Actual OCO reflects the full year Continuing Resolution reduced by sequestration.

2/ The FY 2013 OCO Actual level reflects the transfer of $15 million from the Foreign Military Financing account to the Transition Initiatives account.

3/ The FY 2013 OCO Actual level reflects the transfer of $223.667 million from the Foreign Military Financing account to the Economic Support Fund account.

4/ The FY 2013 OCO Actual level reflects the transfer of $87.14 million from the Foreign Military Financing account to the Peacekeeping Operations account.

5/ The FY 2014 Estimate reflects the estimated funding level for FY 2014 at the Account and Operating Unit level and are subject to change. Detailed allocations below the Account and Operating Unit level are not available.

Foreign Military Financing
($ in thousands)

	FY 2013 Actual[1, 2, 3, 4]	FY 2014 Estimate[5]	FY 2015 Request
PM - Political-Military Affairs	72,386	60,000	63,945
FMF Administrative Expenses	72,386	60,000	63,945

	FY 2013 Actual[1, 2, 3, 4]	FY 2014 Estimate[5]	FY 2015 Request
Total Overseas Contingency Operations - FMF	720,800	530,000	537,000
Near East	434,029	300,000	250,000
Iraq	434,029	300,000	250,000
South and Central Asia	280,171	42,229	280,000
Pakistan	280,171	42,229	280,000
Office of U.S. Foreign Assistance Resources	-	50,000	-
Complex Crises Fund (CCF)	-	50,000	-
Other Funding	6,600	126,771	-
Global Security Contingency Fund	-	25,000	-
To Be Programmed	6,600	101,771	-
PM - Political-Military Affairs	-	11,000	7,000
FMF Administrative Expenses	-	11,000	7,000

1/ The FY 2013 Actual Enduring reflects the full-year continuing resolution, reduced by the 0.032% rescission and sequestration. The FY 2013 Actual OCO reflects the full year Continuing Resolution reduced by sequestration.

2/ The FY 2013 OCO Actual level reflects the transfer of $15 million from the Foreign Military Financing account to the Transition Initiatives account.

3/ The FY 2013 OCO Actual level reflects the transfer of $223.667 million from the Foreign Military Financing account to the Economic Support Fund account.

4/ The FY 2013 OCO Actual level reflects the transfer of $87.14 million from the Foreign Military Financing account to the Peacekeeping Operations account.

5/ The FY 2014 Estimate reflects the estimated funding level for FY 2014 at the Account and Operating Unit level and are subject to change. Detailed allocations below the Account and Operating Unit level are not available.

Foreign Military Financing
($ in thousands)

	FY 2013 Actual[1, 2, 3, 4]	FY 2014 Estimate[5]	FY 2015 Request
Romania	11,391	8,000	5,400
Serbia	1,709	1,800	1,800
Slovakia	949	450	-
Slovenia	427	450	-
Ukraine	6,646	4,200	2,000
Europe and Eurasia Regional	-	3,000	5,000
Near East	4,639,077	4,840,000	4,846,500
Bahrain	12,575	10,000	7,500
Egypt	1,234,259	1,300,000	1,300,000
Iraq	37,291	-	-
Israel	2,943,234	3,100,000	3,100,000
Jordan	284,829	300,000	300,000
Lebanon	71,207	75,000	80,000
Libya	949	-	-
Morocco	7,595	7,000	5,000
Oman	7,595	8,000	4,000
Tunisia	20,554	20,000	25,000
Yemen	18,989	20,000	25,000
South and Central Asia	9,914	248,656	7,900
Bangladesh	2,848	2,500	2,000
Kazakhstan	855	1,500	800
Kyrgyz Republic	655	1,050	-
Maldives	380	400	400
Nepal	2,274	1,300	1,300
Pakistan	-	237,771	-
Sri Lanka	424	450	-
Taj kistan	854	1,500	700
Turkmenistan	-	685	100
Uzbekistan	1,624	1,500	700
Central Asia Regional	-	-	1,900
Western Hemisphere	59,226	60,215	47,100
Belize	807	1,000	800
Colombia	28,862	28,500	25,000
Costa Rica	1,331	1,400	1,200
Ecuador	427	450	-
El Salvador	1,709	1,900	1,600
Guatemala	712	1,740	1,000
Haiti	1,519	1,600	800
Honduras	2,848	4,500	3,100
Mexico	6,646	7,000	5,000
Panama	2,659	2,125	1,800
Paraguay	332	-	-
Peru	1,880	2,500	1,800
Western Hemisphere Regional	9,494	7,500	5,000
Caribbean Basin Security Initiative (CBSI)	*[9,494]*	*	*[5,000]*

International Organizations and Programs
($ in thousands)

	FY 2013 Actual[1,2]	FY 2014 Estimate	FY 2015 Request
TOTAL	326,651	344,020	303,439
IO - International Organizations	326,651	344,020	303,439
International Civil Aviation Organization (ICAO)	940	800	800
International Development Law Organization (IDLO)	590	600	600
International Maritime Organization (IMO)	390	360	360
Intergovernmental Panel on Climate Change / UN Framework Convention on Climate Change	9,500	10,000	11,700
International Chemicals and Toxins Programs	3,470	3,610	3,610
International Conservation Programs	7,750	7,900	7,000
Montreal Protocol Multilateral Fund	25,650	25,500	25,500
Multilateral Action Initiatives	999	-	-
OAS Development Assistance	3,325	3,400	3,400
OAS Fund for Strengthening Democracy	4,275	4,500	2,700
Regional Cooperation Agreement on Combating Piracy and Armed Robbery Against Ships in Asia (ReCAAP)	-	50	50
UN Office for the Coordination of Humanitarian Affairs (UN OCHA)	2,800	3,000	2,800
UN Voluntary Funds for Technical Cooperation in the Field of Human Rights	1,200	1,250	1,200
UN Women (formerly UNIFEM)	7,200	7,500	7,500
UN Human Settlements Program (UN-HABITAT)	700	1,400	1,400
UN Capital Development Fund (UNCDF)	870	900	595
UN Democracy Fund (UNDF)	4,581	4,200	4,200
UN Development Program (UNDP)	78,000	80,000	62,200
UN Environment Program (UNEP)	7,315	7,550	7,550
International Contributions for Scientific, Educational, and Cultural Activities (UNESCO/ICSECA)	-	-	880
UN Population Fund (UNFPA)[1]	28,850	35,000	35,300
UN High Commissioner for Human Rights (UNHCHR)	4,500	5,500	2,000
UN Children's Fund (UNICEF)	125,168	132,000	116,594
UN Voluntary Fund for Victims of Torture (UNVFVT)	5,500	6,350	3,000
World Meteorological Organization (WMO)	1,986	1,650	1,500
WTO Technical Assistance	1,092	1,000	1,000

1/ The FY 2013 Actual reflects the full-year continuing resolution, reduced by the 0.032% rescission and sequestration.

2/ The FY 2013 Enduring Actual level reflects the transfer of $4.4 million from the International Organizations and Programs account to the Global Health Progams - USAID account.